the spirit of the reformed tradition

the spirit of the reformed tradition

by

M. EUGENE OSTERHAVEN

Albertus C. Van Raalte Professor of Systematic Theology
Western Theological Seminary
Holland, Michigan

WILLIAM B. EERDMANS PUBLISHING COMPANY
Grand Rapids, Michigan

Copyright © 1971 by William B. Eerdmans Publishing Company
All rights reserved
Library of Congress Catalog Card Number: 75-127625
Printed in the United States of America

Scripture quotations are taken from the Revised Standard Version Bible, copyright 1946, 1952, and used by permission.

Quotations from *Calvin: Institutes of the Christian Religion,* Volumes XX and XXI, The Library of Christian Classics, edited by John T. McNeill and translated by Ford Lewis Battles; published in the U.S.A. by the Westminster Press; copyright © MCMLX by W. L. Jenkins; used by permission.

Quotations from *The Recovery of the Anabaptist Vision,* Guy F. Hershberger, editor; copyright © 1957 by Mennonite Publishing House, Scottdale, Pa.; used by permission.

Selections from Søren Kierkegaard, *Fear and Trembling and The Sickness Unto Death,* translated by Walter Lowrie (copyright 1941, 1954, by Princeton University Press: Princeton Paperback, 1968), are reprinted by permission of Princeton University Press.

Grateful acknowledgment is also made for permission to quote from the following works: to Abingdon Press, for permission to quote from *Here I Stand,* by Roland H. Bainton; to Barnes & Noble, Inc., for permission to quote from *The Social Teachings of the Christian Churches,* by Ernst Troeltsch; to Harper & Row, for permission to quote from *The Righteousness of God,* by Gordon Rupp; to United Church Press, for permission to quote from *The Heidelberg Catechism, 400th Anniversary Edition,* translated by Allen O. Miller and M. Eugene Osterhaven.

To
the pious memory of
Barnabas Nagy, 1909-1969
and
The Sárospatak Reformed Academy, 1531-1951

pReface

Within the last several years a number of anniversaries have accented the Reformed tradition, beginning in 1959 when several important events were commemorated. That year was the four hundred fiftieth anniversary of John Calvin's birth and the four hundredth anniversary of the definitive edition of his *Institutes of the Christian Religion,* of the founding of the Academy of Geneva, of the first Synod of the Reformed Church of France, and of the adoption of the French Confession of Faith. The year following was the four hundredth anniversary of the "Reformation Parliament" in Scotland and the Scottish Confession of Faith. The quadricentennial of the Belgic, or Netherlands, Confession of Faith was in 1961, followed two years later by the same anniversary of the Heidelberg Catechism. The year 1964 was the four hundredth anniversary of the death of John Calvin, the last of the great Reformers. The year 1966 marked the anniversary of the Second Helvetic Confession, written in 1566; and in 1967 the Hungarian Reformed Church celebrated the quadricentennial of its first national synod. In 1968 the Dutch Reformed Church remembered the quadricentennial of its first national assembly, the Synod of Wesel.

Remembrance of the events we have enumerated prompts one to ask questions about the tradition that has stemmed from them. What is there in the Reformed tradition that is as valid today as it was in the sixteenth century? What in it, if anything, is distinctive? What does the Reformed Church have to contribute to the one holy catholic and apostolic church in an ecumenical era? What are its fundamental emphases? Its inner dynamic? What is the spirit of its tradition?

Questions of this nature have been before me in the preparation of this study. My answer is that at the center of the Reformed tradition there is a profound sense of the presence of God and the

7

consecration of life to him. All else must be seen in relation to this central concept. Some will say that there is nothing uniquely Reformed in that. My response is: indeed! this is simply biblical Christianity. This is the essence of the Reformed tradition. The Reformed Church does not claim to have a revelation from God that other Christians do not have. It claims only that it believes it has by God's grace a relatively clear insight into the revelation he has given the whole church. The Reformed Church makes no claim that it lives up to that revelation as it should. Practice often lags behind principle. Nevertheless, the Reformed Church does believe that God has given it an understanding of the truth. Its task today, as always, is not only to understand God's Word in the midst of his world but to translate it into action. Christian truth must be believed and it must be obeyed.

Among the leaders of the church who have seen this clearly is the Reformer whose life and writings have been the inspiration of much of this study and whose name appears often in the text, John Calvin. I have leaned heavily on him because of his importance to the Reformed tradition and because I know him better than any other writer. The Heidelberg Catechism is cited often for the same reason, my familiarity with it and the place that it has had in the Reformed, particularly the continental Reformed, tradition.

My account begins where much Protestant theology begins, with the Reformation, but I have given full recognition to the fact that the Reformed Church has direct continuity with the mainstream of Christian thought since the time of the apostles and, even further, with Israel. The sequence of the chapters proceeds logically from the introductory chapter on the Reformation to a discussion of the Reformed Church. This leads into a brief treatment of Scripture, inasmuch as the church was reformed according to the Word of God. The fourth chapter treats what I consider to be the center of Christianity for John Calvin and for the Reformed tradition. This is followed by two chapters on ethics, the first on the life of the Christian and the second on the relation of the Christian to the world about him. The conclusion raises the question of the future of the Reformed tradition in the one church of the Lord.

It will be seen that I treat the subject broadly and what I present is brief. Certain topics are included in the treatment because I have met them as problems for elders of the church at one time or another. I have had in mind these elders, students, past and present, and others interested in "what the Reformed Church really stands for." I hope that what I have written is helpful for all of them.

Those who care to pursue certain subjects further may do so in studies referred to in the footnotes.

Some may object that I not only treat the subject broadly but that I have been too broad in my appreciations and too brief in my treatment. To this I can only say that I have not intended to write a treatise on systematic theology or to be exhaustive. Nor have I attempted to write for those who have had formal training in theology. I have touched on many things in a few pages with the hope that information and help may be given. As for the possibility of my being too broad in my understanding of the Reformed tradition, I might say that I rejoice when I see areas of agreement with other traditions. That there are such is as it should be, since there is only one church of our Lord and all Christians are a part of it. Nevertheless, each tradition accents certain emphases and I have tried to point out some of those which have distinguished that tradition of which I am grateful to be a part.

In closing I wish to thank Professors A. A. van Ruler and S. vander Linde of the University of Utrecht for their friendly counsel and advice. I also wish to record my appreciation for a sabbatical year made possible by the Board of Trustees of Western Theological Seminary and the American Association of Theological Schools. The dedication is to a theologian whose friendship meant much to me, and to his venerable alma mater in Hungary. I consider them representative of the best in the Reformed tradition.

—M. Eugene Osterhaven

ABBREVIATIONS

C.R.   *Corpus Reformatorum, Ioannis Calvini opera quae supersunt omnia,* edd. Baum, Cunitz, and Reuss, 49 vols., Brunswick, 1863-1900.

Inst.   John Calvin, *Institutes of the Christian Religion,* ed. John T. McNeill; translated and indexed by Ford Lewis Battles (Philadelphia: Westminster, 1960).

Heid. Cat. *The Heidelberg Catechism* (Philadelphia: United Church Press, 1963), translated by Allen O. Miller and M. Eugene Osterhaven.

table of contents

1

the Reformation of the church

A. THE NEED FOR REFORMATION

The need for reform in the church of the sixteenth century can be illustrated by a series of pictures intimately associated with the life of Martin Luther. The first two are pictures that were impressed upon his mind when he was a fourteen-year-old student at Magdeburg. One of these was on an altarpiece in a church, showing a ship sailing towards heaven. In it were the pope, the cardinals, bishops, monks, and priests. The latter were tending oars and sails and were casting ropes to laymen struggling in the water. Some of the laymen were clinging to the ropes while others were drowning. No layman—not even a king or a prince—was in the ship, and no clergyman was in the water. Hovering over the ship, directing its course, was the Holy Ghost.

The second picture, a living one, was of Prince William of Anhalt who had forsaken rank and inheritance to become a Franciscan friar in a neighboring monastery. Barefooted and emaciated, he walked through the streets carrying his beggar's sack begging alms. His fastings, scourgings and vigils had worn him to skin and bones. Years later Luther recalled the sight:

> With my own eyes I saw him. I was fourteen years old at Magdeburg. I saw him carrying the sack like a donkey. He had so worn himself down by fasting and vigil that he looked like a death's-head, mere bone and skin. No one could look upon him without feeling ashamed of his own life.[1]

Young Martin well understood the meaning of those pictures. The first represented the generally accepted view of the church with the laity utterly dependent on the Roman Catholic hierarchy for salvation. The second shockingly reminded him of the desirability of renouncing this world and all that it offered if one would seek beatitude in the next. The monastic ideal was held before the young men of his day and so spiritually sensitive a boy as Martin had learned the lesson well. It is not surprising then that eight years later in a thunderstorm, when he was already inwardly disposed to go to a monastery, he should cry out: "St. Anne, help! I will become a monk." Luther kept his vow and became a monk because he felt that only a renunciation of the world and the unnatural life of a mendicant would assure him of salvation.

A third picture that illustrates the need for a reformation of the church was the popular conception of God, which Luther shared. God was conceived of as a stern judge who demanded righteousness in men and who was so far removed that he could be approached only through saints or the Virgin Mother. Salvation was thought to be impossible unless one performed works pleasing to God. On the performance of such works religious men set their hopes. But Martin Luther was not a man of ordinary religious interests and inclinations. As an unusually pious monk he set himself to achieving a righteousness that would give him salvation. The story has been told innumerable times.

> I was a good monk and kept my order so strictly that I could say that if ever a monk could get to heaven through monastic discipline, I should have entered in. All my companions in the monastery who knew me would bear me out in this. For if it had gone on much longer I would have martyred myself to death with vigils, prayers, readings and other works.

Again one hears him say,

> I tried to live according to the Rule with all diligence, and I used to be contrite, to confess and number off my sins, and often repeated my confession, and sedulously performed my allotted penance. And yet my conscience could never give me certainty, but I always doubted and said, "You did not perform that correctly. You were not contrite enough. You left that out of your confession." The more I tried to remedy an uncertain, weak, and afflicted conscience with the traditions of men, the more each day found it more uncertain, weaker, more troubled.

Again one reads, "For I hoped I might find peace of conscience with fasts, prayer, vigils, with which I miserably afflicted my body, but the more I sweated it out like this, the less peace and tranquillity I knew." Luther sometimes confessed six hours at a time, carefully going over his sins, racking his memory and searching his conscience until his superior and confessor would rebuke him for his hypersensitivity to sin. He mortified himself in countless ways, sometimes fasting for three days at a time without touching a crumb, keeping long vigils and then sleeping without the few blankets that were given him until he almost froze himself. All of this was required, men of his day thought, to placate God so that punishment might be averted and favor won. How could Luther love this "stern Judge sitting on a rainbow" when he found himself wholly unable to live the perfect life he knew was demanded of him? "I did not love, rather I hated this just God who punishes sinners," he recalled the year before his death. Earlier he had written, "The Law... commanded those things which, even if we had wished, we could not have performed. Then I simply was driven to despair, so that I began to hate and blaspheme God, who seemed to deal so unfairly with me." In 1526 he wrote, "I myself was more than once driven to the very abyss of despair so that I wished I had never been created. Love God? I hated him!"

Luther tells the dramatic tale of his discovery of the gospel in an autobiographical statement written the year before his death. It was one word, *righteousness,* that kept him from understanding the gospel in his early career.

For I hated this word "righteousness of God" which by the use and consent of all doctors I was taught to understand philosophically of that formal or active justice with which God is just and punishes unjust sinners. For however irreproachable I lived as a monk, I felt myself in the presence of God to be a sinner with a most unquiet conscience; nor could I trust that I had pleased him with my satisfaction. I did not love, nay, rather I hated this just God who punished sinners, and if not with open blasphemy certainly with huge murmuring I was angry with God saying: "As though it really were not enough that miserable sinners should be eternally damned with original sin, and have all kinds of calamities laid upon them by the law of the ten commandments, God must go and add sorrow upon sorrow and even through the Gospel itself bring his Justice and his Wrath to bear!" I raged in this way with a fierce and disturbed conscience, and yet I knocked importunately at Paul in this place, thirsting most ardently to know what St. Paul meant.

At last, God being merciful, as I meditated day and night on the connection of the words, namely, "the justice (righteousness) of God is revealed in it, as it is written, the just shall live by faith," there I began to understand the justice of God as that by which the just lives by the gift of God, namely by faith, and this sentence, "the justice of God is revealed in the gospel," to be that passive justice with which the merciful God justifies us by faith, as it is written, "the just lives by faith."

This straightway made me feel as though reborn, and as though I had entered through open gates into paradise itself. From then on, the whole face of Scripture appeared different. . . . And now, as much as I had hated this word "justice of God" before, so much the more sweetly I extolled this word to myself now, so that this place in Paul was to me as a real gate of paradise. Afterwards, I read Augustine, "On the Spirit and the Letter," where beyond hope I found that he also similarly interpreted the justice of God: that with which God endues us, when he justifies us. And although this were said imperfectly, and he does not clearly explain about imputation, yet it pleased that he should teach a justice of God with which we are justified.

Luther had discovered the gospel, the good news that God is a Savior who does not wait for a man to attain a righteousness of his own, but mercifully justifies the ungodly in his grace. This was indeed "more than a new exposition of Romans 1:17; this was the fountain of a new doctrine of God."[2] This new evangelical picture of God was closely bound to the doctrine of salvation. The god whom the young Luther had seen demanded righteousness, but did not give it. Luther wrote: "When I became a doctor I did not yet know that we cannot expiate our sins." So Luther tried the impossible, to expiate them himself. The God he came to know through his study of the Bible and spiritual striving—his *Anfechtung,* as he called it—is a merciful heavenly Father who loves to save, who himself has expiated man's sin and seeks him before man knows himself to be a sinner.

Many other pictures could be drawn to illustrate the utter need for renewal in the church in the sixteenth century. We shall conclude our discussion here with one of the best-known pictures: the hawker of indulgences. The sale of indulgences had been a common practice since the Crusades. For more than a century before Luther the purchase of an indulgence included the presentation of an Indul-

gence Letter, ornamented with the papal signature and seal, so that
the purchaser could have the assurance of his forgiveness in black
and white. Finally, in 1476, the development was complete when
Pope Sixtus IV declared indulgences to be available and valid for the
dead in purgatory as well as for the living. A special form of
indulgence known as "plenary" was sold, which was supposed to
cover every possible sin, past or future. There were Roman Catholic
theologians besides Luther who did not go along with this development, and after Luther's attack the church defined indulgences more
precisely in order to eliminate some of the mischief. Their traffic,
however, had become a scandal while they remained a lucrative
source of income for the church. "They were the bingo of the
sixteenth century," Bainton quips aptly;[3] and many churches had
received papal authorization to get in on the racket.

The castle church in Wittenberg sold an indulgence advertised as
granting full remission of sins upon the payment of a sum of money
and the viewing of certain holy relics. Frederick the Wise, the elector
of Saxony, had dedicated himself to making Wittenberg the most
famous depository of relics in Germany. The collection included

> one tooth of St. Jerome, of St. Chrysostom four pieces, of St.
> Bernard six, and of St. Augustine four; of Our Lady four hairs,
> three pieces of her cloak, four from her girdle, and seven from
> the veil sprinkled with the blood of Christ. The relics of Christ
> included one piece of his swaddling clothes, thirteen from his
> crib, one wisp of straw, one piece of the gold brought by the
> Wise Men and three of the myrrh, one strand of Jesus' beard,
> one of the nails driven into his hands, one piece of bread eaten
> at the Last Supper, one piece of the stone on which Jesus
> stood to ascend into heaven, and one twig of Moses' burning
> bush. By 1520 the collection had mounted to 19,013 holy
> bones. Those who viewed these relics on the designated day
> and made the stipulated contributions might receive from the
> pope indulgences for the reduction of purgatory, either for
> themselves or others, to the extent of 1,902,202 years and
> 270 days. These were the treasures made available on the day
> of All Saints.[4]

It is little wonder that Luther had difficulty with indulgences and
felt compelled to speak against them. A year before the actual
outbreak of the Reformation he had criticized them several times
from the pulpit. The third of these criticisms was delivered on the
eve of All Saints' Day in 1516, exactly a year before he posted his
ninety-five theses on the church door at Wittenberg to strike the

spark that was to set half of Europe ablaze. We can only sketch the picture that aroused his ire in 1517.

Albert of Brandenburg purchased the Archbishopric of Mainz, the most important in Germany, from the pope for the equivalent of about a quarter of a million dollars. The transaction was handled by the Fuggers of Augsburg, the leading banking house in Europe. In order that Albert might repay the Fuggers, the pope granted him the privilege of selling a plenary indulgence in certain German territories. One-half of the proceeds was to go for the building of St. Peter's in Rome and the other half to repay the loan with interest. In a set of printed instructions the Archbishop told his salesmen to stress certain matters, including a plenary forgiveness for sin even for those already in purgatory.

One of the salesmen was a Dominican Monk named John Tetzel, who had been selling indulgences since 1504 and was regarded as a master at the trade. The German Reformer Myconius had heard him preach and relates that Tetzel boasted that he had saved more souls through indulgences than St. Peter had by preaching the gospel. When Tetzel arrived in a town to preach and sell indulgences there was great fanfare and formality. A procession went out to meet him, all the bells in town rang, and as the procession entered the church the organ played. "A red cross was placed in the middle of the church on which the papal papers were hung," Myconius says, adding that "one could not have received and entertained God in a more impressive fashion than this."[5]

Tetzel would preach his first sermon in the town square, where he would attract the largest possible crowd. The subject was "Hell" and Tetzel would be at his best as he pictured the place of the damned. The next sermon, held in the largest church in the community, was on "Purgatory" and he would picture the sufferings of deceased relatives of those present. Playing on the emotions and superstitions of his hearers he would dramatize the cries of their dear departed being purged of their sins in the flames of purgatory. Asking whether sons and daughters could not hear their parents or other relatives crying to them for release while they were calmly enjoying themselves on earth, the preacher would assure his listeners that they were able to secure their release by the purchase of that which he had been commissioned to sell. His third sermon was on heaven and he made the contrasts between heaven and hell, and heaven and purgatory, that one might expect from him. After such exciting conditioning in a day when life was dull the sale began and citizens lined up for their purchases. Payment was according to economic standing, an elaborate classification having been worked out by the Fuggers.

Tetzel did not come to Wittenberg when selling indulgences for Albert because Frederick the Wise had indulgences of his own for sale and electoral Saxony was out of bounds for other salesmen at the time. He was near enough, however, to draw many local towns-people, who came back to Wittenberg with the indulgences they had purchased and tall tales to tell. At least as early as 1512 Tetzel had been saying, "As soon as the *groschen* rings in the bowl, the soul of him for whom it was given rises from the mouth directly into heaven." Bainton relates that Tetzel was reported to have said that "papal indulgences could absolve a man who had violated the Mother of God, and the cross emblazoned with the papal arms set up by the indulgence sellers was equal to the cross of Christ."[6]

The situation was most distressing to Luther. Persons whom he knew to be living evil lives sported indulgences and went on as they pleased. It seemed to him that the cause of Christ in general and the sacrament of penance in particular were being done irreparable harm. The sale of indulgences continued; stories kept coming back to Wittenberg; Luther brooded over it all; the picture of John Tetzel hawking his wares stood out in Luther's mind in ever sharper lines. Finally, just before All Saints' Day in 1517, Luther took up his pen. He set down his convictions in ninety-five propositions, nailed them to the church door, and the Reformation was born.

B. THE CHARACTER OF THE REFORMATION

Something of the character of the Reformation has already been indicated in the pictures that we have sketched of its need. Let us continue with a more precise statement about it, even though it must be a brief one.

The Reformation was described by the pope as a squabble of monks. Others have called it a revolt of the human spirit in the interests of freedom against the absolute power of the church. Some Roman Catholic scholars have described it as a transitional era paving the way for free thinking and unbelief. But the Reformation was altogether different in its inner character. It was a return to the simple, yet sublime, apostolic and scriptural practice of religion that the church had received from its Lord. It was an attempt to recover Christianity in its original purity and to remove from it the beliefs and practices that had become attached to it during the intervening centuries without foundation or support in the Word of God.

The Reformation was first of all, then, a return to the Bible as the only infallible rule for faith and practice. In taking that position, Luther and the other Reformers rejected the belief that the Bible and tradition are the joint rule of faith with the Church of Rome as sole infallible interpreter. The Reformers did not wish to reject the teaching of the church but they felt called to subordinate it to the Word of God as the church of the first Christian centuries had done. Since that early period numerous unscriptural traditions had developed and had become a part of the faith of the church. The Reformation asserted that the church of Christ has no right to impose upon the conscience of man articles of faith for which there is no clear warrant in the Word of God.

In returning to the Bible, the Reformation also emphasized anew two great truths that had been known to the church in former ages, but had been virtually lost in the centuries following: the teaching of the universal priesthood of all believers, and the doctrine of justification by faith alone. With respect to the former, Protestantism came to see that a vast institution, the Church of Rome, ruled by a hierarchy, had placed itself between the individual and God. In reverting to the ancient doctrine of the church the Reformers declared with the New Testament that all believers are saints and priests and that Jesus Christ is the only mediator between God and man.

Concerning justification, the Reformers declared that no "good works" or buying of indulgences have justifying merit, that the "treasury of merit" from which the pope claimed to be able to draw was a fiction, and that salvation is a free gift of God made possible only through a living faith in the righteousness and atoning death of Jesus Christ. Living faith will result in good works, but such works are the fruit, not part of the ground, of the believer's salvation.

Here again the Reformers were not innovators, as has been claimed, but they proclaimed anew what had been the original faith of the church, what pious men had believed in every age, and what they had learned from their own teachers. Luther had learned some of his most valuable lessons in religion from Staupitz, his superior in the Augustinian order; Zwingli, the German Swiss Reformer, had learned at Basel that the death of Christ is the only price of forgiveness and that indulgences are worthless; and Calvin, a Frenchman who was to be associated with LeFevre in Geneva, was only three years old when LeFevre was teaching in Paris that the only good work that justifies sinners has been done by the Son of God. These men were all born, baptized, confirmed and educated in the

Church of Rome. Most of them had served as priests at her altars after taking solemn vows. They had no intention of parting with Christ's church, but because in the critical hour Rome resisted the needed reform with all its might, the Reformers were forced to rebuild the church on the foundation of Christ and the scriptures in harmony with what was best in the medieval tradition. Thus their church came to be called the *Church of Jesus Christ Reformed According to the Word of God.*

C. THE SPREAD OF REFORM

As the Reformation spread, there came to be numerous centers of influence from which its teachings were disseminated. Besides Wittenberg, where Luther had won the entire faculty to his views, there was Zurich, where Zwingli had begun reform. Soon Basel, Strasbourg, Berne, and Geneva—to mention only the most important other cities—came to accept Reformation views. The religious leaders of those cities with their people were at first all a part of one mighty reforming movement as they sought to purify the church of abuses and false teachings. Soon, however, differences in emphasis and even in doctrine were noticeable. Most of these were slight but some were not. Sometimes they existed in the same city, like the difference in emphasis that arose between Carlstadt and Luther, and sometimes they were as distant geographically as Zurich and Wittenberg.

One difference of opinion between Reformation leaders that had far-reaching consequences was that between Luther and Zwingli on the Lord's Supper. In order to understand it, however, one must understand the fundamental differences in training and in outlook of the two men. Luther was a theologian steeped in the traditions of the church, conservative, biblical and uncompromising. Zwingli was first a humanist influenced by the new learning of the Renaissance, *then* a theologian, and a radical in thought. "Zwingli was in fact the most modern in mind of all the Reformers, while Luther was the most medieval."[7] Zwingli's acquaintance with classical writers of antiquity led him to believe that some of them might be saved apart from a knowledge of the gospel. He limited the disturbing effect of original sin and held the power of human reason in high esteem. Luther's views on these subjects were the exact opposite. One or the other of us, Luther once wrote concerning Zwingli, must be the minister of the devil, and Luther was quite certain that it was not himself.

A. M. Fairbairn contrasts them well.

As the one was by disposition and discipline a schoolman who loved the Saints and the Sacraments of the Church, the other was a humanist who appreciated the thinkers of antiquity and the reason in whose name they spoke. Luther never escaped from the feelings of the monk and associations of the cloister; but Zwingli studied his New Testament with a fine sense of the sanity of its thought, the combined purity and practicability of its ideals, and the majesty of its spirit; and his ambition was to realize a religion after its model, free from the traditions and superstitions of men. It was this that made him so tolerant of Luther, and Luther so intolerant of him. The differences of character were insuperable. The two men stood for distinct ideals and different realities; and as they differed so did their peoples. . . .The church adapted to a German kingdom was not suited to the temper and ways of an ancient republic; nor was a system fitted to a despotic State congenial to the genius of a free people.

Hence there emerged a twofold difference between the Reformations accomplished by Luther and by Zwingli: one personal, which mainly affected the faith or creed of the Church, another social or civil, which mainly affected its polity. Luther, a schoolman while a Reformer, created out of his learning and experience a faith suited to his personal needs; but Zwingli, a Reformer because a humanist, came to religion through the literature which embodied the mind of Christ and the Church of the Apostles. Hence, the Lutheran Reformation is less radical and complete and less historical and rational. But the differences due to the political order and the civil usage were, if not deeper, yet more divisive. Luther effected his change under an empire and within a kingdom by the help of Princes and nobles; but Zwingli effected his under a republic by the aid of citizens with whom he had to argue as with consciously freeborn men. Both might organize their respective Churches by means of the civil power and in dependence on it; but the civil powers were not the same, the reigning forces being in the one case the law and the princely will, and in the other case the reason and the free choice of men trained in self government by the usages of centuries. The Lutheran Church was thus more monarchical, the Zwinglian more republican in constitution; the one was constructed by Princes, the other organized by the genius and built by the hands of a free people.[8]

It is understandable then that the Reformation did not express itself in identical forms in all centers where its teachings were accepted. Although Luther and Zwingli had much in common, the differences in their backgrounds, training, and civil and ecclesiastical environments were so great that it is not surprising that there was a difference in their understanding of the Word of God. At Marburg in 1529 that difference was brought into sharp focus when Philip of Hesse arranged a conference in an attempt to bring the Swiss and the German Reformers together in their theological positions. Zwingli was an eager, and Luther a reluctant, participant. Zwingli displayed a conciliatory spirit and made as many concessions as he could conscientiously, but he was unable to accept Luther's position that the physical body of Christ was literally present and received in the supper. To Luther's insistence that the words of the Lord Jesus Christ, "This is my body," be taken literally, Zwingli answered that "is" means "represents" or "signifies," as a portrait represents a person. Christ was only figuratively a "door," or a "vine," and in the Holy Supper his body and blood are only figuratively received as his death is commemorated.

The many scriptural arguments that Zwingli used made no impression on Luther, who wrote on the table *"Hoc est corpus meum"* ("This is my body"), and would not be budged from its literal interpretation. Finally Luther was induced to draw up a series of fifteen articles of faith. Fourteen and one-half of them Zwingli could accept and with respect to the remaining half point the contestants agreed "to show to the other Christian love, as far as conscience permits."

Zwingli felt that the difference of interpretation should be no obstacle to Christian fellowship with the Wittenberg theologians, with whom he said he would rather agree than with any people on earth. Luther, however, rebuffed Zwingli with the words, *"Ihr habt einen andern Geist"* ("You have another spirit"), and refused to take Zwingli's proffered hand although the latter begged him with tears to accept it. The Lutheran theologians soon denied that the Zwinglians were members of the church of Christ and Luther wrote that they were "not only liars, but the very incarnation of lying, deceit and hypocrisy."[9] Thus it was that "the hand which had pulled down the Roman Church in Germany made the first rent in the Church which was beginning to grow up in its place."[10]

Luther was a man of heroic qualities and also of great weaknesses. He could stand alone against church and empire to face almost certain death. He could be used of God as no one else could have been, "to tear up the stumps and dead roots, to cut away the thorns, and to act as a rough forester and pioneer," as he once said of his mission in the church. For this end, he said, he had been born. All of

evangelical Christianity gratefully claims him as its Reformer. Indeed, the entire Christian world including Roman Catholicism is
indebted to him for the reforming influences he set in motion.
Sharp-minded, courageous, heroic, with a great capacity for work,
free from all manner of affectation, with childlike simplicity and
genuineness, impulsive and lovable, Luther was one of history's great
leaders of all time.

But Luther was human and therefore he was subject to human
weaknesses. One of them was an excessive conservatism, which made
him fearful of change even where needed. His tendency was to retain
as much of the old ecclesiastical faith and practice as he could
without being disobedient to scripture. As Fairbairn writes, "he was
a man equally powerful in promoting and in resisting change; he
stood up against forces that would have overwhelmed a weaker or a
smaller man; but as a conservative by nature he professed beliefs that
a man of a more consistent intellect would have dismissed, and
cherished customs which a more radical reformer would have sur-
rendered."[11] Another weakness was his violent temper and in-
creasing irascibility as he advanced in age. This made cooperation
with other reforming leaders difficult and facilitated division within
Protestantism. He hated the Zwinglians as much as the papists and
once declared that he would rather drink blood along with the latter
than wine along with the men from Zurich.[12] Philip Schaff writes
that Luther's last writings against the papists, the Zwinglians, and
the Jews "exceed anything that is known in the history of theological polemics."[13] It is little wonder then that the reforming party in
Switzerland came to feel itself somewhat alienated from the evangelical brethren in Saxony. Nor was it all Luther's fault; Zwingli
himself, as we have seen, entertained unbiblical ideas.

As the Reformation progressed it became increasingly apparent to
some of its leaders that further advances were needed in church
government, worship, discipline, and Christian living. Many congregations seemed only half removed from superstition and, at a time
when Rome was gathering the vast resources she had accumulated
through the centuries to strike a counter blow, half measures could
not win the day. What was needed was further reform, a more
comprehensive understanding of the task to be done if the Reformation were to be a lasting success, and a greater cosmopolitanism.

One attempt at further reform was made by persons who after
1525 came to be known as rebaptizers or Anabaptists. At first a part
of the common evangelical movement associated with Luther and
Zwingli, the Anabaptists became dissatisfied with the nature and

progress of reform and sought to found a church truly Christian. Such a church would not include the whole population of a community, nor would membership in it be signified by a baptism received in infancy. The church of the Anabaptists would be a voluntary association of true believers whose lives would manifest repentance and the fruits of the Spirit. One of their contemporary spokesmen writes:

> The Anabaptists. . .retained the original vision of Luther and Zwingli, enlarged it, gave it body and form, and set out to achieve it in actual experience. They proceeded to organize a church composed solely of earnest Christians, and actually found the people for it. They did not believe in any case that the size of the response should determine whether or not the truth of God should be applied, and they refused to compromise. They preferred to make a radical break with fifteen hundred years of history and culture if necessary rather than to break with the New Testament.[14]

The chief error of the young evangelical movement, the Anabaptist leaders held, was the retention of the state church with its governmental support, so they rejected it. It was the doctrine of the church that separated the Anabaptists from their evangelical brethren, not the doctrine of baptism, as is commonly believed.[15] The baptism of infants was repudiated because the church must be a fellowship of believers only, of which baptism was the sign. The mode of baptism, however, a question of paramount importance to their Anabaptist and Baptist descendants, was evidently unimportant to the first Anabaptists, for they were baptized very simply with water from a dipper.[16]

In attempting to carry forward the work of reform the Anabaptists advocated the separation of church and state and its correlates, freedom of conscience and voluntary religious association. Christianity as a life of obedient discipleship, Christian brotherhood, love, and nonresistance were other teachings of the "Radical Reformation," as this movement came to be called. These latter, with the exception of nonresistance, were also taught by the other Reformers, although insufficiently, the Anabaptists claimed. The former principles, however, were innovations in that day. They were resisted first in Switzerland, where the movement began, then in Germany and elsewhere as it spread. The exemplary lives of many in the movement, however, and their missionary fervor enabled them to triumph over persecution. The principles of religious freedom and voluntary church association for which they contended won gradual acceptance in Europe and came to be written deeply into the foundation of American religious life. Anabaptism, long scorned by the mass of theological scholarship, has received new and appreciative appraisal in our time, as an impressive volume of literature has shown. There was much good in it, as we have seen. In some areas of the reforming church the Anabaptists were among the most Christlike spirits, and in certain convictions they were far ahead of their time.

The Anabaptist story has also another side. Many of its supporters were religious fanatics and troublemakers whose excesses stigmatized the movement as a whole. Bainton summarizes this less happy but intensely interesting and important side of the Radical Reformation as follows:

> Their genius and their experience lay in opposition. They were masters in the art of obstruction. They would shock the community by baptizing adults in the public fountain or by marching in procession through the streets of Zurich crying "Woe, Woe," and proclaiming that Zwingli was the dragon of the Apocalypse. Some in Holland like the later Quakers went naked as a sign in imitation of the prophet Isaiah. Some like Blaurock would interrupt public worship, and attempt to supplant the minister in his own pulpit. Summoned before a court, they might refuse to answer a word or they might wax denunciatory and call their examiners idolaters and heathen. Banished, the Anabaptists refused to stay away. Tortured, they endured without flinching. Executed, they died with a song. Even among themselves there were clashes because rival prophets claimed divergent inspirations from the Lord. And the ideal of perfection led not only to scrupulous self-criticism but also to censoriousness in regard to others. That people with such a temper should have been able to establish a stable community is indeed an amazing achievement.[17]

Their internal community life was also often one of strife and dissension. Bainton's sketch of one phase of the Anabaptist story is no isolated instance:

> In the Hutterian colony at Austerlitz quarrels at once commenced when Jacob Wiedemann selected husbands for the girls. The maidens murmured in spite of his remonstrance that if they did not consent the men would have to marry heathen girls. There were complaints that the children were being too severely disciplined. Positive schisms occurred because of personal rivalries. Räbel could not endure the leadership of Wiedemann and led a seceding group to Auschwitz. This group had as its head Simon Schützinger, when Jacob Huter arrived. He

too was a shepherd and now the community had two shepherds. The confusion was adjusted by making Simon a "shepherd" and Jacob an "apostle" with differentiation of function. But this arrangement was upset when it was rumored that the Schützingers had violated the rule of absolutely no property. Search was made and in their possession were discovered some extra shirts and four pieces of money. Frau Schützinger was consequently a Sapphira and her husband an Ananias. They had to do penance and he was, of course, deposed from the leadership of the community. But a certain Philip suspected that Jacob Huter had engineered this *coup* and therefore seceded. Then Huter received a call from the Lord to go out on the Great Commission which for him ended in martyrdom. Reconciliation was eventually achieved between the Hutterites and the Philipists and under the leadership of Peter Ridemann a spirit of healing prevailed.[18]

D. THE CALVINISTIC REFORMATION

The further reform that was needed to carry forward the good work begun by Luther could hardly have been that of the Anabaptists. Their Radical Reformation, in spite of all the good that can be said for it, was lacking in important details. Besides what has been said above, it was too negative in its attitude towards the state, society, and culture, and towards those outside its own select fellowship. Something else was needed beyond the conservative reformation of Luther and the Radical Reformation of the Anabaptists. This the sixteenth century achieved in the "Second Reformation," as that phase of reform has been called which came to have its center in Geneva. Chief among these second-generation Reformers was John Calvin, the most illustrious of the many in his nation who came to embrace the evangelical views.

Born in the year 1509 at Noyon, near Paris, Calvin received the best legal training of his day, was converted to Reformation views, and soon found it necessary to flee his native land. After a brief sojourn at Basel, where he wrote the first edition of the *Institutes of the Christian Religion,* he settled at Geneva, Switzerland. Evangelical teaching had already been accepted in Geneva, but reform still had far to go. For the rest of his life, except for three years that he was in Strasbourg, where he was associated with its fine-spirited Reformer Martin Bucer, Geneva was the scene of his labors; and Calvin turned it into one of the most remarkable centers of religious influence that the world has ever seen. Geneva became the model

and training center for many of the "Reformed" churches of the
second Protestant generation and Geneva was molded by John
Calvin.

In his characterization of Calvin, Fairbairn states that the Reformed Church

> bore indeed even more than the Lutheran the impress of a
> single mind; but then that mind was as typical of France and
> the second Protestant generation as Luther was typical of
> Germany and the first; and it had come by a very different
> process and way to the convictions which drove it into action.
> Calvin, like Zwingli, was a humanist before he became a
> Reformer, and what he was at first he never ceased to be. On
> the intellectual side, as a scholar and thinker, his affinities
> were with Erasmus, though on the religious side, they were
> rather with Luther; indeed, Calvin can hardly be better de-
> scribed than by saying that his mind was the mind of Erasmus,
> though his faith and conscience were those of Luther. He had
> the clear reason and the open vision of the one, but the
> religious fire and moral passion of the other. The conscience
> made the intellect constructive, the intellect made the con-
> science imperious—at once individual, architectonic, and col-
> lective. In Calvin the historical sense of the humanist, and the
> spiritual passion of the Reformer, are united; he knows the
> sacred literature which his reason has analysed, while his
> imagination has seen the Apostolic Church as an ideal which
> his conscience feels bound to realize.[19]

To this perceptive judgment we wish to add that Calvin also had
before his imagination the picture of the living God presented in the
Old Testament. The apostolic church was not the only ideal that his
conscience felt bound to realize; there was also the ideal of a whole
society of men worshipping and serving the one God in every area of
life. This vision from the Old Testament made a powerful impression
on the Reformer.

The story of Calvin's work has been told often. Briefly, it can be
classified under four topics: writing, preaching, lecturing, and administration. The first includes the *Institutes of the Christian Religion*, the commentaries on the books of the Bible, numerous theological treatises, liturgical writings, and his voluminous correspondence.

The amount and the quality of Calvin's writings are most remarkable in view of the many other demands made on his time. There is a
suggestion of what literary achievement might have been his, if he
had had any leisure during his residence in Geneva, in the quality of

his productions in his three years at Strasbourg. Although he was minister of the French church there and lectured on theology—he tells us that he lectured or preached every day—he yet had time to write the reply to Cardinal Sadoleto, perhaps his most outstanding work, as well as the commentary on Romans, the second Latin edition of the *Institutes*, and its French translation. As Luther was a master of the German tongue, more than any person molding it into a literary vehicle, Calvin shaped literary French and wielded a mighty pen, whose written product was graced by clarity, conviction, and power.

Because the proclamation of the Word of God is the first and most sacred duty of the church, Calvin was an active preacher. The French jurist Colladon, who settled in Geneva, informs us that Calvin "ordinarily preached every day every other week." From 1549 on, when a French refugee named Denis Raguenier took down Calvin's sermons as he preached, they were recorded and some of them were published. Raguenier and those who assisted him were skilled in shorthand and were aided by Calvin's asthma which made him speak slowly. Raguenier devoted all of his time to this occupation, writing the sermons out in full after each presentation.[20] The sermons had an unusual effect on those who heard them, and abroad "in Switzerland, France, England, and Scotland his words had an almost apostolic authority—the whispers of this gasping preacher had (to borrow a phrase from John Buchan) the authority of trumpets."[21]

Throughout his public career Calvin lectured regularly on books of the Bible. Many of his commentaries are composed almost entirely of these lectures recorded by secretaries.[22] With the opening of the Academy in 1559 students came from all over Europe to hear Calvin. From France and Germany, Hungary and Italy, England and Spain, Poland and the Netherlands they came, more than one thousand of them crowding the *auditoire* next to the Cathedral of St. Pierre to be instructed and inspired. Then they returned to their native lands carrying with them the lessons they had learned and enthusiasm for the model of reform that their own eyes had seen.

As an administrator Calvin was concerned with the ecclesiastical ordinances by which he sought to transform the life of the city of Geneva. One of his most important accomplishments, the ordinances were calculated to provide the discipline that would make church and city a model of reform. They were opposed by many but eventually, thanks in part to the large number of religious refugees coming into the city, they were accepted and even made more stringent as the city came increasingly under Calvin's power. The life of church, city, and individuals was regulated in a way that sounds strange to modern ears. Most of the populace tolerated that rule, however, and many came to cherish it when the changed character of the community became apparent.

Besides the ecclesiastical ordinances, which were directed particularly to the life of the church, Calvin was responsible for improvement and legislation in civic life in general. With its geographical location at one of the crossroads in Europe, Geneva had been an immoral and unsanitary city. Prostitution was finally eliminated after the guilty women were made to walk through the streets in a cap of shame and then banished from the city. If they returned they were liable to be drowned in the Rhone. Every house had to have latrine facilities and filth had to be kept from the streets. Inspectors were appointed for the city markets and unhealthy food had to be destroyed. Taverns of bad repute were closed and street-begging was abolished. A hospital and poorhouse were provided. Fires were not permitted in rooms without chimneys. A law required railed balconies around homes for the safety of children; police permission was required for the renting of rooms; and in many other ways municipal regulations circumscribed the lives of the people. There were efforts to provide work for every man. On December 29, 1544, Calvin spoke at length to the city council about the advisability of introducing the silk and cloth industry. Two months later he presented the four city syndics, or magistrates, funds to establish the new venture. An affirmative vote was given and the industry later became the foundation of the city's economy. Geneva's first dentist was not licensed until Calvin had personally tested his skill, McNeill informs us. Although his influence was great, there were occasions, even in his later years when his power was at its height, that the city council and the consistory of the church opposed him. He was no absolute dictator but a respected leader and advisor to the people.[23]

In his planning and administration of Geneva's school system, Calvin's greatness is most clearly seen. For, as Fairbairn has written, "with the insight of genius he perceived that the battle could be won, not by chance recruits, but only by a disciplined army; and, in order that the army might be created, he invented the discipline."[24] Earlier Fairbairn argues that Calvin was greater as a legislator than as a theologian, although he so construed the latter as to make the former "its logical and indeed inevitable outcome." Calvin's legislative powers, he opines, give him a chief place in the history of religion and of civilization.

A study of Calvin's work on behalf of education helps support Fairbairn's contention. In Geneva Calvin created the means whereby the future citizens were to be schooled, catechized, taught to sing Psalms, to believe in the kind of godly life that was set before them in precept and example, and to glorify their Creator whatever their calling in society might be. The excellence of the Genevan schools is attested by numerous scholars. Impartial critics, even persons opposed to Calvin's aims and his interpretation of religion, have acknowledged the uniqueness of the system and its general superiority. After it had been in existence for some years and the populace had come to recognize its effect on the educational level of the city, it was said with justifiable pride that the schoolboys there were so well trained in catechism that each was able to give a reason for his faith "like a doctor of the Sorbonne"; and it was frequently remarked that their training in Latin was so intensive and successful that each pupil who undertook the discipline knew his Latin "like a doctor of the Sorbonne."

The crown of Geneva's school system was the Academy, of which Theodore Beza was the head. On June 5, 1559 the Academy was formally instituted at a great service held in the cathedral. The statutes of the school, prepared by Calvin, were read; and the rector, Beza, and the professors were installed. Beza then presented an address, and Calvin as presiding officer closed the historic meeting with some remarks and prayer. Lectures in the Academy were on theological subjects, law, science, medicine, linguistics and literature. Theology reigned as "queen of the sciences." The success of the Academy was assured from the start. Nine hundred students from all over Europe constituted its first student body. Its historian, Charles Borgeaud, writes that with its establishment "Calvin had achieved his task; he had secured the future of Geneva. . .making it at once a church, a school and a fortress. It was the first stronghold of liberty in modern times."[25]

The overall aim of Calvin in his reforming activity was to transform men into servants of God. A prime reason that the Reformation was not being more successful, he felt, was that profession of the new faith did not always mean a changed life. Fairbairn expresses well the "master problem" before him: "How could the Church be made not simply an institution for the worship of God, but an agency for the making of men fit to worship him?"[26] His solution to this problem is one of history's great achievements and it has brought incalculable blessings to mankind.

Geneva became the fountain sending forth a stream of persons who were to carry the message of the Reformation to the corners of Europe and beyond. The total influence of that small city-state reformed can hardly be exaggerated. John Knox spent some time in Geneva and returned to Scotland to begin its transformation. English Protestantism was imbued with the spirit of Geneva and became a part of the Calvinistic Reformation. In 1549 Zurich, where Zwingli had begun the Swiss Reformation, adopted Calvin's view of the Lord's Supper, which differed from Zwingli's in retaining the mysticism that characterizes the biblical teaching. Soon thereafter most of Switzerland was won. The Rhineland was penetrated and the Palatinate became Reformed under the Elector Frederick III. Its famous university in the capital city of Heidelberg became a center of influence and the Heidelberg Catechism, published in 1563, became the Reformation's most widespread and best-loved creed.

Other German cities and states were won to the Reformed cause; and Bohemia, Moravia, Poland, and Hungary were all influenced. In Hungary the Reformation struck like a "thunderbolt," as one of its chroniclers records, and soon after the middle of the century that country had become Calvinistic. The Reformed Church made rapid strides in France for more than a decade. It threatened to capture the country but then was eclipsed after a long and bitter struggle whose heroic nature is surpassed only by its pathos. The Netherlands became Calvinistic under the stress of persecution when the nation rose against Philip II of Spain and the Duke of Alva, his representative. Its leader, William of Orange, accepted the Reformed faith in 1573. Beginning in 1575, when its first university was founded at Leyden as a thank offering for the deliverance of the city from a long Spanish siege, centers of learning were organized in the spirit of Geneva. In the seventeenth century these universities, at Leyden, Franeker, Utrecht, Groningen, and Harderwijk, became famous as citadels of Reformed theological scholarship and their influence was felt at home and abroad. Among the foreign students who were attracted to them were three thousand Hungarians who, during the next century and a half, made the long trek to Holland to study theology.

E. THE CONTINUING NECESSITY FOR RENEWAL

It is not our purpose in this book to survey the spread of the Reformation since the sixteenth century. Numerous authors have treated this history adequately. Our attempt in the following chapters to capture the spirit of the Reformed tradition will, of course, refer often to events that have taken place throughout the history in which the tradition developed. We shall consider such themes as the return of the Bible as a living witness, the restoration of the individual believer to his proper place in the life of the church, and the development of a scriptural doctrine of the role of the Christian in society. Underlying and giving meaning to all of these areas of reformation is the idea that continuing reform is necessary for the church.

The fathers of the church that was re-formed in the sixteenth century believed that the renewal of the church is a continuing necessity, for they took seriously the reality of sin and of its consequences within as well as outside the body of Christ. They were aware that scripture ever calls man to repentance and renewal, and their experience with Rome and its refusal to engage in the self-criticism it needed confirmed them in their belief. Refusing to absolutize their own position or to claim infallibility for the ecclesiastical structure they were permitted to build, the Reformers found perfection only in the church's head, Jesus Christ, and his Word. The "true church," they held, finds that Word profitable "for teaching, for reproof, for correction, and training in righteousness" (2 Tim. 3:16).

Believing as they did that the church must be conscious of its imperfection and need for renewal if it is to be faithful to Christ, some within the Reformed tradition used an interesting characterization of their church. They spoke of it as the *"ecclesia reformata quia semper reformanda est"* ("the church reformed because it must always be reforming"). There is an important truth here that is worth preserving. Human pride and proneness to error, the tendency to absolutize one's own position, and the failure to recognize one's own shortcomings are constant threats to spiritual vitality. The temptation for the church to become a religious establishment whose leaders become priests interested in personal position and the perpetuation of certain forms of religion instead of prophets dedicated to proclaim the Word that the Spirit gives them is perennial, especially where the institutional life of the church is highly developed. Establishment, institutionalism, bureaucracy are perversions of ecclesiastical life that plague every denomination.[27] Moreover, the values that receive priority among many in the church are evidence of a refined idolatry. The modern churchgoer is too sophisticated to worship relics or dumb idols; his gods are comfort, community status, a rich ecclesiastical and cultural heritage, sophistication, and the plush living made possible by modern science and an expanding economy. He may prate unctuously about sacrifice without any understanding of it. When the church recognizes these dangers it sees the need for grace from day to day, and an ancient admonition takes on fresh relevance:

> Fear the Lord, and serve him in sincerity and in faithfulness; put away the gods which your fathers served beyond the River, and in Egypt, and serve the Lord (Josh. 24:14).

Sometimes a national catastrophe is necessary before the church realizes its plight. When Hitler came to power a small group of leaders in the German church met to assess the situation. The declaration that came from that meeting affirmed that the church has only one God and that it only lives when it is called and sustained, comforted, and governed by that Lord from day to day. Those churchmen learned by experience the true character of the church and the necessity for it to strive to live daily by God's grace. They insisted that the church remember its calling in a world that opposes it, so that it might not lose its character as church. One of that number wrote:

> There are churches which retain a Christ-like form, a reverential reformed appearance, but their message is accommodated to human philosophy, and therefore, in spite of their reformed church order and in spite of their reformed church law, they are dead. . . .An accommodation of the church to the world is no renewal, but a destruction of the church.[28]

The church of God, and in particular the church that calls itself _Reformed,_ must ever remember the need for renewal. _Quia semper reformanda est:_ because it always needs reformation, is the way the fathers put it. The least and the best that their sons and daughters may seek is constant renewal through the Spirit of God. The tendency to despise the old landmarks characteristic of some modern theology and church life; an unreasoned clinging to certain traditions so that they become a fetish; a dead orthodoxy in which one has a form of godliness but in reality denies its power—these and other weaknesses, some of them mentioned previously, witness to the church's need to remember its true character. Particularly where the church claims to be "reformed" it should exert itself to overcome imperfection. In all its members it must strive, says the apostle,

> until we all attain to the unity of the faith and of the knowledge of the Son of God, to mature manhood, to the measure of the stature of the fulness of Christ (Eph. 4:13).

Wherever Christians consider themselves to have arrived at their goal and so resist the demand for continuing renewal, they share the fatal weakness against which Luther and Calvin protested with all their might. They have lost the vision that made them a *Church of Jesus Christ Reformed According to the Word of God,* and, no longer reforming, have forfeited the right to be called Reformed.

NOTES TO CHAPTER I

[1] Roland H. Bainton, *Here I Stand* (New York: Abingdon, 1950), p. 33. The following quotations from Luther are taken from Gordon Rupp, *The Righteousness of God* (London: Hodder and Stoughton, 1953), pp. 103f., 111, 121f.

[2] Karl Holl in *Gesammelte Aufsätze zur Kirchengeschichte*, quoted by Rupp, *op. cit.*, p. 128.

[3] *Op. cit.*, p. 72.

[4] *Ibid.,* p. 71.

[5] Quoted by Ernest G. Schwiebert, *Luther and His Times* (St. Louis: Concordia, 1950), p. 310.

[6] *Op. cit.*, p. 79.

[7] A. F. Pollard, *The Cambridge Modern History* (Cambridge: The University Press, 1934), Vol. II, p. 208.

[8] *The Cambridge Modern History*, Vol. II, pp. 345f. G. W. Bromiley speaks about the "pronounced humanistic colouring" of Zwingli's doctrine of God, *Zwingli and Bullinger, The Library of Christian Classics,* Vol. XXIV (London: SCM, 1953), p. 241; and Gottfried W. Locher, *Die Theologie Huldrich Zwinglis im Lichte seiner Christologie* (Zurich: Zwingli Verlag, 1952), interprets Zwingli less humanistically and more christologically.

[9] This side of Luther is depicted by Philip Schaff, *History of the Christian Church*, 2d ed., rev. (New York: Scribners, 1910), Vol. VII, pp. 654ff.

[10] Pollard, *loc. cit.,* p. 209.

[11] *Loc. cit.*, p. 343.

[12] Schaff, *loc. cit.,* p. 657. A contemporary Lutheran scholar writes similarly: "The Lutheran Church stands closer to the Catholic Church in the doctrine of the Sacrament of the Altar than to the Reformed. And that is true not only for the doctrine of the Lord's Supper of Zwingli, but also that of Calvin." Hermann Sasse, *Was heisst Lutherisch?* (Munich: Kaiser Verlag, 1934), p. 96.

[13] *Loc. cit.,* p. 735.

[14] Harold S. Bender, "The Anabaptist Vision," in *The Recovery of the Anabaptist Vision*, ed. Guy F. Hershberger (Scottdale, Pennsylvania: Herald, 1957), p. 41. Cf. Leonard Verduin, *The Reformers and Their Stepchildren* (Grand Rapids: Eerdmans, 1964).

[15] Fritz Blanke, "Anabaptism and the Reformation," in Hershberger, *op. cit.,* p. 60.

[16] A. H. Newman, *A History of Anti-Pedobaptism* (Philadelphia: American Baptist Publication Society, 1897), p. 107. Cf. William R. Estep, *The Anabaptist Story* (Nashville: Broadman, 1963), p. 32. In later Anabaptist history the mode of baptism became an issue. See, e.g., Ernst Crous, "German Mennonites," in Hershberger, *op. cit.,* p. 242.

[17] "The Anabaptist Contribution to History," Hershberger, *op. cit.,* p. 322.

[18] *Ibid.*

[19] Fairbairn, *loc. cit.,* p. 349.

[20] Of at least forty-four volumes of sermons in manuscript in Geneva at the beginning of the eighteenth century twelve remain! There were 2,304 sermons listed in Raguenier's catalog, not counting the sermons on I Kings and Hebrews, the number of which is unknown. Of these 2,304 sermons there are now only about 680 known plus the 780 sermons published during Calvin's lifetime or shortly after his death, making about 1,460 that have come down to us. Adding the sermons on I Kings and Hebrews it is estimated that about 1,000 have been lost. Bernard Gagnebin, "L'histoire des Manuscripts des Sermons de Calvin," *Supplementa Calviniana* (Neukirchen: Verlag der Buchhandlung des Erziehungsvereins, 1961), pp. XXV-XXVIII. After tracing what is known of the history of the manuscripts and their careless handling Gagnebin understandably describes it as "unbelievable and lamentable." Professor Barnabas Nagy has showed me in Budapest his preparation for publication of the sermons preached on the prophecy of Ezekiel. There are 1,000 pages written in a fine hand by at least twenty different persons who collaborated in this work under Raguenier's direction.

[21] T. H. L. Parker, *The Oracles of God* (London: Lutterworth, 1947), p. 44.

[22] John T. McNeill, *The History and Character of Calvinism* (New York: Oxford, 1954), p. 195.

[23] *Ibid.,* pp. 178-200. Cf. Schaff, *op. cit.,* Vol. VIII, pp. 464, 494.

[24] *Loc. cit.,* p. 370.

[25] Quoted by McNeill, *op. cit.,* p. 196.

[26] *Loc. cit.,* p. 364.

[27] Lewis B. Smedes, "The Establishment," *Reformed Journal,* XV (February 1965).

[28] Wilhelm Niesel, *Was heisst reformiert?* (Munich: Kaiser Verlag, 1934), p. 24.

II

ecclesia reformata

A. THE REFORMED CHURCH

We have already indicated that the name "Reformed" is used to characterize the church that has been renewed by the Spirit of God. It does not refer primarily to personal conversion or renewal, to a way of life, or to a type of Christian person or community. It is important to note this, because "Reformed" has been used so loosely. In his study of the meaning of the word Niesel claims that it has become a word void of meaning, citing as proof the claim of Schleiermacher, the father of theological liberalism, to be a theologian "descended entirely from the Reformed school of thought."[1] *Reformed* means church, and it means church that has been renewed according to the Word of God.

It is appropriate at this stage of our discussion to consider the church, in view of the esteem in which the Reformers, particularly Calvin, held this institution and the place they gave it in their thinking. It is especially appropriate that emphasis be placed on the church as such in a day like our own, when in wide areas there is little appreciation for the church as the body of Christ in the world.

The reasons for the inadequate consideration given the church in much Christian thought are the extreme positions taken by theological liberalism on the one hand and by a significant segment of contemporary fundamentalism on the other. Liberalism, as Anders Nygren has said, viewed the church as "an organization, a human society, a sociological phenomenon. The categories employed—for instance the distinction between *Gemeinschaft* and *Gesellschaft*

37

(community and society)—fit well in the context of sociology but not dogmatics."[2] A definition of the church that illustrates Nygren's point is given by William Adams Brown. After stating that classical liberalism neglected the doctrine of the church and tended to substitute for it the application of the social gospel to society, he offers his own definition:

> The Church is the instrument which preserves and hands down the common symbols through which the conception of God in which Jesus himself believed finds its most significant expression. It is the fellowship through which men become conscious of their intimate relationship with one another, through their experience of a unity which transcends difference. It is the experiment station in which there is being worked out in the relation between different kinds of Christians the way of life that must obtain among all men everywhere if the Kingdom of God is ever to come on earth. Finally, it is the place through which by renewed contact with the great personalities in whom the Christian religion took its rise, the individual may receive the dynamic which alone can give vitality to the social gospel.[3]

Whereas theological liberalism had an aversion to the supernatural and was inclined to see the church as a mere sociological phenomenon, one wing of fundamentalism emphasized the individual's relationship to God at the expense of consideration of the church as a social institution. In large areas of American Protestantism, fundamentalism became un- if not anti-denominational. Its attention was focused on matters of personal salvation and it sought to break completely with the older "apostate" churches, which it believed had compromised the biblical revelation. As the pendulum swung far to the right, groups of believers in multitudes of communities organized "churches," "assemblies," "gospel halls," and Christian fellowships under a variety of names. Many of these groups boasted that they had no membership lists and otherwise sought to keep themselves free from the appearance of a social club, which was all that the "church" down the street seemed to them to resemble.

The Reformed Church sets itself resolutely against both these extremes. Over against theological liberalism it declares the church to be a supernatural phenomenon built upon and by Jesus Christ, God incarnate, and living by his grace from day to day. Over against extreme fundamentalism it declares the reality of the one, holy, catholic and apostolic church, which is in the world and yet is not of the world. Reformed theology reminds liberalism that the church is the body of *Christ;* it would remind fundamentalism that the church is his *body*, which should be cherished and honored as such.

B. THE CATHOLICITY OF THE CHURCH

The dictum of Cyprian in the third century, *extra ecclesiam nulla salus*—outside the church there is no salvation—is taken with utter seriousness in the Reformed tradition, both in the manner in which the doctrine of the church is understood and in the important place given that doctrine. The Reformed Church conceives of the church as the Apostles' Creed expresses it, as "the holy, catholic church," or as the Nicene Creed reads, "one holy catholic and apostolic church."

That the Reformed Church took seriously the characterizations of the church found in those ancient creeds is evident from a study of its confessional statements written during the Reformation period. For example, the first article on the church in the Belgic Confession carries the caption *De Ecclesia Catholica*: Of the Catholic Church. It reads as follows:

> We believe and profess one catholic or universal Church, which is a holy congregation of true Christian believers, all expecting their salvation in Jesus Christ, being washing by His blood, sanctified and sealed by the Holy Spirit.
>
> This Church has been from the beginning of the world, and will be to the end thereof; which is evident from this, that Christ is an eternal King, which without subjects he cannot be. And this holy Church is preserved or supported by God against the rage of the whole world; though it sometimes for a while appear very small, and in the eyes of men to be reduced to nothing; as during the perilous reign of Ahab the Lord reserved unto him seven thousand men, who had not bowed their knees to Baal. Furthermore, this holy Church is not confined, bound, or limited to a certain or to certain persons, but is spread and dispersed over the whole world: and yet is joined and united with heart and will, by the power of faith, in one and the same spirit (Art. 27).

The next article quotes with approval Cyprian's statement that there is no salvation outside the church, and expounds the biblical doctrine of the catholicity of the church; the Heidelberg Catechism defines the church similarly as one organism gathered out of the whole human race throughout the entire history of the world (Q. 54). The Scotch Confession speaks of the church as the spouse of its one head, Jesus Christ, "which Church is catholic, that is universal, because it contains the elect of all the ages."[4] The Westminster Confession likewise specifically mentions the church as "Catholic," and the Second Helvetic Confession bears the title: *Confession and Simple Exposition of the Orthodox Faith, and of the Catholic Doctrine of the Pure Christian Religion.* Chapter 17, which deals with the church, has the caption: "Of the Catholic and Holy Church of God, and of the One Only Head of the Church." The fathers of the Hungarian Reformed Church named their confession simply *Confessio Catholica*—Catholic Confession—and their polemicist during the Counter-Reformation, Alvinczy, gave his chief work the significant title *Itinerarium Catholicum*—Catholic Itinerary.

This point of the catholicity of the church must be stressed because of widespread ignorance or misunderstanding of the nature of the church according to the Reformed confession. In the New Testament the church is present wherever believers assemble in the name of the Lord. The apostle Paul wrote to "the church of God which is at Corinth," to the church in Thessalonica, to the churches in Galatia, or some other place. In each instance it is the body of Christ to which he addresses himself. Whether it be few in members, or large, it is the church. There is only one church and, as Calvin says, it "is called 'catholic,' or 'universal,' because there could not be two or three churches unless Christ be torn asunder—which cannot happen! (*Inst.*, IV. i. 2). Calvin so emphasizes this truth throughout his writings that he may properly be called the most catholic of the fathers of the church in the Reformation era. He felt it to be so important that he included it in a catechism written for children.[5] In answer to the question why the church is called "catholic" or universal, the Geneva Catechism reads: "This signifies that as there is only one head of the faithful so also all ought to be united in one body; so that there are not many churches, but only one, which is spread throughout the world" (Eph. 4:3; 1 Cor. 12:12, 27).[6]

The Reformed creeds, particularly the Second Helvetic Confession, which is more extensive than the others, stress that in spite of the divisions within the church militant the church is one and that the many particular churches "must all be referred to the unity of the Catholic Church."[7] Indeed, the Reformation was needed and continues to be needed because of the lack of catholicity in the church. The Reformers' work was necessary because the church had become too "Roman" in some areas, and too "Greek" in others. The church was no longer "catholic," or universal, in its breadth, outlook, and teachings, but had become provincial and errant. The Reformers sought to restore it to true catholicity.

The need for a restoration of the consciousness of the catholicity of the church remains among us. We need to be reminded that although the church in a particular area receives much from its environment, ideally there is no "Anglican" church or "Dutch" church, no "Eastern" church or "Western" church. Throughout the world there is only one church built on the one foundation "of the apostles and prophets, Christ Jesus himself being the chief corner-stone" (Eph. 2:20). Tempted to conform to cultural patterns around it, that one church, wherever it is found, ever needs to be reminded of its catholicity.

Although this doctrine is written clearly into the creeds and history of the Reformed Church and is a chief feature of its profoundly biblical ecclesiology, it is inadequately understood in areas of the Reformed Church today. The result is a sectarian conception of the church that is in sharp contrast to the broad catholic doctrine held by Calvin and other Reformed fathers. There are many evidences of this narrower conception of the church that might be mentioned. We shall consider only one of these. It is the view held by some zealous Christians that theirs is the only true church in their environment, or that the members of their church are superior to Christians in other churches. In consequence it is held that Christians may be members of these *other* churches but not of *our* church until they have met certain requirements for church membership over and above the requirements of the *other* churches. Confession of faith in Christ and a promise to serve him are insufficient. In addition there must be subscription to a number of other regulations in order to acquire, or retain, membership. These other regulations may have to do with attendance at certain amusements, membership in certain organizations, or the promise to follow a particular pattern of Christian life. If agreement is lacking, prospective members are invited, either explicitly or implicitly, to look for another church home. Their faith in Christ is not questioned; but they are not the kind of Christians desired in the congregation, at least by its officers.

Admittedly, faith in Christ implies obeying him and accepting a life of Christian discipline. As faith apart from works is dead, so confession of faith without acceptance of its implications is impossible. When, however, a congregation through its officers denies membership to one whom it believes to be a Christian because he will not or may not conform to its particular code of behavior, or because he is of another social class or race, that congregation shows that it holds a conception of the church which is uncatholic, sectarian, and un-Reformed. It believes that the candidate for membership is a Christian, that is, that he has been incorporated into Christ, and that by consequence he is a member of the holy catholic church, but it refuses him admission into *its* membership. It thereby demonstrates that it considers itself to be something other than the one holy catholic church of Christ.

The Reformed fathers would contest this inadequate view of the church most vigorously. The Reformed Church is not a sect, nor is it just one among several possible types of churches. Its conception of itself must never be anything less than that it is the one holy catholic and apostolic church. It is catholic because there is only one church, the church of which Jesus Christ is the head, and it is apostolic because it has direct continuity with the church of the first centuries and holds the apostolic doctrines. It is indeed built upon the foundation of the apostles and prophets with Jesus Christ himself its chief cornerstone.

In insisting that the conditions for church membership should be repentance and faith in Jesus Christ as Savior and Lord without extrabiblical requirements, there is no intention of suggesting that matters of Christian behavior and the multitude of problems of which every board of elders is aware are of little consequence. Many of them are, and they should be dealt with by the ministers and the elders of the church. This is the meaning of church discipline, and without it a congregation cannot be healthy. The point of this discussion is that it is dangerous to make these "other" matters a condition for membership when once the officers of a congregation are satisfied as to the genuineness of the confession of faith. The hope and expectation is that as the Christian grows in grace in the fellowship of the church and under the counsel of its spiritual leaders, that which is undesirable will fall away. In the Reformed Church, which is nothing other than the holy catholic church, the requirement for membership is the same as it was in the days of the apostles or as it is in any branch of Christendom when the gospel is proclaimed, repentance toward God and faith in the Lord Jesus Christ.[8]

A popular notion is that a congregation must be a pure church in order to be a true church, and one occasionally hears this idea expressed in discussions of conditions for membership or other aspects of ecclesiastical discipline. The marks of the church are the preaching of "the pure doctrine of the gospel," "the pure administration of the sacraments," and the proper exercise of "church discipline." However, the church reminds her members in the Westminster Confession of Faith that this catholic Church hath been sometimes more, sometimes less visible. And particular Churches, which are members thereof, are more or less pure, according as the doctrine of the gospel is taught and embraced, ordinances administered, and public worship performed more or less purely in them. The purest churches under heaven are subject both to mixture and error; and some have so degenerated as to become no Churches of Christ, but synagogues of Satan. Nevertheless, there shall be always a Church on earth to worship God according to his will.[9]

Calvin argues the same eloquently. When we urge the necessity of the purity of the Word and sacrament in the true church, he avers, we need not infer that the church must be faultless to retain communion with her. It is even possible, he continues, that "some fault may creep into the administration of either doctrine or sacraments, but this ought not to estrange us from communion with the church." The reason for this judgment is that not all articles of our religion are of equal importance. Some are necessary, he goes on to say, such as that "God is one; Christ is God and the Son of God; our salvation rests in God's mercy; and the like. Among the churches there are other articles of doctrines disputed which still do not break the unity of faith." These others he calls "non-essential matters" which "should in no wise be the basis of schism among Christians" (*Inst.*, IV. i. 12).

Calvin continues to develop his point by insisting that Christians must not expect a flawless church in this world, but must love and honor the church in which God has placed them. Agreeing with the purists that it would be well if the situation in the church were other than it is, he presents them, nevertheless, with the judgment of the apostle concerning the church at Corinth. There more than a few had strayed; infection had seized almost all; there were many sins, some of them dreadful crimes; and there was corruption of both morals and doctrine. But what is the response of Paul? Does he pull out? Does he exclude them from the Kingdom or anathematize them?

He not only does nothing of the sort; he even recognizes and proclaims them to be the church of Christ and the communion of saints! Among the Corinthians quarrels, divisions, and jealousies flare; disputes and altercations burgeon together with greed; an evil deed is openly approved which even pagans would detest; the name of Paul (whom they ought to have honored as a father) is insolently defamed; some mock the resurrection of the dead, to the destruction of the whole gospel as well; God's free gifts serve ambition, not love; and many things are done without decency or order. Yet the church abides among them because the ministry of Word and sacraments remains unrepudiated there. Who, then, would dare snatch the title "church" from these who cannot be charged with even a tenth part of such misdeeds? (*Inst.*, **IV**. i. 14).

If these words of Calvin had been taken seriously by his disciples, the Reformed Church, often rent by schism, would have been spared many a heartache.

C. THE CHURCH OF CHRIST

In spite of its imperfection and impurity the church is united in Jesus Christ its head. That makes it a *holy* catholic church, for Christ is a holy Savior. He is the Son of God as well as the Son of Man, and all the treasures of heavenly grace are found in him. One with God so that all power is his and one with man in a complete identification, Christ is the sole mediator. As all things were made through him, so all blessings of revelation and redemption have come through him whom Christians know as Lord. As the Lord and Savior of all who believe, he is faith's center and the one in whom the church finds its meaning. That is why one cannot speak about the church apart from Christ who created it, who washed it in his own blood, and who governs and protects it until he presents it to God the Father. This sharp accent on Jesus Christ lies at the heart of the Reformed tradition and is the foundation of its ecclesiology.

The numerous figures used to describe the church of Christ in the New Testament are rich and varied, but none by itself is adequate. Paul Minear lists ninety-six of them, and shows that none of them dominates the scene.[10] He points out that a proper understanding of them requires at least three types of thinking: (1) *synoptic,* embracing all the images at once; (2) *reciprocal,* thinking "one image into another, to make them almost yet not quite interchangeable, and see how the same meanings flow back and forth from one idiom to the other"; and (3) *retroactive,* or depth thinking, trying to recover the mind of the author when he used the image.[11] All point beyond themselves to that which they signify, the one great reality, the single magnitude that the New Testament designates as the church of Jesus Christ. The greater the number of pointers to that reality, the better our understanding of it becomes.

The metaphors used are often confused:

Paul, for example, could intentionally garble the figure of the body by combining it in a single paragraph with the figures of building, planting, nation, table, and temple. And John could without apparent incongruity visualize the bride, as a city, a temple, a mother, a virgin, and a choir. [12]

Minear then asks the reason for this "literary brigandage, this artistic melange," and answers that it "was made possible by a common perception of a reality that embraced all the images." [13] Whereas Geddes MacGregor has affirmed that the description of the church as "the body of Christ" is most appropriate because of the significance attached to this "root metaphor" in the New Testament, and that it is particularly appropriate in Reformed ecclesiology where it expresses what is "fundamentally important," [14] Minear would question that judgment. The description of the church as "light," for example, "is even more ubiquitous and more subtly influential." The fact is that it is wrong to set these images over against each other, inasmuch as they all point to the same reality and constantly run into each other. [15] In its importance in human history the church stands unique. It is unique because it is the church of the Lord Jesus Christ. That is why no human description is adequate to express it.

D. THE MARKS OF THE CHURCH

The church is not only an organism, a fellowship of believers united to Christ, but it is also an institution in society. Like other social institutions it has certain distinguishing characteristics. These have been called its "marks." Against the background of the controversies of the sixteenth century, the Belgic Confession declared these to be the pure preaching of the gospel, the administration of the sacraments as instituted by Christ, and the proper exercise of church discipline. Where these were in evidence the church was called a "true church"; where they were not it was called a "false church" or a "sect" (Art. 29).

It is quite conceivable that these three are not the only "marks" of the true church today, that there may be others, such as obedience to Christ's command to witness to all men. But these three are the "marks" that were written in the confessional statements and that have come down to us. Hence, they have acquired an important place in discussions about the church, and we shall treat them here.

The Reformed creeds, as we have seen, recognize the imperfect and relative character of the church in this world, yet they insist that she give evidence of being the bride of Christ. Her character must be consistent with her calling and the gift of the Holy Spirit.

(1) *The church must preach the gospel.* By preaching is meant the verbal proclamation of the gospel, or good news, given in the Word of God. Although preaching most commonly takes place on Sunday in a building called a church, it may occur at any time, any place, and under almost any circumstances. Its identification with a certain place one day a week is unfortunate. One would think that this "key" that Christ has given the church could be used more imaginatively.

There are those who scoff at the practice of preaching. Other aspects of the church's ministry may make sense to them but this one seems futile. The Jews may require signs and the Greeks wisdom, but the church preaches "Christ crucified, a stumbling block to the Jews and folly to Gentiles, but to those who are called, both Jews and Greeks, Christ the power of God and the wisdom of God" (1 Cor. 1:22ff.). The reason for this requirement is that it pleases God "through the folly of what we preach to save those who believe" (1 Cor. 1:21). To the mind of the "natural man," whom the apostle mentions in the context, preaching may seem foolish and futile, but unto those who are saved it is "the power of God" (1 Cor. 1:18).

The Reformers restored preaching to the place it had occupied in the early church. Luther began preaching when he was still in the monastery at Erfurt. Then, however, his sermons were given in Latin. Later he changed the form of his preaching to an exposition of scripture delivered in German, the language of the people. For him biblical preaching was the veritable Word of God, whose significance could not be overestimated. Calvin and the Zurich Reformers, Zwingli and Bullinger, held preaching in the same high regard, and the abundance of their pulpit performances confirms their express teaching to this effect. They are representative of the general attitude of the Reformers to this mark of the church. T. H. L. Parker writes,

> In England, France, and Scotland, as well as in Germany and Switzerland, the preaching of the Word was recognized as being the primary task of the ministry. The Mass was dethroned from its usurped reign in the Church, and the sermon was installed in its place. The pulpit, instead of the altar, became the central point in the Lutheran, Calvinist, and Anglican Churches. Preaching was bound to the Scriptures, both in form and in substance. The purpose of preaching, the Re-

formers held, was to lay bare and interpret the Word of God in
the Scriptures. Hence they set up the Scriptures as the criterion by which all their preaching must be judged. Preaching
was the hand-maiden of the eternal Word which God had once
"uttered" and which was witnessed to by the words of the
Prophets and Apostles.[16]

Professor A. A. van Ruler has pointed out an oversimplification in
the above statement. The sermon in the churches of the Reformation did not take the place of the mass in worship, for the liturgical
office of the Lord's Supper held an important place in their worship
also. Some of the Reformation churches continued the practice of a
weekly celebration and, while those who most closely followed
Calvin's teaching were not among these, it is well known that Calvin
himself favored weekly Communion. Nevertheless, it remains true
that preaching was magnified in the Reformed Church, even, on
occasion, at the expense of the rest of worship.[17] One effect of this
development was that the benefit received from church attendance
came to be determined too much by the quality of the sermon.
While the Reformers intended to restore the Word of God to a
central place in the service, they did not intend this. Nevertheless it
is true that the minister was *verbi divini minister*, whose first task
was to expound the Word.

> The Reformed minister was essentially a preacher, intellec-
> tual, exegetical, argumentative, seriously concerned with the
> subjects that most appealed to the serious-minded. Modern
> oratory may be held to begin with him, and indeed to be his
> creation. He helped to make the vernacular tongues of Western
> Europe literary. He accustomed the people to hear the gravest
> and most sacred themes discussed in the language which they
> knew and the themes ennobled the language, the language was
> never allowed to degrade the themes.[18]

To cite one more authority on the importance of preaching in the
Reformed Church in the Reformation era, I refer to a work of the
best-known contemporary Dutch historian, Pieter Geyl, a critic who
has no bias towards the Christian Church. Speaking of the Reformed
Church in the Netherlands, he writes:

> In the Reformed cult the sermon, along with psalm-singing,
> counted for everything. . . .The preachers up and down the
> country expounded to the congregations that Biblical view of
> life which taught the Reformed to look upon themselves as the
> chosen people, as the New Israel. This concept became a
> source of confidence and courage to them, and on it they built

up their strong and narrow national sentiment. The influence
which was thus exercised by the Reformed ministry cannot
easily be overestimated.[19]

(2) *The second "mark" of the church is the administration of the
sacraments as instituted by Christ.* These two, Word and sacraments,
are the means of grace used by the Holy Spirit, who creates faith "in
our hearts by the preaching of the holy gospel, and confirms it by
the use of the holy Sacraments" (Heid. Cat., Q. 65).

From the beginning God gave his people, in addition to the
spoken word, "mystical symbols, or holy rites, or sacred actions
consisting of his Word, of outward signs, and of things signified."[20]
Through their use he reminds his church of his gifts of grace and
confirms his promises. He portrays and seals in an outward, visible
manner the blessings he has given his people, and through them and
the Holy Spirit who accompanies them he strengthens their faith.

Under the new government that Christ instituted, the sacraments
are baptism and the Lord's Supper. Throughout church history there
has been disagreement as to the number of sacraments. In the
centuries preceding the Reformation there had been much confusion
in teaching and practice with respect to the sacraments. Bernard of
Clairvaux, one of the greatest figures in the Middle Ages, listed ten
sacraments; Hugo of St. Victor, another leading theologian, had
thirty; and the Third Lateran Council (1179) included the investi-
ture of bishops and the burial of the dead among them. Finally, the
number seven was settled upon and ingenious arguments were used
to make that number appear correct. Seven was declared to be a
holy number, and the seven sacraments were thought to correspond
with the seven virtues and the seven deadly sins, and also to unite
the number of the Godhead (three) and the number that was said to
stand for the creation (four), thus illustrating the union of God and
man.

The Reformers, examining theory and practice in the light of
scripture, swept aside these and other accretions to the gospel and
proclaimed that the only sacraments of the church were those
instituted by its Lord and that both, baptism and the Lord's Supper,
are divine pledges that signify and seal redemption from sin by Jesus
Christ.

> I say that Christ is the matter or (if you prefer) the substance
> of all the sacraments; for in him they have all their firmness,
> and they do not promise anything apart from him. . . . The
> sacraments have the same office as the Word of God: to offer

and set forth Christ to us, and in him the treasures of heavenly grace (*Inst.*, IV. xiv. 16, 17).

To show their belief that both sacraments find their meaning in the cross of Christ and our redemption thereby, the authors of the Heidelberg Catechism phrased the sixty-ninth and seventy-fifth questions as follows:

> How does holy Baptism remind and assure you that the one sacrifice of Christ on the cross avails for you?

> How are you reminded and assured in the holy Supper that you participate in the one sacrifice of Christ on the cross and in all his benefits?

Baptism in the Reformed tradition is understood to mean cleansing from sin through the blood of Christ and union with him, regeneration and the gift of the Holy Spirit, and the covenant relationship God has established with his people. Each of those significations is meaningful, but the only one on which we shall comment here is the last. We mention it because of its importance to the doctrine of the church and the inclusion of little children among the candidates for baptism, both of which are accented in the Reformed tradition.

John Calvin rediscovered the fact that the church is new Israel, the covenant people of God. God has a people under both covenants and the writings of the New Testament make abundantly clear that there is direct continuity between the two. When God established his covenant with Abraham he made it clear that he intended eventually to include the Gentile nations. His promise to Abraham included the assurance that in him all the families of the earth would be blessed (Gen. 12:3). When the apostle Paul wrote to the Galatians he recalled that promise and wrote,

> So you see that it is men of faith who are the sons of Abraham. And the scripture, foreseeing that God would justify the Gentiles by faith, preached the gospel beforehand to Abraham, saying, "In thee shall all the nations be blessed." So then, those who are men of faith are blessed with Abraham who had faith. . . .Christ redeemed us. . .that in Christ Jesus the blessings of Abraham might come upon the Gentiles, that we might receive the promise of the Spirit through faith. . . . For as many of you as were baptized into Christ have put on Christ. There is neither Jew nor Greek. . .if you are Christ's, then you are Abraham's offspring, heirs according to promise (Gal. 3:7-9, 13f., 27-29).

Paul teaches the continuity of the two covenants through the figure of the olive tree. Some of the branches, the Jews, were broken off, while others, Gentiles, were grafted in. The tree itself, spanning both dispensations, the old covenant as well as the new, is the continuing community of those who know and serve God (Rom. 11:17-24). Jesus' parable of the wicked husbandmen teaches the same truth. Its climax is Jesus' ringing word to the Jewish leaders, "The kingdom of God shall be taken away from you and given to a nation producing the fruits of it" (Matt. 21:33-46). That nation—or people, as the word may be rendered—can be none other than the Christian church, which is now God's covenant community. The new covenant, that is, the new form of the old covenant made with Abraham, has been established with it.

In Jeremiah 31:31-34 God promises that he will make a new covenant with his ancient people. The author of Hebrews quotes that passage to teach that that covenant, *promised to Israel*, has been given to the church (Heb. 8:7-12). The only possible conclusion is that the author understood the church to be the new Israel. And why should he not reason thus? Jesus had instituted the Holy Supper the night before his crucifixion with the words, "This is my blood of the covenant, which is poured out for many for the forgiveness of sins" (Matt. 26:28); the author of Hebrews says that he is "the mediator of a new covenant" (Heb. 9:15; cf. 7:22; 12:24); and Paul reminds the Corinthians that Christ has made them "ministers of a new covenant" (2 Cor. 3:6). The point is that the biblical writers were well aware that a new form of the old covenant made with Abraham had been promised *to Israel.* Yet they claim that it has been given to the disciples of the Lord Jesus, or in other words, to his church. The church then is the Israel of this age.

This teaching is found throughout the New Testament, and it is fundamental to the doctrine of the church. Ephesians 2:11-22 speaks of the "dividing wall of hostility" that had once separated Jews and Gentiles, which has been broken. Gentiles are no longer

> alienated from the commonwealth of Israel, and strangers to the covenants of promise, . . .no longer strangers and sojourners, but . . . fellow citizens with the saints and members of the household of God, built upon the foundation of the apostles and prophets, Christ Jesus himself being the chief cornerstone, in whom the whole structure is joined together and grows into a holy temple in the Lord.

That temple is the holy catholic church. There is a continuous line of spiritual descent, then, from Abraham to believers today. Believers today are the Israel of this age.

The implications of this teaching are clear. Because the Reformed Church believes this to be a teaching of its Lord, it must seek to live as "a people of his own who are zealous for good deeds" (Titus 2:14). Many of the promises given old Israel are fulfilled in the new Israel, the church. Furthermore, in Reformed teaching, children are a part of the family of God today as they were under the old covenant. The Second Helvetic Confession well asks concerning children, "Inasmuch as they are included in God's Church and covenant, 'Why, then, should not the sign of the covenant of God be given to them? Why should they not be consecrated by holy baptism, who are God's peculiar people and are in the Church of God?' "

The practice of baptizing in the Reformed Church follows from its doctrine that the church is the new Israel. As the people of God under the old covenant comprised believers *and their children*, the people of God under the new covenant include the same. The Reformed understanding of the church and the doctrine of infant baptism go together. Others may consider their children to be outside the church of God—which they consider to be the fellowship of believers only—until they arrive at years of discretion and can make their own profession of faith. But the Reformed Church includes the lambs in the flock and considers them to have certain rights and privileges by virtue of their covenant relationship to God. It hears Jesus say, "Let the children come to me, do not hinder them; for to such belongs the kingdom of God" (Mark 10:14). Its teacher, Calvin, writes,

> For when we consider that immediately from birth God takes and acknowledges them as his children, we feel a strong stimulus to instruct them in earnest fear of God and observance of the Law (*Inst.*, IV. xvi. 32).

And another of the fathers of the Reformed Church has written:

> Here certainly appears the extraordinary love of our God, in that as soon as we are born, and just as we come from our mother, he hath commanded us to be solemnly brought from her bosom, as it were, into his own arms, that he should bestow upon us, in the very cradle, the tokens of our dignity and future kingdom. . . .that, in a word, he should join us to himself in the most solemn covenant from our tender years: the remembrance of which as it is glorious and full of consola-

tion to us, so in like manner it tends to promote Christian virtues and the strictest holiness, through the whole course of our lives.[21]

The Reformed conception of the church as new Israel and the inclusion of children in it has implications for the life of the family, for the theory of education, and for the attitude of parents towards their little ones. There is profound theology in the seventeenth-century cradle-song:

> Whilst thus thy lullaby I sing,
> For thee great blessings ripening be;
> Thine eldest brother is a King,
> And hath a kingdom bought for thee.
> > Sweet baby, then forbear to weep;
> > Be still, my babe; sweet baby, sleep.
>
> When God with us was dwelling here,
> In little babes he took delight;
> Such innocents as thou, my dear!
> Are ever precious in His sight.
> > Sweet baby, then forbear to weep;
> > Be still, my babe; sweet baby, sleep.
>
> A little infant once was He,
> And strength in weakness then was laid
> Upon His virgin mother's knee,
> That power to thee might be convey'd.
> > Sweet baby, then forbear to weep;
> > Be still, my babe; sweet baby, sleep.
>
> The wants that He did then sustain,
> Have purchased wealth, my babe, for thee;
> And by His torments and His pain,
> Thy rest and ease secured be.
> > Sweet baby, then forbear to weep;
> > Be still, my babe; sweet baby, sleep.
>
> Thou hast yet more to perfect this,
> A promise and an earnest got,
> Of gaining everlasting bliss,
> Though thou, my babe, perceiv'st it not;
> > Sweet baby, then forbear to weep;
> > Be still, my babe; sweet baby, sleep.[22]

The same abundance of meaning characterizes the understanding of the Lord's Supper in the Reformed Church. Just as baptism is a sign and seal of a relationship with God and of the concomitant blessings he actually bestows on his people, the Lord's Supper is a true communion—*vera communicatio,* Calvin calls it—with Christ in which our souls are nourished for eternal life by his crucified body and shed blood. No doctrine of the Lord's Supper can be accepted as Reformed unless it includes this emphasis on the real presence of Christ in the Supper.[23] Among the Reformed fathers John Calvin and Peter Martyr gave particular attention to this subject.[24] Introducing the subject in his *Institutes,* Calvin writes:

> Since, however, this mystery of Christ's secret union with the devout is by nature incomprehensible, he shows its figure and image in visible signs best adapted to our small capacity. Indeed, by giving guarantees and tokens he makes it as certain for us as if we had seen it with our own eyes. For this very familiar comparison penetrates into even the dullest minds: just as bread and wine sustain physical life, so are souls fed by Christ. We now understand the purpose of this mystical blessing, namely, to confirm for us the fact that the Lord's body was once for all so sacrificed for us that we may now feed upon it, and by feeding feel in ourselves the working of that unique sacrifice; and that his blood was once so shed for us in order to be our perpetual drink (*Inst.,* IV. xvii. 1).

Among the creeds of the Reformed Church the Belgic Confession has a striking section on the Supper. After stating that God has given us material bread for the support of our bodily and earthly life, it goes on to say that Christ instituted the Supper with its earthly and visible elements in order to represent to us the spiritual nourishment, his true body and blood, which he gives and which we truly receive with the "hand and mouth of our souls," which is faith. It continues:

> Now, as it is certain and beyond all doubt that Jesus Christ has not enjoined to us the use of His sacraments in vain, so He works in us all that He represents to us by these holy signs, though the manner surpasses our understanding, and cannot be comprehended by us, as the operations of the Holy Spirit are hidden and incomprehensible. In the meantime we err not, when we say what is eaten and drunk by us is the proper and natural body and the proper blood of Christ. But the manner of our partaking of the same is not by the mouth but by the spirit through faith. Thus, then, though Christ always sits at the right hand of His Father in the heavens, yet does he not therefore cease to make us partakers of Himself by faith. This feast is a spiritual table, at which Christ communicates Himself with all His benefits to us, and gives us there to enjoy both Himself and the merit of His sufferings and death; nourishing,

strengthening and comforting our poor comfortless souls, by the eating of His flesh, quickening and refreshing them by the drinking of His blood (Art. 35).

Whereas the Reformed tradition calls for the baptism of infants, participation in the Lord's Supper is delayed until after the baptized member of the church has been instructed and has made profession of his faith, which usually happens when he is in his teens. The reason for this is to impress upon him when he is old enough to understand them the meaning and implications of membership in the body of Christ. The legitimacy of the distinction between baptized membership and communicant membership has been challenged, and there are churches that admit little children as well as adults to communion. The entire Eastern Orthodox tradition is a case in point. It is reasoned that baptism into Christ admits one into full communion with him including, of course, the Lord's Supper. While there is no biblical warrant for censuring that practice—did not children partake of the Passover feast with their parents and is not the Christian's Passover Jesus Christ (Ex. 12; 1 Cor. 5:7)?—the Reformed Church, in its emphasis on the importance of doctrinal instruction and safeguarding the Lord's Table against profanation or misuse, has traditionally withheld communicant membership from persons until they are able to make their own profession of faith in Christ and promise to live for him.

(3) *To preaching and sacrament, its two means of grace, the Reformed Church added discipline as a third mark of the church.* It did so because of scriptural injunction and because without ecclesiastical discipline Word and sacrament become mockery.[25] Discipline, Calvin declared, forms the "sinews" of the church, holding the members of the body together. There have been debates in the history of the Reformed Church concerning whether discipline belongs properly to the *esse* or the *bene esse*—the being or the well-being—of the church. All, however, have agreed that if the church is to retain its spiritual vitality, the exercise of this third characteristic is necessary. It may take the first form of private admonition; or it may be open admonition, being kept from the Lord's Table, or, in extreme cases, excommunication.

The fundamental reason for discipline is the honor of Jesus Christ, the head of the church, his body. Denial of him or of his gospel by word or deed cannot be tolerated in his body. To fail to exercise discipline where these prevail is to dishonor Christ and to incur his wrath. Yet much of the church, including part of the Reformed Church, is notorious for its utter lack of discipline. It is little wonder, then, that the Lord's blessing is withheld and that, when the condition continues, the church begins to resemble a mere social club bereft of spiritual vigor and the dynamic presence of its Lord.

During the Nazi struggle, writes Niesel, the confessing church in Germany learned anew what discipline is.[26] This was not the first time in history, nor will it be the last, that the church has had to learn the hard way the necessity of exercising this key of the kingdom in order to benefit the erring member, to honor Jesus Christ, and to keep herself his faithful bride. It would be well for some who are of the Reformed heritage to ponder what their spiritual forebear Calvin has to say in the first half of Chapter XII of Book IV of the *Institutes*. They might see that as discipline is necessary in the home, in the club and on the team, it is eminently necessary in the divine society that our holy God has planted in our midst.

E. THE CHURCH'S WORSHIP

Consideration of the marks of the church brings one into the area of the church's worship. "The first point in Christianity," writes Calvin to an adversary in the Church of Rome, "is to worship God rightly." He continues:

> Think for a little on what takes place among you. They adore stone and wood; they invoke the dead; they trust in lying vanities; they would serve God by ceremonies foolishly invented without the authority of His Word. The true doctrine is buried, and if any one wishes to have it brought forth, he is cruelly persecuted. Do you think that God can bear with such pollutions and blasphemies against His own honor?[27]

It was the purpose of Calvin and the other Reformers to restore worship to what it had been in the early church.[28] The title of the book of worship he prepared for the church in Geneva in 1542 is *The Form for Prayers and Ecclesiastical Songs, with the Manner of Administrating the Sacraments and Concerning Marriage According to the Custom of the Ancient Church.*[29] He challenged his opponents "to show us, if they can, if there be anything in the manner of our worship which is not conformable to the institution of our Lord, to the usage of the Apostles, and we are ready to amend our fault."[30] In his instruction for the celebration of the Lord's Supper appended to the liturgical form there are two references to agreement with the customs of the ancient church. The second of these speaks of that body as "the ancient Church of the Apostles, the Martyrs, and the holy Fathers."[31] These witness to Calvin's intense conviction that he was in harmony with the faith and practice of antiquity.

(1) The first principle of Calvin and his collaborators in their reforming of worship was the restoration of worship to conformity with the worship of the ancient church and the norms given in scripture, from which the Church of Rome had deviated.

(2) A second principle invoked in the reformation of this area of the church's life was that worship should be according to the Word of God. *Ad fontes*—"back to the sources"—became the slogan here as elsewhere. Luther and Calvin, at one in most of their reforming activity, differed in their use of the scriptures, and that difference becomes noticeable here. It is well expressed by Davies: "Luther will have what is not specifically condemned by the Scriptures; whilst Calvin will have only what is ordained by God in the Scriptures. That is their fundamental disagreement."[32] With respect to doctrine the two Reformers were in almost complete agreement, but Calvin's application of scripture to the practice of worship differed from Luther's. The latter, Davies argues, was guided by events as well as principles as he broke ground in the reformatory period. His attitude to the reform of worship was partially determined by considerations of expediency.[33] Calvin believed that God has given us in scripture whatever is needed for the proper ordering of worship. Human innovations in worship, as elsewhere, are to be avoided. Much that had come to be accepted in the medieval church in the name of worship both Luther and Calvin abhorred, but Calvin was more rigorous than the German Reformer in excising that which he felt to be extrascriptural. His reason for doing so was his conception of human depravity. Man's sin is such that he cannot properly worship God unless he is guided by the scriptures. Worship, as well as doctrine, needed a thorough reformation based solely on the Word of God.

(3) A third principle of Reformed worship, set forth by Paul and declared by Calvin, is "let all things be done for edification" (1 Cor. 14:26). In his epistle to the reader of the Genevan liturgy of 1542, Calvin speaks of the necessity of "edification" at the beginning and again near the end. There must be instruction and understanding in whatever the church does in its worship in order that there may be edification. The difference between the singing of birds and of men, he avers, is that the former are without understanding while man sings and knows what he sings. A contemporary scholar puts the

matter this way: one of the "essential tenets of the Reformation ...[was] *that no act is to be admitted in Christian worship without its significance being expounded.*"[34]

(4) A fourth principle that the Reformers felt they found in the Bible is that "all things be done decently and in order" (1 Cor. 14:40). What is desirable is an orderly worship in which there is yet freedom. Dignity and decorum are necessary if the sovereign Lord of all is to be worshipped acceptably. There should be thought and something of the artistic if his Spirit is called upon to be present and to bless our service, for he is the Spirit of thought and of beauty. An individual may worship God informally, although, as Henry S. Coffin has said, even then,

> devout souls attain habits in this as in other daily actions. But a group must have an agreed-upon way of doing things together. Whether it be a meeting for singing and impromptu prayers, or a High Mass, there is both a form of service (a ritual), and a method of performing it (ceremonial). Public worship, whether in a hall or a cathedral, cannot escape either. The only options are unconsidered order and slipshod ceremony or a more carefully arranged form and a more effectively conducted ceremonial.[35]

(5) Another principle of Reformed worship is its simplicity. Pre-Reformation worship was complex and ornate. The mass had its officiant, its deacons, subdeacons, acolytes and altar boys. Tapers, censers, and sacred objects were carried and rich vestments were worn. The service was conducted in Latin instead of in the language of the people and was characterized by an elaborate ceremony that had developed over a period of centuries.[36]

The Reformed Church repudiated all this and sought to return to the primitive simplicity of the early church. It would include in its worship only what it felt God had ordained in his Word. It felt that additions were distracting to man and presumptuous before God. In a letter to a priest Calvin acknowledges that Rome has "beautiful general processions." But, he asks, what good do they do, and do the participants believe that thereby they may appease God? And why "place reliance in candles and torches, in beautiful and sumptuous equipment, in images, in reliquaries of the dead?...All that sort of thing smells of rank Judaism and befits Pagan rather than Christian worship."[37]

Reformed worship differed from Lutheran as well as Roman worship at this point. For whereas both Luther and Calvin agreed in the main in their struggle against Rome, Luther retained elements of the Roman worship that Calvin discarded. Luther held that since God has given man five senses it would be ingratitude to worship him with less. Lutheran worship therefore appealed to man's aesthetic sense more than did the Reformed service. Calvin was not lacking in aesthetic appreciation,[38] but believed that worship was to honor God and not to please man's sense of beauty. Moreover, he felt, the latter had often been the reason for the degeneration of worship in time past. For theological, not aesthetic, reasons Calvin and his disciples preferred a relatively unadorned worship. Horton Davies puts the difference baldly as he concludes a chapter on Reformed worship: "The Lutheran *cultus* is rich, the Calvinist bare."[39]

To some, Reformed worship may seem bare compared with the worship of other communions, and in some congregations, unfortunately, the aesthetic quality of worship is indeed poor. But this need not be. The liturgical forms of the Reformed Church are rich and its devotional literature is abundant. For a long time these liturgical forms were hardly known, barely used, and unappreciated.[40] Such neglect, wherever it existed, was in effect a repudiation of that part of the heritage of the Reformed Church and an impoverishment of its chief function. Today, however, there are signs that the church has become more conscious of its rich legacy from the fathers, and nothing is more characteristic of the recent theological revival than the interest in the worship of God.

In the rediscovery of its principles of worship the Reformed Church has found that certain elements that have crept into its worship should not be retained. Here again one encounters extremes. On the one hand, there is a light type of service that makes up in freedom what it lacks in dignity. With bouncy music and an air of informality throughout, the intention seems to be to give everybody a good time. Whether such meetings are in essence worship or entertainment for the benefit of those assembled may be hard to tell. Two things are certain, however: they are a wide variant from anything that the church in the past has considered to be the proper worship of God; and much of the motivation for that type of service is an attempt to attract people to it.

On the other hand, worship in some Reformed congregations has become virtually "high church," with a stereotyped form, abbreviated sermon or sermonette, altar or simulated altar,[41] and other priestly paraphernalia. Whereas the fathers strove to restore worship to its early simplicity, some today have substituted for the theological principles underlying worship a mere hankering for what they believe to be fashionable and enhancing to prestige. So a smoothly conducted and aesthetically appealing service is valued more than the blessing of the Spirit, and the reaction of the hearers more than faithful proclamation of the Word of God. It should not be a case of either-or, for both are legitimate and necessary. The question is one of emphasis. A study of the history of the church may serve to show where the weight ought to fall and should also show a Reformed churchman what constitutes the proper worship of God.

This latter is a good note on which to close this part of our discussion. In the Reformed tradition there is heavy emphasis on the fact that it is *God* who is worshipped. That is why certain embellishments and accoutrements used to adorn worship did not appeal to Calvin but seemed to him to be an impediment to fellowship with God. "A cardinal principle of Reformed worship," writes Maxwell, "is that worship exists for the glory of God rather than the consolation of man."[42] This may be hard to take in a man-centered age, but that is why it is the calling of the Reformed Church to strike this note today. The "approach" to God, another declares, is an "essential part of the tradition of our Reformed churches." So in worship there must be conveyed "an impression of his overwhelming greatness and mystery, along with his graciousness." It is significant, he goes on to say, that "in the finest aesthetic fruit of the Calvinistic Reformation — the religious paintings of Rembrandt — the divine Figure is represented in a point of light emerging from deep shadows. The nearness and the distance of God must both be present to worshippers."[43] If worship succeeds in bringing people face to face with *him,* and if it makes them aware of the fact that they have been in *his* presence, it has accomplished its purpose.

F. THE GOVERNMENT OF THE CHURCH

The drafting of the *Ecclesiastical Ordinances* for the church of Geneva in 1541 was no optional matter. Calvin knew that they were necessary because no church can exist without some form of government by which its life is regulated. The old church order, against which the Reformers felt compelled to protest, had gradually taken shape over long centuries. Finally it assumed the absolute character and power that is best seen in Popes Gregory VII and Innocent III, who could crown and coerce kings and emperors, absolve subjects from oaths of allegiance to sovereigns, and place whole nations under the interdict. It was seen also in the local parish and diocese, where priest and bishop were persons to have on one's side. The experienced emperor Charles V counseled his son, Philip II of Spain, to nominate bishops with the greatest care, for their power rivaled that of the nobility.

The Reformation, besides being a return to the religious teachings of the Bible, was a revolt against the religious authority of the Church of Rome. Prince and peasant, landholder and townsman rejected the rule of the Roman hierarchy for a form of government that they felt would bring blessing to Christians. They did not intend to leave the church of Christ, but they sought to correct those abuses within it which threatened to destroy its character. In order to correct them they had to give particular attention to the manner in which the church was governed. The Reformers felt that there was little chance of success at reform as long as the church was dominated by "the Pope, that pagan full of pride," so they devised a form of government for the church in which the pope and his court were absent. In doing this they succeeded to a degree beyond their fondest expectations and their success, in the Calvinistic part of the Reformation at least, was due in large measure to the new organization of the church and its ministry.

Not the least of Calvin's unusual gifts was his talent for organization. A. M. Fairbairn assesses his legislative and organizational abilities and achievements even more highly than his gifts as a theologian, and regards them as a truer expression of the man than his theology.[44] Whether or not this is correct, it is true that Calvin, with the assistance of others and the favor of providence, succeeded in molding a form of church government that was first seen to be remarkably suited to the Swiss people and was subsequently found to be as well suited for others when carried to their lands. So it was that France and Great Britain, Bohemia and Hungary, Holland, and parts of Germany received a conception of the polity of the church that proved to be one of the most important characteristics of the life of their Reformed churches. John Knox opined after his sojourn in Geneva that, whereas the gospel was preached in other places, nowhere else had it so affected life as a whole as it had at Geneva. There Jesus Christ was confessed to be the truth, indeed, but also the way, and the life. What was true in Geneva came to be true elsewhere, and the accomplishment was largely due to the manner in which the ministry of the church was made effective in the lives of its members. This in turn was done through the organization of church and discipline.

Although church government ought to be administered by the

Lord alone, says Calvin, since he is not visibly among us to give us audible declarations of his will,

> he uses the ministry of men to declare openly his will to us by mouth, as a sort of delegated work, not by transferring to them his right and honor, but only that through their mouths he may do his own work—just as a workman uses a tool to do his work (*Inst.*, IV. iii. 1).

The government and ministry of the church, then, was most important to the Reformer. Calvin's appreciation for them has not been surpassed and his conception of the church and its ministry is as lofty as can be found. This made him unhappy over the lack of regard for the church and its polity among certain extreme groups in the reform movement of his day. He lamented their neglect of order just as he lamented the autocratic rule of Rome. All things in the church are required to "be done decently and in order," writes the apostle, and Calvin adds that

> there is nothing in which order should be more diligently observed than in establishing government; for nowhere is there greater peril if anything be done irregularly (*Inst.*, IV. iii. 10).

Calvin is not making a comparison here between doctrine and church order, but rather a comparison between church government and other aspects of the external ordering of the church. The doctrine, or faith, of the church has had priority in the Reformed tradition since the beginning.[45] But the importance of church order can hardly be overemphasized, and Reformed churches recognize that fact. Moreover, the government of the church in its broad detail is a part of its doctrine.[46] This is made very clear in introductory remarks prefacing the official documents on church order in the various denominations that make up the Reformed Church as well as in the several confessions of faith. These statements make it clear that it has pleased God to use the ministry of men in gathering himself a church from among the lost children of men. The whole church and each member have a ministry to perform. There are also specific offices to which chosen persons are called so that true religion may be preserved and propagated, delinquents chastened, and all things be done decently and in order.

The position that there are specific offices through which God accomplishes his will in the church is being questioned today as it has been in the past. It is being said, with persuasiveness, that the traditional image both of the layman and of the minister must be "shattered" inasmuch as "every member is a minister in the church." No one group of members of the church should be referred to as

> ministers, or as comprising the ministry of the church. Indeed, they are ministers but just as all other members also are ministers. They are not qualitatively or personally different or unique; they are only *functionally* unique. But every other member is also functionally unique in that he shares in one or more forms of ministry that are not shared in by all other members. Not everyone shares equally in every ministry, no one shares in every ministry, everyone shares more intensively in one or several ministries than in others.... The church, therefore, must shatter the traditional image of the pastoral minister as *the* minister. He no more has a peculiar and indelible stamp placed upon his soul or person than any other Christian .... Until this image of the minister is shattered, little progress will be made in shattering the image of the laity as a group of passive, irresponsible, second-rate Christians.[47]

It is true that all Christians are ministers, *diakonoi,* servants of God. It is also true that there is only "one essential ministry, the perpetual ministry of the risen Lord, present, as he promised to be, where his people are gathered in his name, and renewing to each generation the gifts they need to continue *his* ministry."[48] Yet, as he continues his ministry Christ calls persons to offices that he, the chief officebearer, has given the church. At least, this has been the position of the Reformed Church in its interpretation of the relevant New Testament passages where office as well as function have been found. Paul wrote that Christ's gifts "were that some should be apostles, some prophets, some evangelists, some pastors and teachers, for the equipment of the saints, for the work of ministry, for building up the body of Christ" (Eph. 4:11f.).

In addition to the general office of all Christians to discharge their respective ministries, then, Christ has given the church special offices that some, not all, are called to fill. By offices we mean specific positions of trust, ministration, and authority with specified responsibilities and duties. These offices function within the fellowship of believers through the power of the Holy Spirit, whose anointing qualifies those called by the church and consequently by its Lord. Expressing the relationship of the special offices to Christ and the church, A. A. van Ruler writes that when one uses the Pauline metaphor of the church as the body of Christ with Christ its head, he should not only think of the offices "as organs of his body, as functions of that entire living organism, but also as organs of

Christ himself in his body. He himself acts — *within* the totality of his body, to be sure, but it is Christ himself who does it." The offices come from him and not from the body itself. There is not only a line from Christ to the offices by way of the congregation, but also a direct line from him to them. Moreover, this should not be understood as though there are offices in the church because Christ instituted them, or because Christ calls the officebearers to office and bestows gifts on them, but rather in the sense that his spiritual authority is directly given the offices and their holders. "Office-bearers and members of the congregation are both equally related directly to Christ. In him alone they find each other (and their own independence)."[49]

Van Ruler's emphasis on the real presence of Christ among his people is reminiscent of T. W. Manson's retort to the Bishop of Oxford's typical high church claims concerning the episcopate and apostolic succession. When the latter wrote that "our Lord endowed his Church with two great gifts: the means of grace (the word and the sacraments), and the ministry of grace (the apostles and their fellow-labourers)," Manson replied that his complaint was not that this doctrine was too high, but that

> it is not high enough. Our Lord did better than that: he gave the Church himself. His real and abiding presence in the Church is the supreme "means of grace" and the supreme "ministry of grace." Other means of grace there are; but they are derivative and subordinate. Other ministries of grace there are; but they are one and all dependent on this.[50]

In the Reformed Church the special offices are usually considered to be three in number: minsters of the Word, elders, and deacons. Each of these offices is derived from Jesus Christ, the only head of the church and the sole lawgiver in Zion. In his name and by his grace the functions of the offices are discharged so that blessing comes to the church and God's name receives praise.

The office that is most fundamental to the policy of the Reformed Church is that of elder. That is why many of its member churches are called Presbyterian, from the Greek word for elder, *presbyteros.* Coming directly out of the Old Testament, where the elders of Israel are mentioned some one hundred times, and out of the New Testament, from where it was taken over by the early church, the office of elder is that of overseer of the church. The Greek word for overseer is *episkopos,* from which the word "episcopal" is derived. The elder is an overseer, an *episkopos,* a ruler over the church of God (Acts 14:23; 20:17, 28; 1 Tim. 5:17; Titus 1:5, 7). He who resists an elder ministering in Christ's name resists God; he who receives the word of an elder ministering in Christ's name receives the word of God. Of this, the reality, the dignity, and the importance of the office, the Reformed Church came to be fully aware. The office of elder is one of the Lord's gifts to his church and it has been the chief advantage of the Presbyterian system of government over those other systems which do not have that office or, having it, do not allow it to function.

Elders are called and ordained to rule the church of God. Some of them are ruling elders only; others have been set aside to preach the Word and to administer the sacraments so that theirs constitutes a specialized office within the body of elders. They are the ministers of the Word.[51]

The duties of the ministers of the Word are to preach and teach that Word faithfully so that the congregation is edified; to call upon the name of the Lord on behalf of the people; to administer the sacraments; to set forth a godly example; and to govern the church. The nature of their office is such that it requires particular gifts and special training. The presence of the gifts and the training are determined by the church, which has been given the authority to ordain men to office. The specialized theological training that candidates for the ministerial office receive consists of the acquisition of the scholarly tools necessary for an understanding of scripture and the proclamation of its message to the world. In addition to literary, philosophical, and linguistic skills, therefore, the minister must be able to serve the church effectively. That means that he must be able to speak publicly and be a spiritual leader of the people. After the successful completion of his training the candidate is available for a call. Upon receiving and accepting a call, he is ordained by the church with the laying on of hands, which signifies that he is set aside for his special task and offered to God for the work of the ministry.[52]

As one who holds office in the church, the minister, like other officeholders, exercises a spiritual and ecclesiastical authority given by Christ. This authority was given the apostles in the power of the keys (Matt. 16:19; John 20:23) and remains with their successors. The "keys of the kingdom" signify the ability to open and to close heaven through the preaching of the gospel and the exercise of church discipline. The authority of an officeholder inheres in the office and not in the person. As the church can ordain, so it can remove from office when such extreme action is for the well-being of the body of Christ.

Elders who are not called to be ministers of the Word are ruling elders. Having an equal voice with the ministers in the presbytery or body of elders, their function is to oversee the church, to encourage and admonish, to guard the sacraments, to administer discipline, and to receive the penitent back into the fellowship of the church. Furthermore, they are to assist the ministers with their counsel and to give particular attention to their teaching and conduct. Many volumes have been written about the significance of the duties of the ruling elders in a congregation. The office is of such importance to the polity of the Reformed Church that without it the church would lose its character as a Reformed Church. Presbyterianism as a form of church order gives the office of ruling elder its biblical prominence. When the first General Assembly of the Church of Scotland met in 1560, there were thirty-six ruling elders and six ministers of the Word as delegates.[53] The Reformed fathers believed that God's Word prescribes order for the church, and the office set forth most frequently in both testaments is that of elder. Wherever the Reformed Church is conscious of its heritage and responsibilities and the opportunities inherent in the office of elder, that office is given its due.

The third office is that of deacon. Arising out of a need in the early church, the diaconate was established to provide for the wants of some of its members. Certain Greek widows were being neglected, and when this was called to the attention of the apostles an assembly of the church was called. The congregation was asked to select seven men of good reputation who were full of the Holy Spirit and of wisdom to whom these duties could be assigned. The apostles were too busy with their own tasks, the ministry of the Word and prayer, to give attention to these other matters. After the selection was made the candidates were set before the apostles, who ordained them with the laying on of hands and prayer (Acts 6:1-6).

The deacons, then, were appointed to be servants of the church. As the apostles and elders were to rule it, the deacons were to serve it in accordance with its needs. These needs may have been few at first; soon they were to become myriad and they remain so today.

The office of deacon, altogether different from that of elder, is nonetheless essential to the well-being of the church. Deacons are concerned with the financial and material maintenance of the church and its members, which requires instruction in stewardship and the promotion of the denominational program. They study the many requests for financial aid that come to the congregations. Following the example of Christ, they fulfill the ministry of sympathy and service in his name. Considering the range of duties for which the deacons are responsible, one wonders how any healthy congregation can do without them. The fact is that they or their equivalent are found in most churches because of the practical need for a board or committee to discharge the aforementioned tasks.

In the Reformed Church the biblical office of deacon came to be recognized and accepted for its full worth. The manifold, often tedious, details that must be accomplished in the name of the whole church and demand attention are handled by those ordained to the diaconate for that purpose. As Christ came "not to be ministered unto but to minister," the deacons are appointed to minister. They must seek to imitate, as far as they are able, the example of their Lord in providing for the needs of men. There may be a temptation to look on this office as one that, when properly discharged, is concerned with considerable detail, but it is far less time-consuming today than it was when poverty was great and government had not yet engaged in broad programs of social welfare. The history of the church in the Netherlands, for example, records the great usefulness of the deacons in society and also hints at the burdens they bore. This latter fact is borne out in an advice to the church on July 2, 1751, by the theological faculty at Utrecht, who said that the office of deacon is "a ministry in which one usually sees nothing but cares, troubles, work, grief, ingratitude, etc."[54]

The discovery of these and other principles of church government in the sixteenth century provided the Reformed Church with insights that it has been able to offer the whole body of Christ. Because of historical circumstances the Lutherans and Anglicans were unable to develop an adequate polity for their churches. The Lutherans might have achieved something substantial, such as their descendants were one day to do in America, but Luther's experiences with the man on the street or in the field led him to judge that congregations of ordinary Christians were incapable of running their own affairs. Princes were given powers that had previously been wielded by bishops; and the Lutheran Church in Europe, thus bound to the state, had its political development arrested. In England, likewise, the church, dominated by a monarchical state, did not develop a robust polity. The judgment of James I, that Presbyterianism "has no more in common with a monarchy than the devil with God," is indicative of a long-time attitude of the British crown towards a church with an independent government. For in Geneva certain ideas were set in motion which were to have far-reaching consequences, as James correctly saw. In the *Consistoire* Calvin had a representative body of men, independent of king, priest, or prelate, who were called upon to exercise their talents and make judgments on questions of vital importance. When this example was imitated in thousands of congregations, each of which had its own "consistory" or "session," there came to be a powerful incentive to democracy in civil government as well.[55]

NOTES TO CHAPTER II

[1] Cf. Niesel, *Was heisst reformiert?*, pp. 5ff.

[2] *This is the Church* (Philadelphia: Muhlenberg, 1952), p. 6.

[3] In *Liberal Theology: An Appraisal*, edd. D. E. Roberts and H. P. Van Dusen (New York: Scribners, 1942), pp. 269f.

[4] Schaff, *The Creeds of Christendom* (New York: Harper, 1919), Vol. III, p. 458.

[5] *C.R.* 34,3.

[6] *C.R.* 34,39.

[7] Schaff, *loc. cit.*, p. 869. "In spite of the divided state of Christendom, the Church of Scotland considers herself a part of the Church Universal, and that her ministry and worship are valid, catholic and in agreement with Holy Scripture. . . .In its worship the Church of Scotland believes that the local worshipping company is united with the whole Church in heaven and earth, and the worshippers are deeply conscious of this unity. This fact has been repeated in all her standards and it is evident in her practice. At Holy Communion her table is open to all Christians. Moreover, it is interesting to observe that the Church of Scotland has never used the description 'Protestant' but always 'Reformed.' The Church of Scotland is not a new protesting Church formed at the Reformation, but she is the ancient Church of Scotland, Catholic and Reformed." W. D. Maxwell, "The Elements of Liturgy: Reformed," in *Ways of Worship: The Report of a Theological Commission of Faith and Order*, edd. P. Edwall, E. Hayman and W. D. Maxwell (London: SCM, 1951), p. 122. Cf. W. Nijenhuis, *Calvinus Oecumenicus* ('s Gravenhage: Nijhoff, 1958); J. T. McNeill, "The Church in Sixteenth-Century Reformed Theology," *Journal of Religion*, XXII (1942), 251-269; R. Stuart Louden, *The True Face of the Kirk* (London: Oxford University Press, 1963), pp. 16, 25f. Louden asserts that "the designation 'catholic' has always been very precious to the Church of Scotland" (p. 16); T. F. Torrance, "What is the Reformed Church?" *Conflict and Agreement in the Church* (London: Lutterworth, 1959), Vol. I, pp. 76ff.

[8] Cf. Harry R. Boer, *That My House May Be Filled: A Study of Evangelism in the Christian Reformed Church* (Grand Rapids: Eerdmans, 1957), pp. 18ff.

One practical reason for the validity of the position here taken is the following: At one time or another elders or ministers of congregations within the Reformed Church have expressed the opinion that persons who play cards, dance, attend the theater, are divorced, drink or sell alcoholic beverages, belong to secret societies or to the AFL-CIO, bathe, picnic, or play ball on Sunday, or smoke should not be allowed membership in a Reformed church. Excessive use of make-up, or a career on the stage or in certain sports has been considered by others as sufficient reason for exclusion from the church. One can imagine the situation in which the church would find itself if all these, and others unmentioned, were made conditions for church membership. It helps little for the individual to reply that *he* would only insist on abstention from one or a few of the practices mentioned above. The point is that *others* would insist on *their* personal preferences with respect to extrabiblical requirements for church membership. In its teaching ministry the church must seek to bring the gospel to bear on every aspect of life; its requirement for membership in the holy catholic church, however, should remain the same the world over in every generation.

9 Schaff, *loc. cit.,* p. 658.

10 *Images of the Church in the New Testament* (Philadelphia: West-minster, 1960), pp. 222, 268f.

11 *Ibid.,* p. 221.

12 *Ibid.,* pp. 224f.

13 *Ibid.,* p. 225.

14 *Corpus Christi: The Nature of the Church According to the Reformed Tradition* (Philadelphia: Westminster, 1958), pp. 174, 145, 170, 227.

15 Minear, *op. cit.,* p. 129; cf. pp. 188f., 225.

16 Parker, *The Oracles of God,* p. 21.

17 James H. Nichols cites as an instance of this the title of Leo Judea's liturgy in which worship is built around sermons: *Order for Opening and Closing of Sermons.* "The Liturgical Tradition of the Reformed Churches," *Theology Today,* XI (1954), 217.

18 Fairbairn, *The Cambridge Modern History,* Vol. II, p. 373.

19 *The Revolt of the Netherlands* (New York: Barnes & Noble, 1958), p. 262.

20 The Second Helvetic Confession, Schaff, *loc. cit.,* p. 884.

21 H. Witsius, *The Oeconomy of the Covenants Between God and Man* (London: Dilly, 1763), Vol. III, p. 1235.

22 Quoted by W. F. Flemington, *The New Testament Doctrine of Baptism* (London: S.P.C.K., 1953), pp. 143f.

23 MacGregor goes so far as to say, "The doctrine of the Real Presence of Christ in the Eucharist is so vital to the Reformed tradition that even the slightest neglect of it leads rapidly to catastrophic decline in the life of the Church," *op. cit.,* p. 195.

24 See Joseph C. McLelland, *The Visible Words of God: An Exposition of the Sacramental Theology of Peter Martyr Vermigli* (Grand Rapids: Eerdmans, 1957).

25 Cf. MacGregor, *op. cit.,* pp. 176, 249.

26 Niesel, *op. cit.,* p. 45.

27 *C.R.* 39, pp. 484, 486.

28 Horton Davies, *The Worship of the English Puritans* (Glasgow: Dacre Press, 1948), pp. 14f.

29 *C.R.* 34, p. 161.

30 *C.R.* 39, p. 487.

31 *C.R.* 34, pp. 193, 195.

32 *Op. cit.,* p. 16.

33 *Ibid.,* pp. 16ff.

34 G. vander Leeuw, "The Inner Meanings of Word and Sacrament," in Edwall, Hayman, and Maxwell, *The Ways of Worship,* p. 227. Italics his.

35 *The Public Worship of God* (Philadelphia: Westminster, 1946), pp. 43f.; cf. p. 33.

36 L. Duchesne, *Christian Worship: Its Origin and Evolution* (London: S.P.C.K., 1949).

37 *C.R.* 39, p. 488.

38 See McNeill, *The History and Character of Calvinism,* p. 231: "In nothing, perhaps, has Calvin been more misjudged than in the view that he lacked any aesthetic sense." Cf. L. Wencelius, *L'Esthetique de Calvin* (Paris: Societe d'Edition "Les Belles Lettres," n.d.).

39 *Op. cit.,* p. 24.

40 C. W. Baird, *The Presbyterian Liturgies* (Grand Rapids: Baker, 1957), p. 252.

41 A development within the Reformed community in America that speaks eloquently of a lack of theological sensitivity, if not ignorance, is the introduction of altars or near-altars into Reformed churches. Altars, in which were lodged the bones of the saints, had replaced communion tables during the Middle Ages and on them the sacrifice of the mass was performed for the living and the dead. Since it was thought that the bread and the wine were miraculously changed into the whole Christ, "body and blood together with the soul and divinity" (*The Canons and Decrees of the Council of Trent,* Sess. XIII, Canon I), this whole, living Christ was thought to be offered to God on the coffin-altar as a re-enactment of the sacrifice on Calvary. Thus Trent declared that "this sacrifice is truly propitiary, and that by means thereof this is effected, that we obtain mercy and find grace. . . .For the victim is one and the same, the same now offering by the ministry of priests, who then offered himself on the cross, the manner alone of offering being different" (*ibid.,* Sess. XXII, Chap. II). With the center of Roman Catholic worship being a sacrifice, it was natural that its officiant was called a priest and that the sacrifice was performed on an altar. When Protestantism repudiated the mass and its priesthood for good, biblical reasons, the retention of altars in its churches was an incongruous carry-over from pre-Reformation worship. Coffin-altars were removed from Reformed churches, therefore, and the Lord's Table was reintroduced into the sanctuary and worship. Commenting on contemporary developments in the architectural setting for worship, Nichols and Trinterud remark that "today we have the curious situation that it is the most advanced and religiously most powerful sections of Roman Catholicism and Anglo-

Catholicism which come nearest to a fresh representation of the Reformed tradition, while Presbyterian churches right and left are dressing themselves up in the shopworn and cast off church furniture of the Anglo-Catholic movement a century back. The modern Catholic liturgical revival nourishes itself especially on the church of the Fathers, and since. . .the Reformed tradition is the closest akin of all the major modern traditions to patristic practice, the Catholics often approach Calvin and Bucer, and are notably closer to them than their contemporary heirs." *The Architectural Setting for Reformed Worship* (Chicago: The Presbytery of Chicago, 1961), p. 18. I would commend this and another excellent study by Donald J. Bruggink and Carl H. Droppers, *Christ and Architecture: Building Presbyterian/Reformed Churches* (Grand Rapids: Eerdmans, 1965).

42 Edwall, Hayman, and Maxwell, *op. cit.,* p. 119.

43 Coffin, *op. cit.,* p. 17.

44 Fairbairn, *loc. cit.,* p. 364.

45 For a statement of this principle see Marcel Pradervand, "The Eighteenth General Council: A Report by the General Secretary," in *Reformed and Presbyterian World,*XXV, No. 7 (September 1959), 294.

46 Torrance, *op. cit.,* Vol. I, pp. 87-89.

47 Arnold B. Come, *Agents of Reconciliation* (Philadelphia: Westminster, 1960), pp. 117ff.

48 T. W. Manson, *The Church's Ministry* (Philadelphia: Westminster, 1948), p. 81.

49 A. A. van Ruler, *Bijzonder en Algemeen Ambt* (Nijkerk: G. F. Callenbach, 1952), pp. 58f.

50 *Op. cit.,* p. 23; cf. Torrance's answers to high-church Anglicanism, *op. cit.,* Vol. I, pp. 23-75.

51 For a good discussion of this office see Harry G. Goodykoontz, *The Minister in the Reformed Tradition* (Richmond: John Knox, 1963).

52 In the debate over whether the imposition of hands at the ordination of a minister should be by ministers alone or also by elders, Goodykoontz favors the practice of the Presbyterian Church in the United States (Southern) in which the latter prevails. Granting the logic of the other position, that only those who hold a particular office can induct another into that office, he argues that psychologically the inclusion of elders in the laying on of hands has much to commend it. "In a democratic world where anti-clericalism already exists in too many places, the Presbyterians can do much to lessen this anti-clericalism by allowing the ruling elders to impose hands as well as judicially to determine that a man is worthy of being ordained. Theologically something can be said for the concept that ordination as an act of the whole church calls for the participation of ruling elders. . .ruling elders are truly representatives of the people. . . .It is good, then, for the entire body to participate in ordination, and this can best be done symbolically by the representatives of the people, the ruling elders, participating in the imposition of hands." *Ibid.,* pp. 125f. Professor A. A. van Ruler has told me that he favors this same position.

53Louden comments: "This historical background, which gave so large a place in Church government to representatives of the people as a whole, cannot be over-emphasized in an understanding of the development of the Scottish eldership." *Op. cit.,* p. 41.

54 Quoted by J. A. Cramer, "Protestantsch Kerkelijk Leven in Oud-Utrecht," *Nederlandsch Archief voor Kerkgeschiedenis,* XXX (1938), 72.

55 The above discussion touches only the essential question of the three offices of the Reformed Church and omits the question of graded judicatories and the problems raised in controversies over presbyterianism versus congregationalism versus episcopacy.

III

REFORMED ACCORDING TO THE WORD OF GOD

When the church was re-formed in the sixteenth century its doctrine and government, worship and way of life were not re-designed according to its own preconceived ideas of what ought or ought not to be. Its reformation was according to a standard, a "rule of faith," by which it could measure itself. It was reformed according to the Word of God. For this reason the full name by which it has often been called is *The Church of Jesus Christ Reformed According to the Word of God.* It is a name peculiarly appropriate for the Reformed Church because of the position that scripture has had in it. It is indeed a church that has been measured and molded by the Bible.

For this reason the exposition of the Word of God has had a prominent place in the worship of the Reformed Church, and family Bible reading became a daily habit in Reformed homes. The Reformed confessions of faith, unlike some creeds, include a statement on scripture, usually near the beginning. An exception is the Heidelberg Catechism, which has no such formal statement but which fortifies each of its one hundred twenty-nine answers with an array of texts, follows the main outline of Paul's Epistle to the Romans, and is guided throughout by the biblical perspective.

Because the churches of the Reformation sought to give scripture its proper place some have said they substituted another external authority for the pope, so that instead of being emancipated in the spiritual and intellectual upheavals of the sixteenth century, they

72

were bound to a "paper pope." Although that epithet is not intended complimentarily, it may serve that end nevertheless. For the Reformed Church, like Luther at Worms, confesses itself to be held captive by the Word of God. Its bondage, however paradoxically it may seem, is not a burden but an emancipation, for it is bondage to him whose service is perfect freedom.

There would be strength in the "paper pope" charge if subjection to scripture meant the abandonment of scientific investigation and blind submission. Obviously, this was far from the mind of Calvin and those who wrote the confessional statements. Free inquiry and learning were a passion with them and are honored by their spiritual descendants today. The choice now is as it was then: the acceptance or rejection of scripture as a revelation from God. The church has made its choice; that is why it is still the church. For if it should abandon scripture as the light of God by which it finds its way through the uncertainty and confusion of the world, it would abandon God and destroy its own character as the church. The church is the body of Christ and lives by union with him, hearing his word from day to day. It does not find that word in the depths of its own being but in the historical record of God's past association with his people, a record that he is pleased to keep alive and meaningful for them today.

> Because he saw the minds of all men tossed and agitated, after he chose the Jews as his very own flock, he fenced them about that they might not sink into oblivion as others had. With good reason he holds us by the same means in the pure knowledge of himself, since otherwise even those who seem to stand firm before all others would soon melt away. Just as old or bleary-eyed men and those with weak vision, if you thrust before them a most beautiful volume, even if they recognize it to be some sort of writing, yet can scarcely construe two words, but with the aid of spectacles will begin to read distinctly; so Scripture, gathering up the otherwise confused knowledge of God in our minds, having dispersed our dullness, clearly shows us the true God. This, therefore, is a special gift, where God, to instruct the church, not merely uses mute teachers but also opens his own most hallowed lips. Not only does he teach the elect to look upon a god, but also shows himself as the God upon whom they are to look. He has from the beginning maintained this plan for his church, so that besides these common proofs he also put forth his Word, which is a more direct and more certain mark whereby he is to be recognized (*Inst.*, I. vi. 1).

> Daily oracles are not sent from heaven, for it pleased the Lord
> to hallow his truth to everlasting remembrance in the Scrip-
> tures alone. Hence the Scriptures obtain full authority among
> believers only when men regard them as having sprung from
> heaven, as if there the living words of God were heard (*Inst.*, I.
> vii. 1).

This is a startling claim. To believe that God speaks through the
Bible today as clearly and audibly as he did when the message was
originally given, and that the Bible is the means by which he
instructs his people, may be hard to believe. Yet the Christian
church, and in particular the Reformed Church, accepts that claim.
What then is the teaching about scripture?

The first element in the Reformed doctrine of scripture is the
necessity of scripture. Apart from scripture man is hopelessly lost.
Created in the divine image, good and holy, and with knowledge of
his creator, man has fallen and darkness has engulfed him. Luther
and Calvin had much to say on this theme, and it has become a
distinguishing tenet of the churches that have sprung from their
teaching. Man in sin is not only spiritually ill, but dead. He is not
only confused in his pilgrimage through this world; he is lost. He is
like a person in a forest, without map, compass, or guide and no idea
which way to go. Far from the nearest help, he heads off in what he
hopes is a consistent direction only to discover that he has made a
circle. When he starts off again he finds a river blocking his path here
and a swamp or mass of rock thwarting him there. With limited
strength and rations he will soon be a victim of the wilderness unless
help comes from the outside.

To be sure, there is a revelation in creation. God continues to
speak to all men in spite of their sin, but the consequences of sin are
such that men cannot hear. Other sounds distract them and drown
out the call of God. The revelation in nature (Ps. 19; Acts 14:17;
17:27; Rom. 1:9f.) is insufficient to lead most men out of the
wilderness of ignorance and sin. They hear its call but indistinctly.
The calls of the world and of self are too strong. Without someone
to come and lead them they will never find their way to the Father's
house. They are not even sure who their Father is until they are told
(John 8:42-44; 14:6). That is why salvation from God is necessary.
Apart from it, the apostle declares in shocking language, men are
"separated from Christ, alienated from the commonwealth of Israel,
and strangers to the covenants of promise, having no hope and
without God in the world" (Eph. 2:12). Such is the need for a word
from God and that message has come through scripture.

The nature of scripture, as the Reformed Church understands it, can be described according to its divine-human character, its perspicuity or clarity, its unity, its sufficiency, and its self-authentication.

A. ITS DIVINE-HUMAN CHARACTER

The divine-human character of scripture means that it was composed by men in human language as they were motivated and guided by the Spirit of God. Because God has used the medium of human language to make his will known and has employed men to put his message into writing, there is variety in the literary form of the Bible. Individual styles and the culture and background of human authors can often be detected, as well as the historical setting out of which the particular writing comes. These are not new discoveries but are as old as the writings themselves, although for a time they were lost to the church. Calvin was very much aware of them, as his commentaries on the books of the Bible show.[1] Moreover, modern biblical scholarship has contributed greatly to our appreciation of the Bible as a human and historical document.

There are those who object to the characterization of the Bible as a human book. In the interests of its sacred character the only adjective they will ascribe to it is divine. The humble manner in which most of it came into being would be an offense to them, if they were to reflect on it, just as the manger in Bethlehem and the cross on the hill have been an offense to others. The communication of God's will in the midst of thunder and lightning, as at Sinai, is understandable, but that it should come through an obscure prophet or in the drafting of an apparently ordinary letter is hardly worthy of the nature of revelation.

The reply to such reasoning is that this is the nature of revelation. In most instances God has not made his will known in a spectacular manner but in a quiet, unostentatious way. In the time of crisis in his life the prophet Elijah stood on Mount Horeb, as Moses had done earlier, to receive a message from God. First a powerful wind tore rocks loose from the mountain, but God's word did not come in the wind. After that there was an earthquake, but the word did not come through the earthquake either. Then there was a fire, but neither was it the bearer of the message. After the fire there was "a still small voice" and this was the voice of God (1 Kings 19:12).

Paul, who was aware of the divine manner of action and was

himself a chosen vessel, writes that among those who were called there were not many who were

> wise according to worldly standards, not many were powerful, not many were of noble birth; but God chose what is foolish in the world to shame the wise, God chose what is weak in the world to shame the strong, God chose what is low and despised in the world, even things that are not, to bring to nothing things that are, so that no human being might boast in the presence of God (1 Cor. 1:26-29).

Revelation has come in this manner likewise. It was not given to the priest Amaziah, or to King Jeroboam of Israel, but to Amos who was neither a prophet nor the son of a prophet, but a herdsman and a dresser of sycamore trees. The Lord took him from following the flock and said, "Go, prophesy to my people Israel" (Amos 7:14f.).

Amos' message was cast in human speech so that both he and Israel could understand it. It is as clearly and fully human as a message can be. It passed through Amos' mind and his vocal organs framed it. Moreover, it must have been presented with all the power of his person. It was indeed *Amos'* message. But it was more than that. It was divine. It had originated with God, and what Amos spoke was precisely what God had commanded. As it was fully human, it was also fully divine. That is the character of the inscripturated Word of God likewise. It is the Word of God in and through the words of men, God lisping to us, his children, as Calvin puts it, as a nurse lisps to a little child to make him understand. The appearance of the sacred record is like that of any other book but its content is a message from God. That message is found *in* the Bible and the Bible *is* the Word of God.

The divine-human character of the Bible is the offense of particularity that was a stumbling block to the great German thinker Lessing and a host of others. That God's revelation should have occurred in certain times and at certain places and that the record of those once-for-all experiences has been deposited in a book was too much for Lessing and many of his eighteenth-century contemporaries. If there is any revelation of God, these men reasoned, it must be in the laws of nature and the general principles existing in the minds of all men, or at least of the philosophers. The most amazing assumption and express teaching of the literature of that period is man's innate ability to know whatever needs to be known about God. Belief in the Bible as a necessary, special revelation from God was folly to these men and they weakened it by argument when they were able or treated it with outright contempt.

B. ITS CLARITY

In his discussion of Calvin's "three essential characteristics" of the Bible—its necessity, clarity, and sufficiency—Doumergue cites the second as most important. For, he asks, "how would it be necessary if it were obscure?" Moreover, its sufficiency, according to Calvin, follows its clarity.[2] The question concerning the clarity of scripture (or perspicuity, as it is known in theological discourse) at bottom is whether or not the central message of the Bible can be understood by the man on the street. The discussion concerning scripture turned around this point in the Reformation era and it continues to be a major hurdle in Roman Catholic-Protestant theological conversation until our day.

According to historic Roman Catholic teaching, modified in our time, scripture is difficult to understand; and so a qualified interpreter is needed, which is the Roman church. The church here refers not to the church of the sheep, but of the shepherds; and by shepherds, one learns if he presses the argument, is not meant all the clergy, but rather the bishops and prelates of the church assembled in council; even more particularly the pope, as the infallible head and spokesman of the church.[3] To allow every person to be his own interpreter and to decide what he will believe is to bring chaos into the church. As the Dutch proverb states, *ieder ketter heeft zijn letter*—every heretic has a text to support his position. Rome argued, with much to be said for it, that the idea that every man with a Bible in his hand can determine what he should believe is individualism run wild. It is the duty and prerogative of the church through its trained hierarchy to define the truth and it is the duty of the faithful to receive it obediently. Knowledge of biblical languages, history, and other scientific tools is necessary for biblical interpretation and the laity are not in possession of these.

The Protestant answer to this position of Rome was as follows: God gave *his people* the Word; and not only their spiritual leaders but they, too, are able to understand its message. The law was given all Israel; the prophets addressed all who would hear in the name of the Lord; Jesus spoke to the common people and they heard him gladly; the apostles wrote to whole congregations of Christians expecting them to understand the message. Thus scripture witnesses to its own clarity and shows that it was not intended for a favored few but for all to understand. There are passages, to be sure, that are difficult, but even these may be understood by reading them in the light of other passages whose meaning is clear. By this principle of comparing scripture with scripture, many difficulties are removed and those that remain are not sufficient to render our salvation uncertain.[4] Moreover, the Reformation said, by affirming the clarity of scripture there is no intention of minimizing the necessity of a learned ministry. For the *public* interpretation of scripture a trained ministry is necessary, for scripture testifies that not all have equal gifts but to some it is given to be "apostles, some prophets, some evangelists, some pastors and teachers, for the equipment of the saints, for the work of the ministry, for building up the body of Christ."[5]

Bible reading was encouraged everywhere and by all means in the Reformation church. Ministers assumed that their flocks were composed of Bible-reading Christians. When a certain "learned man" said in 1520 that it would be better to be without God's laws than the pope's, William Tyndale responded, "If God spare my life, ere many years I will cause a boy that driveth the plough shall know more of the Scripture than thou doest." When he finished translating the Bible into English that boast may have been realized. Calvin insisted on attendance at worship so that the exposition of the Bible would be heard. He assured his listeners and readers that scripture is intelligible, that it was their duty to read and ponder it, and that nothing necessary for their salvation would be withheld from them. Spiritual food was as necessary as food for the body, it was reasoned, so the common man was encouraged, even required, to read, think, and learn. What this meant in the way of intellectual and spiritual advance can be imagined. "Here we have the beginning both of general education and of that awakening of the mind of the average man which is the foundation of democracy," writes Dakin. He then quotes Milton in the *Areopagitica,* who says, "For now the time seems come wherein Moses the great prophet may sit in heaven rejoicing to see that memorable and glorious wish of his fulfilled when not only the seventy elders but all the Lord's people are become prophets." Dakin rightly singles out Calvin for this remarkable phenomenon, claiming that "his view of Scripture contained in it this great possibility of development...which makes it so interesting and important for a study of the shaping forces of the modern world." He concludes with the reminder that Calvin's *Institutes* was written as "an easy introduction" to the sacred scriptures to help the believer to "ascertain both what he ought principally to look for in Scripture, and also to what head he ought to refer whatever is contained in it."[6]

Rome's historic answer to the Protestant position, that it entails hopeless diversity of opinion, is not altogether incorrect. Yet the advantages of the Protestant position far outweigh the disadvantages. Denial of the doctrine of the clarity of the scriptures, as Herman Bavinck affirms, means the subjection of the layman to the priest and the conscience to the church. Acceptance of it means freedom for religion and conscience, church and theology.[7] The church does not have the last word in theological matters; that prerogative belongs to the Word of God. For Rome there is no appeal beyond itself: *"Roma locuta, causa finita"* ("Rome has spoken, the matter is settled"). Protestantism affirms that church interpretation is not magisterial but ministerial. It can only bind the conscience insofar as the individual is convinced that its interpretation is in agreement with the Word of God. The individual may be excluded from a given church but he knows that he stands before God who alone is the Lord of the conscience. When necessary he may challenge a church with the Bible in his hand, as Luther did, for while churches and church councils have erred and do err, the Word of the Lord remains forever.

C. ITS UNITY

By the unity of the scriptures is meant their presentation of one message of salvation. Both testaments point to Jesus Christ, the Old Testament by prophecy and preparation for his coming, the New by the presentation of the gospel and its interpretation. Christ is the key to understanding both (Matt. 1:1; John 20:31; Acts 1:1; Rom. 1:3; 2 Cor. 3:13-15; Rev. 1:1). In the ancient church Augustine said that the New Testament lies hidden in the Old and the Old becomes manifest in the New. The Puritans said it in the couplet:

> The New is in the Old contained;
> The Old is by the New explained.

Each testament is incomplete without the other. Together they furnish one history of salvation (Luke 24:44; Acts 3:24; 8:30-35). Calvin never tires of emphasizing this important fact and the broad biblical teaching on which it rests. There are more similarities than differences between the testaments, he avers. "The covenant made with all the patriarchs is so much like ours in substance and reality that the two are actually one and the same" (*Inst.*, II. x. 2). There are the same blessings in both covenants; only the mode of dispensation is different (*Inst.*, II. x, xi). The reason for the similarity is the same in Calvin's thought as in Reformed theology in general, namely, that Christ is the mediator of the old covenant as well as the new. This is stated forcefully in the discussion of the means of grace God has given the holy catholic church:

> First, if what Christ says is true—"No one sees the Father except the Son and anyone to whom the Son chooses to reveal him"—surely they who would attain the knowledge of God should always be directed by that eternal Wisdom. For how could they either have comprehended God's mysteries with the mind, or have uttered them, except by the teaching of him to whom alone the secrets of the Father are revealed? Therefore, holy men of old knew God only by beholding him in his Son as in a mirror. When I say this, I mean that God has never manifested himself to men in any other way than through the Son, that is, his sole wisdom, light, and truth. From this fountain Adam, Noah, Abraham, Isaac, Jacob, and others drank all that they had of heavenly teaching. From the same fountain, all the prophets have also drawn every heavenly oracle that they have given forth.

> For this Wisdom has not always manifested itself in one way. Among the patriarchs God used secret revelations, but at the same time to confirm these he added such signs that they could have no doubt that it was God who was speaking to them. What the patriarchs had received they handed on to their descendants. For the Lord had left it with them on this condition, that they should so propagate it. The children and children's children knew when God dictates within that what they heard was from heaven, not from earth (*Inst.*, IV. viii. 5).

Calvin's position on the unity of scripture and on the significance of Christ for the Old Testament was long unpopular in theological circles, but recently it has been championed by a large number of scholars in the forefront of contemporary biblical study.[8] The Bible is again seen to be one book with the one message of man's redemption from sin through Jesus Christ running throughout it.

D. ITS SUFFICIENCY

The sufficiency of scripture means that everything necessary to believe for salvation is found in it. This position, like that of the clarity of the Bible, was taken in opposition to Rome, which taught that scripture is incomplete and requires the traditions of the church in order to complete it. Tradition, the Council of Trent declared, is to be received reverently and venerated equally with scripture.[9] The grounds offered by Roman Catholic theology to substantiate this position have been summarized by Bavinck. They are, in brief, (1) that the church before Moses lived wholly by tradition; (2) that many from then until today live and die by tradition with little knowledge of scripture and yet are saved; (3) in law and morals, art and science, family and commerce, tradition is fundamental to life. The same must be true of the church. Moreover, here it is surer and safer because Christ gives and preserves it; (4) scripture recognizes the presence of tradition; (5) orally and by his Spirit Jesus gave the disciples much that is unwritten; (6) church fathers, councils, and popes have received and recognized tradition; (7) the apostles were told to witness but they were not told to write. Their writings were produced by historical circumstances and much is omitted. Tradition, therefore, is necessary alongside scripture, since the latter is insufficient by itself.[10]

Over against this position the Reformation held to the sufficiency of scripture. It said that the greater the distance in time between the early church and the apostles the greater the difficulty in determining whether a given tradition is apostolic. It is necessary to limit tradition, therefore, and to indicate its characteristics. According to Vincent of Lerins, the criterion of tradition is that a doctrine must have been believed everywhere, always, and by everyone. This formulation was accepted by Rome, but it presented a number of difficulties. First of all, there was always a question as to the precise doctrines and usages so accepted. In addition, there was disagreement about whether antiquity and universality were both necessary. It was decided that one, but not both, of these might be needed. Moreover, Protestantism felt that the decision ultimately made by the pope as to the validity of a given tradition has often been arbitrary. For these reasons, and because of the shocking examples of extrascriptural traditions being held, the Reformers set themselves over against Rome and held to the doctrine of the sufficiency of the scriptures. They did not thereby deny the existence of tradition or that much of what Christ and the apostles said and did is not in the canonical scriptures (John 20:30). They held rather that Rome could not prove that alleged extracanonical traditions actually were apostolic, and they affirmed that in Jesus Christ the revelation of God is complete. Moreover, they held that there is a distinction between apostolic tradition, which is certain and in the canon of the Bible, and ecclesiastical tradition, which may be interesting and is sometimes important, but which is not to be regarded as the Word of God.[11]

The Belgic Confession expresses succinctly the position and the

temper of the Reformation church on the doctrine of "the sufficiency of the Holy Scriptures to be the only rule of faith":

> We believe that those Holy Scriptures fully contain the will of
> God, and that whatsoever man ought to believe unto salvation
> is sufficiently taught therein. For since the whole manner of
> worship which God requires of us is written in them at large, it
> is unlawful for any one, though an apostle, to teach otherwise
> than we are now taught in the Holy Scriptures: *nay, though it
> were an angel from heaven,* as the apostle Paul says. For since
> it is forbidden *to add unto or take away anything from the
> word of God,* it does thereby evidently appear that the doc-
> trine thereof is most perfect and complete in all respects.
>
> Neither may we consider any writings of men, however holy
> these men may have been, of equal value with those divine
> Scriptures, nor ought we to consider custom, or the great
> multitude, or antiquity, or succession of times or persons, or
> councils, decrees or statutes, as of equal value with the truth
> of God, since the truth is above all; *for all men are of
> themselves liars, and more vain than vanity itself.* Therefore,
> we reject with all our hearts whatsoever does not agree with
> this infallible rule which the apostles have taught us, saying,
> *Prove the spirits whether they are of God.* Likewise, *if any one
> cometh unto you, and bringeth not this teaching, receive him
> not into your house* (Art. 7).

E. ITS SELF-AUTHENTICATION

The self-authentication of scripture is concerned with the witness
of the Holy Spirit and the problem of biblical authority. The
consideration of it takes us into an area of utmost importance in the
doctrine of scripture. Here, if anywhere, one's theological prejudices
are likely to show. If he is inclined towards an excessive exaltation
of reason, that may come out in a weak treatment of the work of
the Spirit in the hearts of men, particularly in relation to scripture.
If feeling plays a strong role in his religious life, that may be evident
in his exaltation of the work of the Spirit at the expense of the
written Word of God. The history of theology demonstrates that
both tendencies are continuously present in the church.

It is generally recognized that here, in the authenticating of
scripture by the Holy Spirit in the hearts of believers, the Reformed
Church has made one of its finest contributions to theology. It is
also generally recognized that the person responsible for working out
the doctrine is Calvin. Once the Protestant churches saw the truth

and the necessity of the position taken, it became a common possession of them all. The dangers of an exaltation of reason on the one hand, and of feeling on the other, are always present in the church as it moves through history, as is Rome's claim to have exclusive right to authenticate the Bible. The necessity for the church to understand the ground and nature of biblical authority, therefore, can hardly be exaggerated. Because Calvin saw this problem clearly, and because he had an unusual insight into the teachings of scripture and an unusual ability to put them together into a meaningful pattern, he was able to formulate an answer that has not been surpassed. His work on the Holy Spirit was probably his most important single theological contribution and in this particular aspect of the Spirit's work his service to the church in the formulation of its theology is evident.

The problem before Calvin was one of religious authority: how one could rest assured that what he believed from scripture was the truth of God? Before the break with Rome there had been no problem, at least outwardly. One believed what the church through its hierarchy told him to believe. Or, to put the matter differently, one accepted the authority of the church and, by implication, its *corpus fidei,* or body of faith, which he might know or, as was more common, might not know. One believed explicitly or implicitly what the church in its teaching office declared. Thus the question of religious authority was settled.

Once the authority of the Church of Rome was repudiated, however, the fundamental question of by what authority Christians believe the gospel demanded an answer. The obvious response is that they believe by the authority of God who spoke through the prophets and the apostles; and the early Reformers, on the whole, took their stand here. The further question of inner assurance remained unanswered, however. Who is to certify to the Christian that the Bible is indeed the Word of God, the only proper religious authority? *By what authority* can he believe that? That this is no sham question is demonstrated throughout the history of the church. There is no question more fundamental than that of the grounds on which the Christian believes, for if he is uncertain here he will have little peace.

Calvin's answer is significant for two reasons. In the first place, there is an appeal to the objective Word of God, the inspired witness in scripture to the revelation given once for all by the Holy Spirit. Secondly, there is an appeal to the subjective witness to the scriptures by the Holy Spirit in the hearts of Christians. By the first he established the external authority by which one could measure belief. The Bible was declared to be the norm, the criterion by which all should be judged. By the second appeal he emphasized the internal reason for faith, the testimony of God within the heart that his Word is true. What more adequate reason can one have for belief than this?

> The testimony of the Spirit is more excellent than all reason. For as God alone is a fit witness of himself in his Word, so also the Word will not find acceptance in men's hearts before it is sealed by the inward testimony of the Spirit. The same Spirit, therefore, who has spoken through the mouths of the prophets must penetrate into our hearts to persuade us that they faithfully proclaimed what had been divinely commanded (*Inst.*, I. vii. 4).

To that statement one should add another in the same context.

> Those whom the Holy Spirit has inwardly taught truly rest upon Scripture, and that Scripture indeed is self-authenticated; hence, it is not right to subject it to proof and reasoning. And the certainty it deserves with us, it attains by the testimony of the Spirit. For even if it wins reverence for itself by its own majesty, it seriously affects us only when it is sealed upon our hearts through the Spirit. Therefore, illumined by his power, we believe neither by our own nor by anyone else's judgment that Scripture is from God; but above human judgment we affirm with utter certainty (just as if we were gazing upon the majesty of God himself) that it has flowed to us from the very mouth of God by the ministry of men. We seek no proofs, no marks of genuineness upon which our judgment may lean; but we subject our judgment and wit to it as to a thing far beyond any guesswork! (*Inst.*, I. vii. 5).

This is the answer to the widely prevailing "pernicious error" that the authority of scripture depends upon the superior authority of the church.

> As if the eternal and inviolable truth of God depended upon the decision of men! For they mock the Holy Spirit when they ask: Who can convince us that these writings come from God? (*Inst.*, I. vii. 1).

> It is as if someone asked: Whence will we learn to distinguish light from darkness, white from black, sweet from bitter? Indeed, Scripture exhibits fully as clear evidence of its own truth as white and black things do of their color, or sweet and bitter things do of their taste (*Inst.*, I. vii. 2).

It is fair to ask whether Calvin indulges in overstatement here for the sake of emphasis. This is particularly relevant when one considers the questions of Calvin's opponents to which he feels he has given an adequate answer. They include such inquiries as: "Who can assure us that scripture has come down whole and intact even to our very day? Who can persuade us to receive one book in reverence but to exclude another, unless the church prescribe a sure rule for all these matters?" (*Inst.*, I. vii. 1). If one subjects the question of the canon to the exclusive test of the witness of the Spirit in this fashion, is not an injustice done to historical considerations? Moreover, is it not asking too much of the doctrine of the internal testimony of the Holy Spirit when one applies it indiscriminately to all scripture in this fashion? Is every part of scripture as different from all other literature as white is from black, sweet from bitter? Or, must other tests be used also?

In fairness to Calvin certain considerations must be kept in mind when answering these questions. First, here as always Calvin is thinking of scripture as an organism, and the witness of the Spirit is to the various parts of that organism, considered as one whole. It would hardly be fair then for the critic to isolate a passage and ask if the witness of the Spirit were there. Scripture is a unity and every part is related to all of the rest. Second, it is evident elsewhere that Calvin is well aware of historical considerations in the formation of the canon, for he quotes from Cyprian and Jerome to support the contention that II Maccabees does not belong in the Old Testament (*Inst.*, III. v. 8). Moreover, his commentaries show clearly that he does not wish to slight historical considerations. Third, immediately after the chapter on the testimony of the Holy Spirit there follows a discussion of the rational arguments for an acceptance of the Bible among which are a number from history. Even though these are mere "secondary aids" unable to create faith (*Inst.*, I. viii. 13), he must have felt that they were worth considering or he would not have given them the attention that he does. So Calvin may not fairly be charged with subjectivism, mysticism, or obscurantism in his appeal to the Spirit for authentication of the Word. Nevertheless his primary concern, even in the discussion of the secondary aids, is to insist on the necessity of God's own witness to himself in his Word as it is read and pondered in the heart of the Christian. This is the one foundation for faith and for assurance—that the message is from God. Thus, the Westminster Confession likewise says concerning scripture that "our full persuasion and assurance of the infallible truth and divine authority thereof is from the inward work of the

Holy Spirit, bearing witness by and with the Word in our hearts." [12]
And the Belgic Confession reads as follows after the listing of the
books of the canon:

> We receive all these books, and these only, as holy and canon-
> ical, for the regulation, foundation, and confirmation of our
> faith; believing without any doubt, all things contained in
> them, not so much because the Church receives and approves
> them as such, but more especially because the Holy Spirit
> witnesses in our hearts that they are from God, and because
> they carry the evidence thereof in themselves (Art. 5).

The authoritative character of the message is implied in its inspiration and self-authentication. When men are convinced that God
speaks in scripture they seek to understand and obey it as readily as
if he were visibly present. That is the way Calvin regarded the
Bible;[13] that has been the position of the Reformed Church as
attested in its creeds; and that is the position of the church today.
For God *is* there in the midst of his people. That is why his Word is
no ordinary word but a dynamic, creative power that renews and
strengthens, kills and makes alive. The prophets of the Old Testament were not claiming too much when they described the action of
the Word in such language. For the Word that goes forth out of the
mouth of God does not return to him empty but it accomplishes his
purpose. Used by the Spirit it has in times past renewed and
empowered the covenant community to make it a redemptive instrument in the world. When it pleases him again to renew his people it
will be through that same Word, so that they may become in a fresh
sense *the church of Jesus Christ reformed according to the Word of
God.*

NOTES TO CHAPTER III

[1] J. A. Cramer, *De Heilige Schrift bij Calvijn* (Utrecht: A. Oosthoek,
1926), pp. 30, 116-138.

[2] *Jean Calvin: Les Hommes et les choses de son temps* (Lausanne: Georges
Bridel & Cie, 1910), Vol. IV, pp. 79, 82.

[3] H. Bavinck, ed., *Synopsis Purioris Theologiae, per J. Polyandrum, A.
Rivetum, A. Walaeum, A. Thysium, Editio Sexta* (Leiden: Didericum Donner,
1881), p. 43 (V, xxi).

[4] *Ibid.,* p. 44 (V, xxiii); cf. Calvin, *Inst.*, "Prefatory Address to King
Francis."

[5] *Synopsis Purioris Theologiae*, p. 46 (V, xxxii).

[6] *Calvinism* (Philadelphia: Westminster, 1946), pp. 171-179.

[7] *Gereformeerde Dogmatiek* (Kampen: Kok, 1928), Vol. I, p. 449; cf. the dissertation by H. W. Rossouw, *Klaarheid en Interpretasie* (Amsterdam: Jacob Van Campen, 1963).

[8] Yet Dakin laments that Calvin "makes Christ central in the whole of Scripture in a way that is scarcely possible to a modern thinker." *Op. cit.*, p. 177.

[9] See Schaff, *The Creeds of Christendom,* Vol. II, p. 80.

[10] Bavinck, *op. cit.,* Vol. I, p. 452.

[11] For a contemporary statement see Oscar Cullmann, "Tradition," *The Early Church* (Philadelphia: Westminster, 1956), pp. 59-99.

[12] Schaff, *The Creeds of Christendom,* Vol. III, p. 603.

[13] In addition to the above, see his exposition of 2 Tim. 3:16 in the commentaries, where he says that we must give scripture the same reverence that we give God.

IV

in the presence of god

Our discussion has brought us to the heart of the Christian faith. Having begun with the Reformation of the church and the rise of the Reformed tradition, we observed that the name "Reformed" refers primarily to the church of Christ reformed according to a standard, the written Word of God. In this chapter we shall discuss the fact that it is *God's* Word that addresses us, that our ultimate concern is not with what Luther or Calvin said about this or that, nor with theories about the church or the inspiration of the Bible, but with God. For if God is what, or whom, the Christian faith claims him to be, everything else is secondary and the one matter of consuming importance is knowledge of him. Moreover, this knowledge must not only be an intellectual awareness of certain facts about him, but a knowledge of the heart, which is inclusive of the whole person.

The center of Christianity is the relation of man to God. This relationship is more than theology; it is more than philosophy or science. It is the living encounter of a creature with his creator. If man were an ordinary creature there would be no occasion for concern; but inasmuch as he has been made like his creator with intellectual and spiritual gifts and a personal existence that will continue forever, his relationship to God is superior to the other relationships in his life.

The two facts that overshadow all others then are the existence of God and our relationship to him. Elijah put them together during two crises in his life, when he exclaimed, "As the Lord, the God of Israel, lives before whom I stand!" (1 Kings 17:1; cf. 18:15). This formula conveys the essence of true religion, God's reality and man's

88

Ron Snyder

James Smith
Ralph Smith

Louis Snedeker
e Snedeker

Ysbrand Sprik
trating

Greg Steenbergen
Larry Steenbergen

Harold Steenbergen
Rich Steenbergen

Harold Strating
Richard Strating

Richard Stratton
Harold Stratton

Rich Steenbergen
Harold Steenbergen

Terry Steenbergen
Greg Steenbergen

Martin
Raymond Spink

e Snedaker
Louis Snedaker

Ralph Smith
James Smith

standing before him. The realization of this was necessary to make a lone individual strong before Ahab and Jezebel and the prophets of Baal. Once, in a life and death contest, Elijah faced those four hundred and fifty prophets; on other occasions he stood before the hostile king. But because he knew that he also stood in the presence of the living God before whom whole "nations are like a drop from a bucket" (Isa. 40:15), he was equal to the challenge and fulfilled his ministry.

Other prophets had similar experiences; that is why they were prophets. Isaiah saw the Lord in the temple and was overwhelmed with a sense of mission (Isa. 6). Micah said that he was "filled with power, with the Spirit of the Lord, and with justice and might, to declare to Jacob his transgression and to Israel his sin" (Mic. 3:8). Jeremiah was set "over nations and over kingdoms to pluck up and to break down, to destroy and to overthrow, to build and to plant" (Jer. 1:10). He might be ridiculed and cast into a dungeon for a time but he could not fail. For God had made him "a fortified city, an iron pillar, and bronze walls against the whole land, against the kings of Judah, its princes, its priests, and the people of the land." They would fight against him but they could not prevail because God was with him (Jer. 1:18f.). The divine word given to Jeremiah was like fire, like a hammer that breaks the rock in pieces (Jer. 23:29).

Israel's greatest king is another unusual instance of a person with an acute awareness of God's presence. The clearest testimony to this is the many spiritual songs that he wrote, of which the best known is Psalm 23, where David, the shepherd, tells of his fellowship with God.

> The Lord is my shepherd,
>   I shall not want;
> He makes me lie down in green pastures.
> He leads me beside still waters;
>   He restores my soul.
> He leads me in paths of righteousness
>   for his name's sake.
> Even though I walk through the valley
>   of the shadow of death,
>   I fear no evil;
> For thou art with me;
>   thy rod and thy staff,
>   they comfort me.
> Thou preparest a table before me
>   in the presence of my enemies;

> Thou anointest my head with oil,
>   my cup overflows.
> Surely goodness and mercy shall follow me
>   all the days of my life;
> And I shall dwell in the house of the Lord forever.

When David's son, one greater than David, appeared, God manifested his presence in the midst of his people more clearly, more palpably, than ever before or since. Jesus Christ was Immanuel, God with us, and when men had been with him they knew that they had been with God (1 John 1:1-3). Before his return to heaven he promised that he would always be with them in the Holy Spirit (Matt. 28:20; John 14:16-18, 25f.; 16:7-14). The church soon learned the reality and the rich meaning of that gift (Acts 2; 1 Cor. 12).

Thereafter a marked awareness of being in the presence of their Lord has been the experience of his people. Not all have felt this presence or exercised this power as dramatically as Elijah, Jeremiah, David, or the first disciples, but they are there nevertheless. And he is there! That is why his presence and power are experienced.

Luther and Calvin are particularly good examples of men who sensed the living presence of God. We saw this in Luther's sharp struggle for an assurance of salvation. "However irreproachable I lived as a monk," he said, "I felt myself in the presence of God to be a sinner with a most unquiet conscience; nor could I trust that I had pleased him with my satisfaction."[1] The Latin expression that Luther used to represent his sense of standing in the presence of God, *coram Deo*, has come to signify that sense of the divine presence of which the Reformers and their associates were aware.

Luther felt himself always to be standing before the Lord. This was an overwhelming conviction with him. He felt that God is present immediately in the conscience, Karl Holl writes, and this is the proof for his being. He is not just the god of reason; if so, he would only be a god of works-righteousness who would not bother himself with a sinner.[2] The living God, however, knows us and graciously makes himself known as the one before whom we spend all our days. Moreover, Luther believed that in our *Anfechtung,* the spiritual struggle that Christians must wage, we wrestle not only with the devil but, like Jacob at Jabbok, with God also. He is present even in our darkest and apparently most God-forsaken moments.[3]

There were Christians before the Reformation who experienced a profound sense of the divine presence. Francis of Assisi and other Christian thinkers and mystics of the late Middle Ages are evidence of that. But this experience became characteristic of the Reformation begun and dramatically represented by Martin Luther. Throughout wide areas of the church there came to be a new sense of the presence of God in human affairs, and this conviction contributed heavily to the success of the Reformation.

Calvin's belief that he stood *coram Deo* was as real as Luther's and it is as fundamental in his writings. It is this conviction from which all his theology proceeds, and to which it all returns again, like the waters of a fountain. As Calvin has been described as "the theologian of the Holy Spirit par excellence,"[4] he can be characterized with equal propriety as the theologian who lived and labored conscious of the presence of God. As the doctrine of the Christian's union with Christ is central to Calvin's teaching on the application of salvation, this conception that man's whole existence is lived before the Lord forms the foundation of all his work. In discussing *coram Deo* as the heart of Christianity and, in particular, of the Reformed tradition, we can do no better than to follow Calvin's discernment of this great biblical truth. It is especially prominent in his treatment of the following subjects:

1. Providence. God maintains and governs all things, including man. Inasmuch as in him we live and move and have our being, we are ever before him. Two matters related to this broad topic should be mentioned here. One is Calvin's frequent reminder to his hearers and readers that man's "business is with his Maker and the Framer of the Universe" (*Inst.,* I. xvii. 2).[5] The other is God's special relation to his children who have been reconciled in Christ. Through him, says Calvin, we approach more nearly to God than the Levites formerly did. "We are therefore enjoined to 'walk before him,' as if we were under his eye, that we may follow holiness and justice with a pure conscience. We are enjoined to walk before him, and always to consider him as present, that we may be just and upright."[6] All men live their lives before God, but he is especially near those who know him in Christ.

2. The divine image in man. Having been created in God's "image" and "likeness," man bears a relationship to his creator that is not shared by any other creature. Although sin has defaced that image, it has not obliterated it. Man still shows that he excels in some faculties and should therefore be thought of as "the reflection of God's glory" (*Inst.,* I. v. 1). Through salvation the image of God in him is restored so that he reflects the image more perfectly. As the crown of creation man reflects something of God's glory and lives before his face from day to day.

3. Creation. Because God "daily discloses himself in the whole workmanship of the universe. . .men cannot open their eyes without being compelled to see him. . . .Upon his individual works he has engraved unmistakable marks of his glory, so clear and so prominent that even unlettered and stupid folk cannot plead the excuse of ignorance" (*Inst.*, I. v. 1). The case for general revelation is pressed at length here and elsewhere in the author's writings. The point of the teaching is that inasmuch as God presents himself to us in his works we should recognize that fact, contemplate him, and thereby advance in piety.

4. Vocation. Every man has been appointed certain duties in this life by God. These "various kinds of living are called 'callings,' " and this means that "each individual has his own kind of living assigned to him by the Lord as a sort of sentry post so that he may not heedlessly wander about through life" (*Inst.*, III. x. 6). His task is significant, whatever it be, because it is done "in God's sight."

5. Blessings. Since these are an evidence of God's paternal relationship to men, their lives should be a "sacrifice of praise" to him.[7]

6. Spiritual struggle. Like Luther, Calvin emphasized God's presence in temptation. "The Lord daily tests his elect, chastising them by disgrace, poverty, tribulation, and other sorts of affliction." Unlike Satan, whose design in temptation is destruction, God's purpose is to prove and to strengthen his children. Since one can never overcome the devil without God's help, Christians are exhorted to pray daily for it. They must see God's Spirit with and in them so that they can cast off all weakness and win the victory. That is why the prayer Christ taught his disciples includes the petition "lead us not into temptation, but deliver us from evil" (*Inst.*, III. xx. 46).

7. Prayer is a daily practice of the Christian in which he pours out his heart to the Father, lays his desires before him, thanks him for his gifts, and confesses his sin. It presupposes a filial relationship of the child to the Father, who sees, who knows, and who loves. Here, in particular, the intimate relationship between God and man must be appreciated, for the possibility and reality of prayer are dependent on it (*Inst.*, III. xx. 37).

8. Suffering. In his exposition of the Christian life Calvin also teaches the necessity of denying oneself (*Inst.*, III. vii) and of bearing one's cross (III. viii). Inasmuch as "Christ our head had to submit," he reasons, why should we be exempted? (III. viii. 1). Properly understood, suffering is reason for joy, for it is a means towards our spiritual development (III. viii. 2-4). It reminds us that we are indeed children of our Father, whose kindness and generosity ought to be recognized in it (III. viii. 6). Hence Christians do not rebel under divine chastisement but they go to their Father and find their consolation and joy in him (III. viii. 8, 11).[8] Suffering then brings them close to God.

9. *Meditation* is a spiritual exercise of the Christian to clear away the mist and enable him to see God with the eye of faith. As God presents himself to men they are confronted by his presence. Because of the darkness of their hearts and the perversity of their wills, however, they fail to see him in his work until he enables them to do so by a special act of grace. When their eyes are opened they behold him in all things and especially in what he has done for their salvation. Then, in the realization of what the Lord has laid up for them in the future, they project their thoughts to that happy estate. They begin to see the vanity of this earthly life (*Inst.*, III. ix. 1, 2) and to long for that which is to come where shadow is exchanged for substance and Christians stand visibly before their Lord. Such meditation, Calvin reasons, causes us "to raise our eyes to heaven" (III. ix. 1).

In the chapter on this topic Calvin uses Paul's expression that while we are in the body "we are away from the Lord," in order to enhance the expectation of the life to come. He does not mean to minimize thereby the fact of present fellowship with God but to emphasize the superiority of that which still awaits the faithful who labor in this world (III. ix. 4). In the same context he speaks of living and dying unto the Lord while waiting for his call from this life. The practice of meditation then is another area of the Reformer's teaching where our present relationship to God is suggested.

10. *Word and Sacraments.* In these God confronts us, speaks to us, and shows us his mercy. It is a "settled principle that the sacraments have the same office as the Word of God: to offer and set forth Christ to us, and in him the treasures of heavenly grace" (*Inst.*, IV. xiv. 17).[9] The point to be noticed here is that Christ is present in the sacraments. Through them more particularly than in any other means his presence is announced and his life shared by Christians. Word and sacrament to Calvin were not bare signs void of power but mighty instruments in which God is veritably present and through which he performs daily miracles of salvation and grace.[10]

11. *Salvation.* At his creation man knew God and lived in perfect relationship to him, a relationship that would have continued "if Adam had remained upright" (*Inst.*, I. ii. 1). Calvin conceives this to

be so important that he mentions it at the beginning of the *Institutes:* "Our very being is nothing but subsistence in the one God" (*Inst.,* I. i. 1). This relationship, disturbed by sin, is reconstituted in salvation. The heart of salvation is union with Christ through the Holy Spirit, and this means life in fellowship with God.[11]

A. "WHO IS THE LORD?"

It avails little to speak about God and man's existence before him until the meaning of the word "God" is made clear. When Moses and Aaron informed Pharaoh that they were addressing him in the name of the Lord his response was, "Who is the Lord, that I should heed his voice and let Israel go? I do not know the Lord, and moreover I will not let Israel go" (Exod. 5:2). Pharaoh's question was to the point. Its weakness was the spirit in which it was spoken. He was not honestly inquiring in expectation of a helpful reply. Rather, he was expressing sarcastically the scorn he felt for the Yahweh of the Hebrews and his religious traditions. His question, however, is as valid today as it was then: Who *is* the Lord? It brings to mind Elijah's challenge to Israel at another crisis in its history: "If the Lord is God, follow him; but if Baal, then follow him" (1 Kings 18:21).

In answer to this question the church goes back to the canonical scriptures that have come out of the Hebrew-Christian tradition. In them it learns about God because they are a message that he gave to his people. It learns first that, unlike the gods of the nations round about Israel, he is the living God.

> Why should the nations say,
> "Where is their God?"
> Our God is in the heavens;
> he does whatever he pleases.
> Their idols are silver and gold,
> the work of men's hands.
> They have mouths, but do not speak;
> eyes, but do not see.
> They have ears, but do not hear;
> noses, but do not smell.
> They have hands, but do not feel;
> feet, but do not walk;
> and they do not make a sound in their throat.
> Those who make them are like them;
> so are all who trust in them.

O Israel, trust in the Lord!
He is their help and their shield (Ps. 115:2-9).

The utter folly of idolatry is similarly described in the prophecy of Isaiah in a classical passage. After extolling the sovereignty of Yahweh the prophet asks: "To whom then will you liken God, or what likeness compare with him?" This is followed by a scornful description of idolatry and a comparison of it with knowledge of the true God:

The idol! a workman casts it,
    and a goldsmith overlays it with gold,
    and casts for it silver chains.
He who is impoverished chooses for an offering
    wood that will not rot;
he seeks out a skilful craftsman
    to set up an image that will not move.

Have you not known? Have you not heard?
    Has it not been told you from the beginning?
    Have you not understood from the foundations of the earth?
It is he who sits above the circle of the earth,
    and its inhabitants are like grasshoppers;
who stretches out the heavens like a curtain,
    and spreads them like a tent to dwell in;
who brings princes to nought,
    and makes the rulers of the earth as nothing....

To whom then will you compare me,
    that I should be like him? says the Holy One.
Lift up your eyes on high and see:
    who created these?
He who brings out their host by number,
    calling them all by name;
by the greatness of his might,
    and because he is strong in power,
    not one is missing.

Why do you say, O Jacob,
    and speak, O Israel,
    "My way is hid from the Lord,
    and my right is disregarded by my God"?
Have you not known? Have you not heard?
The Lord is the everlasting God,
    the Creator of the ends of the earth.
He does not faint or grow weary,
    His understanding is unsearchable (Isa. 40:18-23, 25-28).

This is the answer to the question: "Who is the Lord?" The Lord is the living God. He is the everlasting God, the creator of the ends of the earth. In other words, he is the only God; none other exists. All that lives owes its being to him. By an act of will God brought forth something other than himself which had no previous existence. In his wisdom and power he fashioned it with all its wonderful properties so that now *it is*. This is the great burden for independent human reason to accept. More fundamental than the coming of God into human life in the person of Christ, it is harder to believe. For when a person believes that "in the beginning God created heaven and earth," belief in other miracles may follow. The incarnation, the resurrection, and the consummation of all things may be seen as mighty works of God. As the fountain and bestower of life, he can give new life to man who has lost it in sin. Once this first article of the creed becomes credible and its significance for the rest of one's view of life has been pondered, the other articles may be credible also. That God is the creator, this is the first truth to be believed about him, and it is also the most difficult.

It is also difficult not to believe it! If belief in creation is hard on reason, the alternatives are no more satisfying. Volumes, hundreds of them, have been written on the alternatives during the history of the church, most of them in the last few generations. Is one to believe, with some of them, that reality is meaningless? Or, with others, that it is eternal with divinity somehow animating ,it as the soul of the world? Those alternatives, like others, were known millennia ago. To believe any alternative to the biblical position requires faith, only faith of another kind. Nor is there rest in agnosticism, for it has always left the soul dissatisfied. Man has been so created that he yearns to rest his soul in that which is real, true, and permanent. Only God meets those conditions, and God is the creator of heaven and earth.

He is also their sustainer and providential Lord. Scripture makes that as clear as it does the fact of creation. God does not desert his universe after he has brought it forth. Nor is he an absentee Lord as some have fancied. They cannot believe that God "upholds, as it were by his own hand, heaven and earth together with all creatures, and rules in such a way that leaves and grass, rain and drought, fruitful and unfruitful years, food and drink, health and sickness, riches and poverty, and everything else, come to us not by chance but by his fatherly hand" (Heid. Cat., Q. 27). But, as might be expected, half-gods do not last long. Inasmuch as they do not trouble their heads much over men, their devotees cease being concerned about them and soon run off into atheism, skepticism, or some other point of view. What men need, and what at bottom they desire, is a God who is worth having and loving and serving with all their heart. Religions lacking here do not understand the true nature of God. They cannot believe that he associates with creatures whom he has made, that he watches over them, and cares for them, and that he is the Lord of history in any personal sense. Yet these positions are a part of the biblical answer to the question that we have been considering.

B. THE NATURE OF GOD

Men are not satisfied to know only that God is their creator and preserver. They wish to know more about him. What is Almighty God like? What may we know about this fearful one with whom we have to do?

The biblical answer to this question is rich. It tells first of all that God is merciful. He has forgiven the sins of men and taken them into covenant with himself so that they may know him and be his people. Although they have not always remained faithful, he has kept his covenant. After Israel rejected God at Sinai he renewed the covenant with his people. While Moses stood on the mountain with two new tables of stone in his hands we read that God stood with him there and proclaimed,

> The Lord, the Lord, a God merciful and gracious, slow to anger, and abounding in steadfast love and faithfulness, keeping steadfast love for thousands, forgiving iniquity and transgression and sin, but who will by no means clear the guilty, visiting the iniquity of the fathers upon the children and the children's children to the third and the fourth generation (Exod. 34:6f.).

God showed his mercy to Israel and his covenant faithfulness is with the church today. Reformed theology has always made much of this fact. With its sensitivity to sin and to the holiness of God, it has seen that only through God's mercy can men have fellowship with him. Mercy is an attribute, a characteristic of God. There are others as well. Scripture eulogizes these divine perfections constantly. "For the Lord is good, his steadfast love endures forever, and his faithfulness to all generations" (Ps. 100:5). Likewise it says that he is just:

O Lord, thou God of vengeance,
thou God of vengeance, shine forth!
Rise up, O judge of the earth;
render to the proud their deserts!
. . . .
Justice will return to the righteous,
and all the upright in heart will follow it (Ps. 94:1, 2, 15).

Scripture also ascribes other characteristics to God, too many to treat here. Those we have mentioned suggest the fullness of the treatment. Nothing in the entire sweep of religion or life is of more vital interest to men than this, for here they consider the nature of him before whom they stand. Although attempts to describe him are finite and fallible, they are not without meaning, for they are based on the revelation God has given. Because he has spoken we can speak, and that which is most important is his word about himself.

The best word that God has spoken was given in Jesus Christ. There his nature is most clearly seen. For Christ does not only express an idea about God but, as Paul has put it, "in him all the fulness of God was pleased to dwell. . . .[in him] are hid all the treasures of wisdom and knowledge" (Col. 1:19; 2:3). He is more than *a* word about God; he is the eternal Word of God himself who makes all of our words about God and every created thing meaningful. The word of God in its most sublime expression is not paper and ink, nor an idea audibly expressed one way in one language and another way in another tongue. In its highest representation the Word of God is a person. It is the "person of the speaking God," as Calvin expressed it.[12] God's revelation came through him. In both testaments Christ, the eternal Word of God, is the revealer.[13] He is the mediator of revelation as well as of creation and redemption.

Christ could be the full and perfect revelation of God because he and the Father are one. Here we approach another truth about God that lies at the center of the biblical teaching about him. It is that God is to be thought of as a plurality of persons. He is one; that was the chief lesson taught Israel when surrounding nations wandered in polytheism: "Hear, O Israel: the Lord our God is one Lord" (Deut. 6:4).

But God is not only one. In the divine being there is more than one person. There are Father, Son and Holy Spirit and these three are one God. In the days of the Old Testament it was seen that there is a glorious fulness of being in God, which approaches the conception of a plurality of persons within the Godhead. But not until God came into the world in a particular manner was the full truth known.

After salvation had been accomplished in the life, death, resurrection, and ascension of the Son of God, and after the Spirit had been sent at Pentecost, the church quietly and unhesitatingly accepted the fact that the God whom it knew and worshipped must include Jesus Christ and the Holy Spirit. Yet the church retained its conviction that the Lord is one God.

The doctrine of the trinity that the church accepted is an attempt to relate the threeness and oneness of God into a meaningful pattern. It does not at all claim to have explained this mystery of God's person, but it states certain truths about him that should be believed in fidelity to revelation. Forever God has been Father, Son, and Holy Spirit, a society of persons within himself. In the person of the Son he has entered into our human existence, having truly become one of us. In the person of the Holy Spirit he has made his abode with us, gives us the spiritual gifts with which we are blessed, and witnesses to us concerning the things of God. God is also our Father whom we can trust "so completely that we have no doubt that he will provide us with all things necessary for both body and soul. Moreover, whatever evil he sends upon us in this troubled life he will turn to our good, for he is able to do it, being Almighty God, and is determined to do it, being a faithful Father (Heid. Cat., Q. 26).

In the last paragraphs several new ideas about God have been introduced. We have mentioned God's fatherhood. Many would begin a discussion of the nature of God with this doctrine because it is so close to the heart of the Christian. Its uniqueness and comfort can be seen by contrasting Christianity with leading non-Christian religions, which have no such teaching. Islam, one of Christianity's great rivals for the souls of men, is an outstanding example. Its icy deity sustains no paternal relationship to his creatures, nor is he considered to be the overflowing fountain of love. This latter concept is another Christian idea. To say that God is love is sheer heresy to some Moslems. Rather he is sovereign will and power.

Christianity, however, while being equally insistent on emphasizing the sovereign will of God, lays great stress on his fatherly mercy and love as well. It does not do so arbitrarily but because God has thus revealed himself in unveiling his nature to men.

> As a father pities his children,
>> so the Lord pities those who fear him.
> For he knows our frame;
>> he remembers that we are dust (Ps. 103:13f.).

God's fatherly compassion is strikingly exhibited in the salvation of mankind. Men who were once "estranged and hostile" (Col. 1:21), who were, as the apostle calls them elsewhere, "sons of disobedience" (Eph. 2:2), are made sons of God who come to know him as their Father. Writing to some of them, Paul says: "You did not receive the spirit of slavery to fall back into fear, but you have received the spirit of sonship. When we cry, 'Abba! Father!' it is the Spirit himself bearing witness with our spirit that we are children of God, and if children, then heirs, heirs of God and fellow heirs with Christ" (Rom. 8:15-17).

Because he is a merciful Father, God saves men. It is customary to refer salvation to Jesus Christ and, indeed, he is the Savior. But it must be added that salvation is through the triune God, for the Father and the Spirit as well as the Son are active participants in salvation. The Father sent the Son into the world and the Spirit applies salvation to men so that they may believe and that believing they may see (John 9:39ff.). While Christians properly relate their salvation to the Lord Jesus Christ, it is equally necessary for them to relate it to God their Father and to the Spirit whom he has given them. This is a truth which needs emphasis in our time when both a shallow fundamentalism and a sophisticated school of theology tend to subordinate the doctrine of God to the person of Christ. Christ is God and we know God the Father only through him. Nevertheless everything, even the Son of God, must be subjected to the Father. "When all things are subjected to him, then the Son himself will also be subjected to him who put all things under him, that God may be everything to everyone" (1 Cor. 15:28). In the person of the Son, God has become our elder brother as well as Redeemer. His work having been accomplished, he has been highly exalted and has been given the name "above every name, that at the name of Jesus every knee should bow, in heaven and on earth and under the earth, and every tongue confess that Jesus Christ is Lord." Yet this is all to redound "to the glory of God the Father," the apostle informs us (Phil. 2:9ff.). To subordinate one person in the holy trinity to the others with respect to divine essence is heresy; to subordinate certain persons to the other with respect to rank is good theology (John 14:28; cf. *Inst.*, I. xiii. 26).

C. THE ALPHA AND OMEGA OF FAITH

In his study of the thought of Calvin, Doumergue divides the discussion of God into two parts. The first is devoted to the doctrines comprehended under the first article of the creed, which speaks of God the Father Almighty, maker of heaven and earth. The second part of the discussion concerns the sovereignty of God and predestination. The author introduces this latter discussion with the following comment:

> At the end of Calvinistic dogmatics we find the same idea as at the beginning: the idea of God. In a particularly profound sense Calvinism is a theocentric theology. For the Calvinist the doctrine of God is the doctrine of doctrines, in a sense the only doctrine. [14]

There is no need to confirm Doumergue's judgment by a citation of passages from other writers. It is shared by representative spokesmen from the Reformed tradition. What we shall do rather is illustrate its truth by the example of three doctrines.

The first is the doctrine of predestination. Simply stated this doctrine means that God is sovereign Lord, who has determined whatever comes to pass, yet not so as to destroy the reality of man's free agency and responsibility. Undeniably, this doctrine brings with it certain intellectual difficulties, but those difficulties are shared by all persons who believe in an almighty, infinite God and the reality of evil in his world.

There are various ways that men have tried to solve these problems. One is to deny predestination in any except a very general sense, so that the decisions of men are untouched and free. This is an attempt to preserve human responsibility at the expense of divine sovereignty. Another proposed solution denies both foreordination and foreknowledge to God inasmuch as acceptance of one of them seems logically to lead to an acceptance of the other. But this position is even worse than the other, for in taking away God's foreknowledge as well as foreordination one removes the possibility of prophecy, a divine purpose in history, and the Lordship of God. Then God lives from day to day as we do, and there is no assurance that he will prevail in the end. Besides contradicting the clear teaching of scripture, both of these alternatives to the doctrine of predestination create more problems than they solve.

The Reformed Church has not resorted to either of these or other expedients in the face of the admittedly difficult problems that the acceptance of the doctrine of predestination raises. It refuses to try to limit the sovereignty of God in any degree. Rather, it proclaims his absolute Lordship over men and nations while it also holds to its belief in man's responsibility and the reality of evil in the world.

Where reason finds difficulties, faith believes, and following faith, reason often finds its own problems reduced. In his famous doctrine of "antinomies," the philosopher Kant showed long ago that reason has its limitations, and that apparently contradictory conclusions about fundamental questions can be drawn from the same premises. Concerning the main point of Kant's argument there is hardly room for debate. Reason *does* have its limitations. It cannot give us answers to certain questions, and the question of predestination is one of these. The fact that God is sovereign Lord *and* the facts of evil and man's free agency and responsibility are paradoxical realities that can be received and held only by faith. But when a person in faith accepts these apparently contradictory ideas and holds them together, even while he is unable to explain them, he may find his own frustration lessened and a satisfaction in humbly acknowledging his reason's subordination to faith's God.

The Reformed fathers accepted scripture's teaching about man and God and they found themselves in respectable company when they did so. In the doctrine of God's sovereignty and predestination they were in agreement with Augustine and Aquinas and most of the great theologians of the old church, and with Luther and the creed of the Church of England as well. Predestination is one aspect of the Reformed understanding of the doctrine of God and it serves to enrich that doctrine by showing that God acts in creation, providence, and redemption in accordance with an eternal plan that he purposed in Christ Jesus our Lord. In accepting it in obedience to scripture the Reformed Church witnessed to its belief that God is the beginning and the end of theological discussion as well as the Alpha and Omega of faith.[15]

(2) The doctrine of the work of the Holy Spirit in the application of salvation to men is another proof of the theocentric character of the teaching of the Reformed Church. How are men saved? By God, say all Christians. How is the salvation that has been accomplished by Jesus Christ outside a person applied to his heart so that he becomes a new man in Christ? Here answers differ. Some hesitate to give all the glory to God but desire to keep some, perhaps a very little, for themselves. The Reformed faith, however, ascribes all to God. That is why it has spoken in terms of total depravity and sovereign grace. These expressions insist on God's priority and sovereignty in bestowing salvation on creatures wholly unable to save themselves.

The understanding of some believers leaves much to be desired here. They have a sound apprehension of the goodness and love of the Father in sending the Son into the world for their salvation, and they hold orthodox views on the person and work of Christ. Their conception of salvation ends there, however, with no appreciation of the work of the Holy Spirit, or how the salvation that has been wrought outside them is going to be worked within so that those who were once dead in trespasses and sins are made new creatures in Christ. At this point Calvin, the theologian of the Holy Spirit, has given the church much valuable help in interpreting the Word of God.[16] It is from within the Reformed tradition that the most significant treatises on the place and function of God the Holy Spirit in the salvation of men have arisen.[17] Moreover, in its struggle with Arminianism, which reached its climax at the great Synod of Dordrecht in 1618-19, the Reformed Church put in creedal form a statement of the application of salvation that honors the initiative and efficacy of divine grace. What was said by the church at Dort was no optional matter. It had to be said to preserve the sovereignty of grace so that in man's salvation God might continue to have the glory. In its teaching on the application of salvation the overarching interest of the Reformed Church in the doctrine of God is clearly seen. As Doumergue has said, it is "the doctrine of doctrines, in a sense the only doctrine."

(3) The same emphasis is seen in the teaching on the purpose of creation. While all of Christianity acknowledges that "the earth is the Lord's and the fulness thereof, the world and those who dwell therein" (Ps. 24:1), the Reformed faith has stressed the truth that the purpose of creation is the glory of God. This means that the earth is not only the Lord's but that he manifests his perfections—his wisdom, his goodness, his power, his grace, in a word, his *glory*—in it; that he blesses it and receives its praise; that man's highest purpose and greatest blessing is to live in love for and obedience to his creator and redeemer. Man's comforts and interests are subordinated to the end that he serves. In carrying out that service man finds joy and comfort that he could not find elsewhere. For he has been made for God and his heart cannot be at rest until it finds its rest in him, as Augustine said long ago. In declaring God to be the center of creation man is not slighted but given his rightful place as a servant. When he sees himself in that light he can rejoice in God and receive his blessings, but only then. For God is God and he will not, nor can he, give his glory to another.

> Glory and honor and thanks to him
> who is seated on the throne,
> who lives for ever and ever. . . .

> Worthy art thou, our Lord and God,
> to receive glory and honor and power,
> for thou didst create all things,
> and by thy will they existed and were created (Rev. 4:9, 11).

The Westminster Shorter Catechism begins by stating that the chief end of man is "to glorify God and to enjoy him forever." It is not surprising that this is the first question and answer of a Reformed confession, for there is a God-centeredness in Reformed theology and life. It is proper that it come to expression here.

D. A THREEFOLD IMPLICATION

The exclamation of Elijah that we observed at the beginning of this chapter called attention to God and it said something about the prophet himself. It mentioned the Lord and the fact that he, Elijah, stood before him. Because Elijah knew that God *is* and that he had been called to be God's prophet, life had a meaning for him that it would not have had otherwise. If God lives and if we stand before him, everything else derives its significance from these primary truths. They bear a threefold implication that is relevant for all the rest of life.

(1) We have already alluded to the first implication, that life has a meaning that is determined by God. Because he knew this, Elijah was a power to be reckoned with in Israel. If he had not had this assurance there would have been little reason for him to risk his life contending against the prophets of Baal or to challenge the evil king and queen. The decisive event in his experience was the revelation of God, which gave him knowledge of both God and himself. Through that revelation Elijah learned the meaning of his own existence. As he reflected he became convinced that neither Ahab, in his weak wretchedness, nor Jezebel, in her heathen hate, nor the pitiful prophets of Baal, were to determine the course of his life, but that he was wholly in the hand of God. His enemies might rage against him if they wished, but Elijah would go on living confidently before the face of the Lord.

This question of meaning is the great question of our time. The most important intellectual and spiritual battle today is not what it was in the sixteenth century. Then it was between Protestantism and Rome, both of which, in spite of their wide differences in other matters, shared a common belief in God and creation. Today these latter fundamental truths are denied or questioned, and that struggle is being carried on in classroom and club, in the pulpit and on the printed page, and in the minds of millions of men. There is evidence of the struggle in literature, in the fare of public entertainment, in the subtle assumptions of much of modern advertising, and in the confused lives of men.

Where is meaning to be found? That is the question. Does it lie hidden in our little comforts and pleasures or in financial security? These can be snatched from one in a moment. Does Communism have the answer? Racism? Sex? A chauvinistic Americanism? Or the struggle for national or racial equality? These are the gods of millions of people in our time. Others, weary of the search for meaning in a world that thwarts their independent attempts to understand it, declare dogmatically that human existence is at bottom meaningless and that we should have the courage to recognize that fact. Eloquent statements of this contemporary "faith" are not wanting. Jean Paul Sartre's repeated affirmation that man is a useless passion and that life is absurd, by which he means meaningless, is a fair example. The only adequate answer to such bold declarations is given by him who said, "I am the Lord thy God....Thou shalt have no other gods before me." If that categorical statement is accepted life has one meaning; if it is not, it has another. The struggle continues between faith in God, on the one hand, and atheism, theoretical or practical — they are equally destructive — on the other.

Discussing this problem, A. E. Loen affirms that the fundamental category with which thought is concerned is man's "there-ness over against the word, that is, existence."[18] This relationship means that there must be hearing and answering. Hearing may not be perfect, for there is the possibility of enmity toward the word. Nevertheless, hearing and answering are the fundamental conditions of life. This hearing must be conscious and the answer must be given in freedom; otherwise hearing and answering would not be real. In order to find its true nature, however, the self that consciously hears and freely answers must give up its independence and be reconciled to the word, so that it comes to sustain another relation to it. The self must die to itself in order to live unto God. Before this actually occurs, being oneself without independence is wholly unacceptable to the self. It cannot give up its independent status because it lives in it. Thus the maintenance of independence is precisely the repetition of the original sin: it is a desire to be oneself apart from God. After the death of the self and reconciliation with the word, existence acquires new meaning. "It is no longer a there-ness over against the word, but a there-ness in the word, in Christ, in the Holy Spirit. It is an existence in gladness, in love, in faith. Its gladness is God's joy, its love is God's love, its faith is God's faithfulness in the Holy Spirit. The Spirit is the miracle of the self existing as that which is God's."[19]

The original possibility for such meaningful existence was creation in the image of God. God fashioned man like himself. That does not mean that "the infinite qualitative distinction" between creator and creature was done away — that would be impossible — but it does mean that man was given capacities and abilities and a relationship to God that no other creatures were able to enjoy. Not even the angels were related to God in the position of privilege enjoyed by man. For, what are the angels? "Are they not all ministering spirits sent forth to serve, for the sake of those who are to obtain salvation?... Surely it is not with angels that God is concerned but with the descendants of Abraham" (Heb. 1:14; 2:16). Abraham was the friend of God; Moses saw God face to face; David was a man after God's own heart. We, like them, can have fellowship with God because he has created us with such possibilities. "Our fellowship is with the Father and with his son Jesus Christ" (1 John 1:3).

(2) This leads us to the second implication of our living *coram Deo:* that man has been given a high privilege. This was anticipated in the remarks above. Man occupies a unique position in creation. No angel enjoys the blessings that God has reserved for him. None of them has been made a child of God and a brother of Jesus Christ, but men have been granted both of these relationships (Rom. 8:16f.; Heb. 2:11-17).

> O Lord, our Lord,
>> how majestic is thy name in all the earth!....
> When I look at thy heavens, the work of thy fingers,
>> the moon and the stars which thou hast established;
> what is man that thou art mindful of him,
>> and the son of man that thou dost care for him?
>
> Yet thou hast made him little less than God,
>> and dost crown him with glory and honor.
> Thou hast given him dominion over the works of thy hands;
>> thou hast put all things under his feet,
> all sheep and oxen,
>> and also the beasts of the field,
> the birds of the air, and the fish of the sea,
>> whatever passes along the paths of the sea.

O Lord, our Lord,
how majestic is thy name in all the earth! (Ps. 8:1, 3-9).

As a lord in God's world, man has been given vast privileges. He may reflect on the meaning of reality and seek to unlock its secrets. He can soar to the moon and examine the starry heavens, or study particles of life whose minuteness staggers the imagination. He can become an abode for the Holy Spirit and, with his help, believe the gospel. In nature and in the gospel man is able to think God's thoughts after him because it has pleased God to endow his favorite creature with such blessings. In all his thinking and living man is encountered by his maker. Each day, each moment, he is being addressed by him: "I am the Lord thy God; give me thy heart."

(3) Privilege implies responsibility. From him to whom much has been given, much shall be required. This is the final implication of our living before the face of God. When God put man in the garden and told him to dress it and to subdue the earth, man could obey or disobey that command. Whatever he did, however, would be an answer to his maker. God speaks and we answer in one way or another, for hearing and answering are primary conditions of our life. To be answerable is to be responsible; the words are synonymous. This motif of responsibility runs throughout scripture from the account of man's creation to the vision of his glorification in heaven. God's sovereignty and man's responsibility are the two fundamental truths in human existence, as in the Bible, and neither of them may be emphasized at the expense of the other or neglected.

There are high points in the history of redemption when responsibility is emphasized dramatically. Joshua's call to Israel is an illustration of this. Summoning all Israel, their elders and chiefs, their judges and officers, he called on the people to choose that day whom they would serve. If they were unwilling to serve the Lord they should choose whether they would serve the gods whom their fathers had served beyond the river or the gods of the Amorites. "But," declared Joshua, "as for me and my house, we will serve the Lord" (Josh. 24:15). In calling the people to decision he was only reminding them of a responsibility that had always been theirs but which they often forgot, denied, or sought to evade.

The message of the prophets was likewise a summons to responsible living. When Israel went astray it was told to return to the Lord who would one day make a reckoning with all people including his own. The message of the New Testament is the same. Since "we must all appear before the judgment seat of Christ, so that each one may receive good or evil, according to what he hath done in the body" (2 Cor. 5:10), it is necessary for each to discharge his responsibility acceptably before the Lord. It is before him that we stand or fall. Therefore Peter and John had to speak what they had seen and heard even though they were threatened by the Jewish council (Acts 4:20), and Paul so sensed his responsibility that he wrote in a letter, "Woe to me if I do not preach the gospel!" (1 Cor. 9:16). The same compulsion drove Luther to declare before church and empire that he could not recant, and it motivates the simplest believer today. For all Christians are aware of the fundamental conditions of existence declared by Elijah when he exclaimed about the living God and added the pregnant expression "before whom I stand."

The Reformed Church shares this sense of Christian responsibility and proclaims it along with the sovereignty of God with equal power. Both doctrines are necessary, and together they form the foundation for biblical faith. Faith is not arid, speculative discussion about this or that theory of theology, philosophy, or life, but it is devout living before the face of the Lord in the consciousness of responsibility to him.

NOTES TO CHAPTER IV

1 Quoted by Rupp, *The Righteousness of God*, p. 121.

2 Karl Holl, "Was verstand Luther unter Religion?" *Gesammelte Aufsätze zur Kirchengeschichte*, Vol. I, pp. 36f.; cf. J. T. Bakker, *Coram Deo: Bijdrage tot het Onderzoek naar de Structuur van Luthers Theologie* (Kampen: J. H. Kok, 1956).

3 Holl, *op. cit.*, p. 69.

4 B. B. Warfield, quoted by Doumergue, *Jean Calvin*, Vol. IV, p. 426.

5 Cf. I. xvi. 6; III. iii. 6, 16; III. vii. 2. John T. McNeill writes: "For Calvin, every man in all circumstances has dealings with God (*negotium cum Deo*). . . .This conviction was held by him in a very personal sense. For example, in his letter to Farel when in the stress of decision regarding his return to Geneva: 'I am well aware that it is with God that I have to do.' " *Inst.*, I. xvii. 2, note 2 (Vol. I, p. 212).

6 "*Itaque iubemur coram ipso ambulare ac si essemus sub eius oculis ut pura conscientia sanctitatem et iustitiam colamus. Iubemur enim coram ipso ambulare, ipsumque semper considerare praesentem, ut iusti atque integri simus.*" *Commentary on the Book of the Prophet Isaiah* (Edinburgh: Calvin Translation Society, 1851), p. 162. Ronald S. Wallace remarks concerning the

special relationship believers sustain to God in Calvin's thought as follows: "God acts towards them providentially in a special way, and throughout their life in this present world they are specially protected from evil, specially provided for and specially blessed." *Calvin's Doctrine of the Christian Life* (Edinburgh: Oliver and Boyd, 1959), p. 132.

7 See Wallace's rich collation of references, *op. cit.,* pp. 284f.

8 Cf. Wallace, *op. cit.,* pp. 258ff.

9 Again: "God himself is present in his institution by the very-present power of his Spirit" (*C.R.* 30, 953f.).

10 Besides Calvin's own writings see Ronald S. Wallace, *Calvin's Doctrine of the Word and Sacrament* (Edinburgh: Oliver & Boyd, 1953), and Parker, *op. cit.*

11 Another aspect of salvation in which man's life before God is stressed is the doctrine of justification. In one paragraph in the discussion of this topic in the *Institutes* (III. xi. 2) the expression "in God's sight" occurs three times. Equivalent expressions are used more often as Calvin drives home the personal character of man's relationship to God.

12 *"Itaque summa Scripturae probatio passim a Dei loquentis persona sumitur." Inst.,* vii. 4.

13 Cf. *Inst.,* I. xiii. 7-10; II. ix. 1.

14 *Op. cit.,* Vol. IV, p. 361.

15 "I maintain that predestination is not the formative principle of Reformed Protestantism, although it is, of course, an essential element in our system. The character of our theology is preeminently theological. This is the reason why the doctrine of the decrees is looked upon by some as the material principle of Reformed theology. This doctrine is an important part of theology proper. But it is not the whole of it. The doctrine of God is the basis on which our theology rests." N. J. Steffens, "The Principle of Reformed Protestantism and Foreign Missions," *The Presbyterian and Reformed Review,* 1894, p. 244.

16 See S. van der Linde, *De Leer van den Heiligen Geest bij Calvijn* (Wageningen: Veenman, 1943); Werner Krusche, *Das Wirken des Heiligen Geistes nach Calvin* (Göttingen: Vandenhoeck und Ruprecht, 1957).

17 E.g., John Owen, *The Works of John Owen, D.D.,* ed. W. H. Goold (London: Johnstone and Hunter, 1952), Vols. III and IV; Abraham Kuyper, *The Work of the Holy Spirit* (New York: Funk & Wagnalls, 1900); A. A. van Ruler, *De Vervulling van de Wet* (Nijkerk: G. F. Callenbach, 1947).

18 A. E. Loen, *De vaste Grond* (Amsterdam: H. J. Paris, 1946), p. 132.

19 *Ibid.,* p. 160.

V

the life of the christian

The central truth in Christianity and in all human existence is that man is *coram Deo:* in the presence of God. No other consideration can stand alongside this most important one; all else must be subsumed under it. Luther and Calvin rediscovered this scriptural teaching and worked it into their thinking, as can be seen frequently throughout their writings. Man is no lord of creation sufficient unto himself, they asserted, but he stands as a creature before his creator on whom he is dependent and before whom he is responsible. This Lord, having made man like himself, "in his own image" (Gen. 1:27), calls man to live his life consciously before him. As man stands *coram Deo,* so he must live, remembering that he is not his own but that he has been bought with a price and that therefore he must glorify God with his whole being (1 Cor. 6:20).

No one has given this theme fuller and more eloquent treatment than the Genevan Reformer. One need only read the chapters on living the Christian life in the third book of the *Institutes* to observe how large a place *coram Deo* occupied in Calvin's thinking. His discussion of the life of the Christian, self-denial, cross-bearing, the right use of the present life, and meditation on the future life, his broad treatments of faith, justification, prayer, and Christian freedom, is that section of the *Institutes* which is closest to Calvin's heart. Contrary to some opinion, John Calvin was no armchair theological strategist, no mere theoretician who had little practical interest in the day by day life of men. "Empty speculations which idle men have taught apart from God's Word" (*Inst.,* I. xiv. 4) held little interest for him. Since "empty speculation merely flits in the

110

brain" and is not "sound and fruitful" (I. v. 9), he repeatedly warns his readers against it. The "Sophists of the Sorbonne" may engage in this fruitless exercise, but those who have come to know God in his Word should not be deceived by "the senseless ravings of certain monks" or by "Schoolmen's follies" (II. iii. 13; III. iv. 39).

From the time of Calvin an emphasis upon practical Christian living has characterized the Reformed Church. Man was created and redeemed, it was reasoned, to "glorify God, and enjoy him forever," as the Westminster Shorter Catechism says. Right doctrine is necessary so that man may serve the Lord. It is no end in itself, but is a help to the realization of life's purpose as the loving service of God and man. "That truth is in order to goodness; and that the great touchstone of truth is its tendency to promote holiness," is the expressed presupposition of the polity of Presbyterianism[1] and a proposition etched deeply into the life of the Reformed Church.

This practical, utilitarian character of faith is seen in no confessional statement of the Christian church more clearly than in the Heidelberg Catechism. So, for example, the motif of the Christian's comfort with which the catechism begins in the first question and answer prevails throughout. The question and answer on providence read:

> Q. What advantage comes from acknowledging God's creation and providence?
>
> A. We learn that we are to be patient in adversity, grateful in the midst of blessing, and to trust our faithful God and Father for the future, assured that no creature shall separate us from his love, since all creatures are so completely in his hand that without his will they cannot even move (Q. 28).

The Christian is taught to seek the "benefit" in each article of the faith, in Christ's sacrificial death on the cross (Q. 43), in his resurrection (Q. 45), ascension (Q. 49), glorification (Q. 51), and even in his "holy conception and birth" (Q. 36; similarly, the Westminster Shorter Catechism asks about the benefits of faith in Q. 32, 36, 37, 38, and 88). He is asked "what comfort" he receives from the doctrines of the second advent of the Lord (Q. 52), the resurrection of the body (Q. 57), and the life everlasting (Q. 58). Most striking of all is the question after the exposition of the Apostle's Creed: "But how does it help you now that you believe all this?" (Q. 59). The intention is to emphasize the very practical and useful consequences of Christian faith. A later question asks how baptism reminds and assures the Christian that the one sacrifice of Christ on the cross "avails" for him (Q. 69), and a question on the Lord's Supper asks how we are reminded and assured thereby that we "participate" in the one sacrifice of Christ on the cross and in all his benefits (Q. 75). In addition, the answers to other questions are deliberately given a practical turn, following the Reformed emphasis upon Christian living and making the catechism a relevant instrument in both preaching and teaching. The place of the law in the catechism, in the last part so that it may assist the Christian in his life of gratitude for salvation, is further evidence of the practical bent of Reformed theology. The underlying conviction is that Christianity is a life to be lived before the face of God and that the catechism, like scripture, should serve that end.

A. LIFE IN THE HOLY SPIRIT

Man can live before the face of God only on the condition that he receive grace. Because he is a sinner he needs the salvation worked out by God in history and its application to him through the Holy Spirit. Presently we shall consider the work of the Savior as the motive for Christian living. Suffice it to say now that redemption was accomplished in Jesus Christ through the power of the Holy Spirit. It was through the Spirit that Jesus was conceived in Mary's womb (Matt. 1:18; Luke 1:35), that he was anointed and began his ministry (Luke 4:1, 14, 18), that he performed his work (Matt. 12:18), and that he offered himself as a sacrifice to God (Heb. 9:14). The work of the Holy Spirit, often slighted and misunderstood among Christians in even its most obvious New Testament teaching, the application of salvation to the elect, is virtually unknown in its relation to the person and work of our Lord. Yet, as Van Ruler has shown, the work of the Spirit is equally important as and more comprehensive than the work of the Messiah.[2]

If one is to receive the benefits the Father bestowed upon the Son, he must receive them through the same Holy Spirit in whom they were acquired. By nature man is unable to desire or understand spiritual truth, for it is foolishness to him; he can accept it and recognize Jesus as Lord only by the Holy Spirit (1 Cor. 2:14; 12:3). One must be "born of water and the Spirit" in order to enter the kingdom of God (John 3:15); he is sealed with the Holy Spirit (Eph. 1:13; 4:30); the Spirit, who searches the deep things of God, reveals them unto believers (1 Cor. 2:10). John writes concerning God's presence with his people: "By this we know that he abides in us, by the Spirit which he has given us" (1 John 3:24). Later he comments: "By this we know that we abide in him and he in us, because he has given us of his own Spirit" (1 John 4:13). The life of the Christian, then, is life in the Holy Spirit, who also dwells with him, is in him, and instructs him in the things of God (John 14:17, 26; 16:13).

With the Reformation the biblical teaching about the Holy Spirit again found its true place in the teaching of the church. The most important theological contribution Calvin made is probably his teaching on the Spirit.[3] One finds the greatest concentration of this teaching in the first chapters of the third book of the *Institutes*. The Spirit is shown to be the bond that unites believers to Christ and gives them whatever gifts they possess. One of these, fundamental to the others, is faith, which cannot be considered apart from him: "What else is it, then, than to do injury to the Holy Spirit if we separate faith, which is his peculiar work, from him?" (*Inst.,* III. ii. 39). He is the person of the Godhead who abides with us and unites us to Christ, our head.

This biblical emphasis on the Holy Spirit was transmitted from Calvin to the Reformed tradition. It is seen in the Heidelberg Catechism, where the person and work of the Spirit receive treatment commensurate with the place given them in the written Word of God.[4] It was observed also in other creedal statements, theological writings, and devotional literature until the antimystical spirit of rationalism weakened this part of the church's witness. One can see it further in the Puritan and Methodist movements, not to mention other, lesser known, forms of pietism that also arose within the Reformed Church. It can be said that no major tradition of the church has been more conscious than the Reformed of the biblical teaching of the Holy Spirit or more concerned about realizing his presence in the lives of believers.

In its recognition of the Christian life as life in the Holy Spirit the Reformed Church avoided the error of "perfectionism," the teaching that a Christian can live without sin in this life. The church was aware of the call to holiness, of course, and set it forth as the ideal to be sought. For the scriptural injunction to sanctification could not be missed by a church particularly interested in Christian living. But it also understood the doctrine of sin as the Bible presents it, as a part of man's present nature from which he is not completely set free as long as he is in this life. The difficulty with perfectionist teaching, it saw, is its superficial conception of sin, which it tends to spell in the plural, *sins,* and define as voluntary transgressions of known law. Sin is looked at as something which can be taken out of a man here and now if only he tries and then waits upon the Holy

Spirit for the "second blessing." This teaching is found in John Wesley, one of the greatest Christians of the eighteenth century, and among "holiness people" today. Saddened by the plight of the church in his day and quickened to a high level of spiritual life and achievement, Wesley rang the changes on the biblical theme of holiness. That his intention was good and his work of inestimable benefit to the church is indisputable. This does not void the error in his teaching, however, as some of his most able disciples have seen. R. Newton Flew, a leading Methodist theologian, has written the following concerning Wesley's teaching on sin:

> Inheriting as we did the Augustinian doctrine of original sin, Wesley tends to speak of sin as a *quantum,* or hypostasis; as a substance which might be expelled, or rooted out, or as an external burden which might be taken away. As Dr. Sugden has pointed out, he never quite shook off the fallacious notion "that sin is a *thing* which has to be taken out of a man like a cancer or a rotten tooth" .... But sin is not a mere *thing.*[5]

The dangers of perfectionism are evident. Besides the weakness mentioned above, it leads to a false belief in victory over sin with consequent disillusionment. It easily begets spiritual pride, that prolific father of the sins of arrogance, self-sufficiency, hypocrisy, pharisaism, lack of love, and harsh criticism of other Christians. Commenting on spiritual sins of this nature, Stephen Neill remarks that "they are far worse sins than the everyday failings of stealing and lying. It might almost seem as though under the judgment of God, the highest claims prepared the way for the deepest falls."[6]

Because they have felt that the claim to sinlessness is unrealistic, certain groups of holiness people have modified their teaching to allow for minor imperfections. These latter are no longer considered to be sins, but of a less serious character. Among some adherents of the "higher life" or "victory" movements they are spoken of as belonging only to the old nature that has been crucified with Christ, so that the Christian, who has risen with Christ into newness of life, has not "really" committed them and therefore is not responsible for them. But this is also unsatisfactory. "These reductions of perfection to something less than perfection are an evasion of the issue," says Bishop Neill, agreeing with Warfield who writes,

> Nothing can be more important than that the conception of perfection be maintained at its height....The habit of conceiving of perfection as admitting of many imperfections — moral imperfections, glossed as infirmities, errors and inad-

vertences — not only lowers the standard of perfection and with it the height of our aspirations, but corrupts our hearts, dulls our discrimination of right and wrong, and betrays us into satisfaction with attainments which are very far from satisfactory. Such compromises lull men to sleep with a sense of attainments not really made; cut the nerve of effort in the midst of the race; and tempt men to accept imperfection as perfection — which is no less than to say that evil is good.[7]

The biblical answer to perfectionist thinking entails a more adequate conception of sin. If sin is thought to lie near the surface of human nature, so that it may be eradicated root and branch in this life, complete deliverance from it may seem possible. If, however, it is considered to have sent its roots deep into our inner being, its removal will be seen to be another matter. To change the metaphor, if sin is seen to have poisoned our nature so that its last vestiges are not removed nor the waters fully purified until our redemption is complete at death or the end of the age, perfectionist doctrine will seem shallow and dangerous. Sin is a condition of our present existence. The redemption of the world of which we are a part is not yet complete. Christ has performed his perfect work, but we are yet awaiting the final day. "We ourselves, who have the first fruits of the Spirit, groan inwardly as we wait for adoption as sons, the redemption of our bodies" (Rom. 8:23). Our present lack of love is sinful. Our omissions as well as our transgressions make us cry out for forgiveness. Sin requires the forgiveness of God himself, and the death of the Son of God. It is the dark mystery within, against which men must contend all their days lest, thinking that the fight is past, they lay down their arms and lay themselves open to the machinations of evil.

In its objection to perfectionism the Reformed Church is not indifferent to the call to holiness in Christian living. Indeed, its rejection of certain perfectionist doctrine is in the interest of true holiness. This latter, however, cannot be achieved with an inadequate doctrine of sin and an abundance of exhortation. What is required is an understanding of scripture, prayer, and earnest endeavor, all blessed by the Spirit of God.

Perhaps the sons of the Reformed tradition in another age made greater use of these spiritual weapons than their descendants today. History records that in places where it might least be expected the fear of God and a Christian life were much in evidence. In seventeenth-century Britain this came to be true in Oliver Cromwell's army, composed of some of the finest male citizens. Its soldiers boasted that they were putting their lives in jeopardy for the sake of the Christian faith and the political freedom of the land they loved and over whose welfare they were the watchmen. Macaulay writes about Cromwell's army as follows:

> It never found, either in the British Isles or on the Continent, an enemy who could stand its onset. In England, Scotland, Ireland, Flanders, the Puritan warriors, often surrounded by difficulties, sometimes contending against threefold odds, not only never failed to conquer, but never failed to destroy and break in pieces whatever force was opposed to them. They at length came to regard the day of battle as a day of certain triumph, and marched against the most renowned battalions of Europe with disdainful confidence....The banished Cavaliers felt an emotion of national pride when they saw a brigade of their countrymen, outnumbered by foes and abandoned by allies, drive before it in headlong route the finest infantry of Spain, and force a passage into a counterscarp which had just been pronounced impregnable by the ablest of the marshals of France....That which chiefly distinguished the army of Cromwell from other armies, was the austere morality and the fear of God which pervaded the ranks. It is acknowledged by the most zealous Royalists that, in that singular camp, no oath was heard, no drunkenness or gambling was seen, and that, during the long dominion of the soldiery, the property of the peaceable citizen and the honor of woman were held sacred....No servant girl complained of the rough gallantry of the redcoats. Not an ounce of plate was taken from the shops of the goldsmiths.[8]

Does the quest for holiness continue in our day? There are those who believe that it is no longer to be found in the Reformed Church, so they have left its denominations. The following letter undoubtedly expresses the sentiments of many who have left the older, established communions for others in which they have sought a more satisfying emphasis on Christian living. It cannot be dismissed glibly as a "crank" letter, for there are too many "good" people who, like the writer of this letter, are no longer in the older churches. It reads in part:

> The trouble in the lukewarm church groups in these last days of this dispensation is that there is too much pussyfooting which is greatly hindering the cause of Christ (2 Tim. 4:3, 4; Rev. 3:14-22)....I understand your difficulty, for it is only a few short years ago that I was as much in the dark as you are.

First of all, I will give my testimony. I was in the Reformed Church for about thirty-one years; that is where I was saved, but there was no growth in my spiritual life. We got very good spiritual preaching from the pulpit; Jesus was real from the pulpit, during most of these years. But as soon as I'd take my eyes from the pulpit to the congregation Jesus seemed to fade away. In other words, Jesus is not real to the individuals in the congregation. This was something I could not understand. I took my burden to the Lord, and my blessed Lord led me into a group where Jesus *is* real. I praise His wonderful name! He truly becomes sweeter as the days go by....I thank my lovely, precious Jesus for having given me an opportunity to witness to you....Please, Brother, seek the Lord on this matter; you will never be sorry. All my words are of no avail unless you seek the Lord.

No church is stronger than the blessing it has received from God. Certainly the Reformed Church has received a rich measure of grace in its history; whether its strength is as great today is not easy to determine; and what lies in its future no man knows. It appears, however, that it does not hold the lead in spiritual advance as it once did if missionary zeal, stewardship, witnessing, and growth are adequate criteria. Christians from other, less "solid, respectable" communions now lead the way. The Reformed Church continues to enjoy its rich theological heritage and to furnish leadership for the ecumenical movement, one of the remarkable phenomena of our time, but a more accurate measurement of its vitality is the commitment of the rank and file of its membership to Christ and their resolution to live for him by the power of the Holy Spirit from day to day. If a large number of its people are too sophisticated to witness for its Lord, if half-veiled unbelief accepts only what pleases it in the Word of God, if selfishness and complacency dim the fires that burn within it, others will lead the way. The warning given the church at Ephesus that its lampstand might be removed because it had abandoned its first love is intended for us also (Rev. 2:4f.). It is possible for one part of the church to be passed by as the Holy Spirit carries forward his work of salvation. During the evangelical revival of the eighteenth century, when the British church was receiving a rich flow of new life from God, the Bishop of London wrote a pastoral letter in which he commented as follows: "I cannot imagine what persons mean, by talking of a great work of God at this time. I do not see any work of God now, more than has been at any other time." John Wesley, the leader of that great revival, replied, "I believe it: I believe the great man did not see any extraordinary work of God. Neither he, nor the generality of Christians so-called, saw any signs of the glorious day that is approaching."[9]

The venerable bishop has his counterpart in the historic churches of our society, including the Reformed Church. It is found in those whose confidence is in privileged position and social standing instead of the power of the Holy Spirit, or in church members who take pride in the better part of their church's history but lack the will and the faith that, in other persons and in another day, made their church great. Respectability is no adequate substitute for a spirit-filled life, and knowledgeable ministers are no guarantee of heaven's blessing. Nor does an inspiring past make the future sure. As the church is always one generation away from extinction, so every part of it must wait earnestly upon the Lord for the gifts that give labor lasting value. There is wisdom in an ancient Reformed slogan: *nisi Dominus, frustra:* without the Lord all is in vain.

B. THE ORDERING OF THE LIFE OF THE CHRISTIAN

Life in the Holy Spirit has order. This means first that there is conscious motivation for seeking to live as a Christian. That motivation is twofold; it consists of gratitude and expectation, both of which have God as their object.

Gratitude becomes a powerful factor in discipleship because the Christian knows that his salvation has come to him as a free gift from God. He did not earn it or deserve it. Rather, he deserved the worst because of his rebellion and sin.

> But God, who is rich in mercy, out of the great love with which he loved us, even when we were dead through our trespasses, made us alive together with Christ (Eph. 2:4f.).

Salvation is an objective accomplishment and a subjective experience: it happens outside the sinner and is applied to him inwardly by the Holy Spirit. The believer's union with Christ, in whom he has been chosen from eternity (Eph. 1:4), underlies both and binds them together. His justification and sanctification are the two sides of the coin of salvation and a person cannot have the one without the other. It is important to emphasize this point because extreme positions have been taken emphasizing one doctrine at the expense of the other and consequently falsifying both.

An example of an exaggerated teaching of justification is found in Herman F. Kohlbrügge and Eduard Böhl. Reacting against the prevalent liberal theology of the nineteenth century which substituted

Dear Teachers:

As I am now beginning to fe
want to begin to learn more abo
a whole. Some of you have alre
information I requested, which
tached form for providing this
so already. After I receive th
any questions. The comment col
information which might not be
vorced, mother remarried, stude

I also would like to have s
Please fill out the questionnai
may use my mailbox). Thanks fo

NAME _____

1. Do you have an aide in your
   one?

2. How long have you been teach

ethical for legal categories, this father and son-in-law proclaimed the truths of law, guilt, and justification. Their fear of pietism and any subjective undermining of the objective, forensic side of the gospel was so great that they denied altogether the reality of spiritual growth in the life of the Christian. Bohl, for example, rightly shows the sinner's need of forgiveness and the imputation, or reckoning, of Christ's righteousness if he is ever to stand before God, but he leaves no room for a subjective work of the Holy Spirit in his heart. There is only outward, objective imputation. In his *Dogmatik* he holds that

> in regeneration man's substance is unchanged. An infusion of new powers, religious qualities, and dispositions in no way exists....The converted person as little bears an inward holiness in him as an infused righteousness.[10]

In his monograph on justification he objects to those who hold that in sanctification there is a "renewal and a transformation of the whole inner man through faith, in contradiction to justification." Some speak of a "gradual dying of the old man and of a gradual increase of the new man in the same proportion," but this is inadmissible in view of Romans 6:10. For there we read that we "died to sin," and

> that does not mean that sin is expelled from within us by a certain process...but rather in virtue of imputation, according to which, sin, even though it be present, is at the same time not present and has no right to exist in those that are by faith in Jesus Christ. The other one that has died (i.e., the one having been justified) has thus been perfected before the divine tribunal, so that sin has no more to do with him and he needs not to be mortified gradually a second time, through the law.

> Since everything is brought to pass by imputation, since in no other way another's possession could be made ours, so likewise, the new man is present, merely by imputation. The man who had just stood before God as old, He looks upon as new.[11]

In answer to the question whether there is "no restoration of the image of God" in the Christian, "no development of the new man already present in germ," Böhl thunders:

> No, a hundred times no. This would destroy the imputation, for this cannot have anything as a consequence which would essentially destroy justification by faith alone. In short, all the

relations of this cardinal doctrine must be in perfect harmony with it.[12]

This last comment shows that justification is raised to the central position. It is, as with Luther, "the article of a standing or a falling church."[13] Every other doctrine is subordinate to it and affected, if not its meaning determined, by it. The new life in Christ is understood only imputatively (there is no development within), the idea of good works becomes a terror to the theologian, and the doctrine of sanctification is relegated to limbo.

Completely antithetical to the above position is the teaching of some who follow John Wesley's reluctance to ascribe the imputation of Christ's righteousness to the sinner. The sinner must achieve his own righteousness by a process set up within him by the Holy Spirit. The biblical doctrine of justification disappears and the hope of the Christian with it. Thus, Vincent Taylor can write:

> Imputation...can never be anything else than an ethical fiction ....Righteousness cannot be transferred from the account of one person to another. Righteousness can no more be imputed to a sinner than bravery to a coward or wisdom to a fool. If through faith a man is accounted righteous, it must be because, in a reputable sense of the term, he is righteous, and not because another is righteous in his stead. Although, then, Reformation teaching is much nearer the Pauline doctrine than Catholic theology, it cannot be said to have been successful in surmounting the ethical difficulties of justification.[14]

The definition of justification given later envisions it as a work within man, similar to sanctification.

> It is the divine activity in which God gives effect to His redeeming work in Christ by making possible that righteous mind necessary to communion with Himself.[15]

Curiously, after this emasculation of the doctrine of justification, the author closes the chapter by quoting in both Latin and English the Lutheran articles which call justification "the article of a standing or a falling church," and Luther's enthusiastic judgment that

> the article of justification is master and chief, lord, ruler and judge above every kind of doctrine, which preserves and directs every doctrine of the Church.[16]

Turning from these extreme positions, which do violence to the biblical doctrine of salvation, the Reformed faith lays emphasis on both the objective work of Christ outside us *(extra nos)* and the subjective work of his Spirit within us *(in nobis)*. With respect to the former, it insists that justification consists of both forgiveness of sins and the gracious reckoning of Christ's righteousness to the sinner. Thus it is set forth in scripture, and with this understanding the Reformers contended against Rome, who proclaimed a righteousness obtainable by works. The only righteousness that can stand before the judgment of God is one which is "absolutely perfect and wholly in conformity with the divine law. But even our best works in this life are all imperfect and defiled with sin" (Heid. Cat., Q. 62). If God marks iniquities, who can stand? But he forgives and *reckons* sinners righteous. Paul declares in the most forceful manner that God did that with Abraham. Abraham "believed God and it was reckoned to him as righteousness" (Gen. 15:6; Rom. 4:3; Gal. 3:6). Moreover, after a disquisition on the importance of imputation, or "reckoning," the apostle writes that

> the words, "it was reckoned to him," were written not for his sake alone, but for ours also. It will be reckoned to us who believe in him that raised from the dead Jesus our Lord, who was put to death for our trespasses and raised for our justification (Rom. 4:23ff.).

Inasmuch as Abraham's justification "was a gracious declaration of pardon rather than a reward for achievement,"[17] God reckoned to him a righteousness that, strictly speaking, was not his own. It became his by faith and thereafter

> he received circumcision as a sign or seal of the righteousness which he had by faith while he was still uncircumcised. The purpose was to make him the father of all who believe without being circumcised and who thus have righteousness reckoned to them (Rom. 4:11).

In his argument for justification by the gratuitous reckoning of righteousness to the sinner Paul discourages the attempt to work it out for oneself. If one seeks to do so, what he receives is not a gift but what he has coming. But, he continues as he drives his point home, "to one who does not work, but trusts him who justifies the ungodly, his faith is reckoned as righteousness" (Rom. 4:5). The imputation of the righteousness of Christ, then, as the Reformed Church conceives it, does not mean that God observes how well we have done and then declares us to be fit citizens of his kingdom. Rather, scripture invariably sets forth the thesis that God justifies the ungodly, the sinner (e.g., Rom. 5:6, 9f., 16-21). Christ came not to call the righteous but sinners to repentance (Matt. 9:13). The publican who smote his breast asking God to be merciful to him, a sinner, went home justified rather than the self-righteous Pharisee (Luke 18:14). Sinners are justified freely, as a gift, through the redemption that is in Christ Jesus, says the apostle, after which he can throw out the challenge, "Then what becomes of our boasting?" and answers,

> It is excluded. On what principle? On the principle of works? No, but on the principle of faith. For we hold that a man is justified by faith apart from works of law. . . .The wages of sin is death, but the free gift of God is eternal life in Christ Jesus our Lord (Rom. 3:24-28; 6:23).

The Reformed Church stands shoulder to shoulder with the Lutheran Church in upholding this cardinal biblical and Reformation doctrine of justification by faith. Like Luther, it has taken the apostle's words in Galatians at face value. The churches of Galatia had been lapsing into a sub-Christian legalism and works-righteousness. That prompted Paul to write:

> We ourselves, who are Jews by birth and not Gentile sinners, yet who know that a man is not justified by works of the law but through faith in Jesus Christ, even we have believed in Christ Jesus, in order to be justified by faith in Christ, and not by works of the law, because by works of the law shall no one be justified (Gal. 2:15, 16).

The Reformed Church then holds with Paul and Luther that the righteousness that justifies must be a righteousness "apart from law," i.e., it must be the righteousness of God himself given through faith in Jesus Christ (Rom. 3:21f.). This discovery, as we saw in Chapter One, gave Luther a new conception of God and became the heart of the great religious awakening of the sixteenth century.

There is little need to demonstrate Calvin's complete oneness with scripture and Luther in this matter. The eight chapters on justification in the *Institutes* speak for themselves. He gives it thorough treatment because we must

> bear in mind that this is the main hinge on which religion turns, so that we devote the greater attention and care to it. For unless you first of all grasp what your relationship to God is, and the nature of his judgment concerning you, you have neither a foundation on which to establish your salvation nor one on which to build piety toward God (*Inst.*, III. xi. 1).

His consuming interest in justification is practically motivated, as it was with Luther. "The point involved is peace of conscience," he insists.[18] This can only be acquired when we seek our righteousness "outside ourselves [*extra nos*] because we are righteous in Christ only," he writes in his "antidote" to the sixth session of the Council of Trent which was meeting at the time. He continues:

> Let them produce evidence from Scripture, if they have any, to convince us of their doctrine. . . .We have no alternative but to flee to Christ alone, that we may be regarded as righteous in him, not being so in ourselves. Will they produce to us one passage which declares that begun newness of life is approved by God as righteousness either in whole or in part? . . .Can anything be clearer than that we are regarded as righteous in the sight of God because our sins have been expiated by Christ, and no longer hold us under liability.[19]

The word "regarded" is important in the above statement and Calvin used it or its equivalents frequently in his expositions. God graciously regards believers *as though* they were righteous for Jesus' sake. Christ's righteousness is imputed to them so that they may stand before God justified, accepted by him. The denial of this biblical teaching Calvin considered a shocking, arrogant error. Do men think that they can stand before holy God on the platform of an indwelling righteousness of their own? Will they try to play a kind of "do-it-yourself" game in religion? "If strict justice decide, an eternal curse awaits every man who fails in one single iota. . . .The salvation of men turns on this question." We are saved because God "justifies us freely by imputing the obedience of Christ to us. . .only by faith alone" which is not "bare and frigid knowledge" but a resting in the saving work of God. Calvin continues:

> As the Son of God expiated our sins by the sacrifice of his death, and, by appeasing his Father's wrath, acquired the gift of adoption for us, and now presents us with his righteousness, so it is only by faith we put him on, and become partakers of his blessings.[20]

These passages we have cited are from Calvin's lesser known writings, but they are stated as clearly elsewhere. Moreover, the same emphasis on objective, gratuitous justification is found in other chief writings in the Reformed tradition. I cite just two, one from the heart of that tradition and the other from near its periphery but which is yet, in this and other teaching, near the center. The

Heidelberg Catechism asks: "How are you righteous before God?"
The celebrated answer has brought comfort to millions:

> Only by true faith in Jesus Christ. In spite of the fact that my
> conscience accuses me that I have grievously sinned against all
> the commandments of God, and have not kept any one of
> them, and that I am still ever prone to all that is evil, neverthe-
> less, God, without any merit of my own, out of pure grace,
> grants me the benefits of the perfect expiation of Christ,
> imputing to me his righteousness and holiness as if I had never
> committed a single sin nor had ever been sinful, having ful-
> filled myself all the obedience which Christ has carried out for
> me, if only I accept such favor with a trusting heart (Q. 60).

Although some would consider the polity of the Church of
England sufficient reason for classifying that church as a non-Re-
formed church—Calvin himself, however, having approved bishops
for England—and although certain other developments in its history
might seem to confirm that conviction, the truth is that a large part
of the theological heritage and contemporary witness of the Angli-
can-Episcopalian communion is similar to or identical with what we
call Reformed. Perhaps the most representative writer in the long
history of Anglicanism is Richard Hooker. A sharp critic of Puritanism and a defender of reason, Hooker nevertheless writes with power
on matters that lie at the heart of the Christian faith. In a discourse
on justification by faith he speaks of his need for a righteousness
which is not, strictly speaking, a Christian's own:

> The righteousness wherein we must be found, if we will be
> justified, is not our own; therefore we cannot be justified by
> any inherent quality. Christ hath merited righteousness for as
> many as are found in him. In him God findeth us, if we be
> faithful; for by faith we are incorporated into Him. Then,
> although in ourselves we be altogether sinful and unrighteous,
> yet even the man which in himself is impious, full of iniquity,
> full of sin; him being found in Christ through faith, and having
> his sin in hatred through repentance; him God beholdeth with
> a gracious eye, putteth away his sin by not imputing it, taketh
> quite away the punishment due thereunto, by pardoning it;
> and accepteth him in Jesus Christ, as perfectly righteous, as if
> he had fulfilled all that is commanded him in the law: shall I
> say more perfectly righteous than if himself had fulfilled the
> whole law? I must take heed what I say; but the Apostle saith,
> "God made him which knew no sin, to be sin for us, that we
> might be made the righteousness of God in him." Such we are
> in the sight of God the Father, as is the very Son of God

himself. Let it be counted folly, or phrensy, or fury, or whatsoever. It is our wisdom, and our comfort; we care for no knowledge in the world but this, that man hath sinned, and God hath suffered; that God hath made himself the sin of men, and that men are made the righteousness of God. [21]

Along with Calvin, the Heidelberg Catechism, and Hooker, the Reformed tradition has emphasized that the sanctification of the Christian through the Holy Spirit is coordinate with justification. Finding his primary motivation for Christian living in gratitude for a salvation freely given in Christ, the Christian expresses that gratitude in the seriousness he gives the call to service. The attempt to live the good life succeeds the reception of forgiving grace. The foundation of Christian ethics is the doctrine of justification by faith. The close relation of justification to sanctification is well expressed by Brunner:

> In the acquittal and encouragement of justification, therefore, the Word of God becomes to us who are constantly standing alongside of faith the claim of sanctification. The indicative of the Divine promise becomes the imperative of the Divine command. [22]

The reference to the two grammatical moods, frequently made in evangelical discussions of Christian ethics, is well taken. The indicative tells what God has done, is doing, and will continue to do for his people. It gives motivation for Christian action. The imperative sets forth Christian duty predicated on redemption in Jesus Christ. The first gives a statement of fact, the second a statement of the expected Christian response to it.

Sanctification, the work of the Holy Spirit within the believer, is closely associated with justification in the Reformed tradition. Calvin shows it frequently and clearly. One example will suffice:

> It is not to be denied that the two things, justification and sanctification, are constantly conjoined and cohere; but from this it is erroneously inferred that they are one and the same. For example:—The light of the sun, though never unaccompanied with heat, is not to be considered heat. Where is the man so undiscerning as not to distinguish the one from the other? We acknowledge, then, that as soon as any one is justified, renewal also necessarily follows: and there is no dispute as to whether or not Christ sanctifies all whom he justifies. It were to rend the gospel, and divide Christ himself, to attempt to separate the righteousness which we obtain by faith from repentance. [23]

The Heidelberg Catechism puts the matter as plainly after the teaching on justification:

> Q. But does not this teaching make people careless and sinful?
> A. No, for it is impossible for those who are ingrafted into Christ by true faith not to bring forth the fruit of gratitude (Q. 64).

This emphasis in the catechism does not end with the above question and answer, however. It is taken up again in the introduction to the third and last part, which sets the tone for the remainder of the exposition:

> Q. Since we are redeemed from our sin and its wretched consequences by faith through Christ without any merit of our own, why must we do good works?
> A. Because just as Christ has redeemed us with his blood he also renews us through his Holy Spirit according to his own image, so that with our whole life we may show ourselves grateful to God for his goodness and that he may be glorified through us; and further, so that we ourselves may be assured of our faith by its fruits and by our reverent behavior may win our neighbors to Christ (Q. 86).

The primary motivation for Christian service is gratitude for salvation. As the New Testament conceives it, salvation is a past accomplishment, a present experience, and a future hope. We have touched upon the first two of these but so far we have said nothing about Christian hope or expectation. Yet this is an important part of the gospel and of the believer's motivation as he lives *coram Deo*, in the presence of God, and is a welcome new emphasis in some contemporary theology.

The habit of looking ahead for divine deliverance was early learned by God's people under the old covenant. The prophets had taught Israel that the Lord, who had called his people, would save them and use them as a blessing for all nations. Moreover, they had prophesied a "day of the Lord" when God would execute just judgment on the earth; and they had told of the coming of one, the messiah, through whom he would deliver his people. Thus the covenant community had been schooled to look to the Lord for help and salvation, which, though it might tarry, would not tarry long.

With the coming of Christ and the accomplishment of redemption the powers of the new age were ushered into human experience. The kingdom of heaven was established among men and the signs of that kingdom were offered to be seen. Those who were enlightened by

the Spirit knew that they were already living in the last days and
that they had tasted of the good things to come in their fellowship
with the risen Savior and each other. The resurrection and ascension
of their Lord and the gift of the Holy Spirit had convinced them of
that. However, Jesus had also told them that the drama of redemption was not yet complete. The gospel must be preached to all
nations, after which he would return to bring an end to the present
age. There would be a resurrection of all men; Christ would judge
them and separate good and evil forever (Matt. 25:31-46; John
5:25f.; 2 Cor. 5:10; 1 Thess. 4:13—5:11). Until his return and the
consummation of the present age his disciples were exhorted to
witness and to watch (Acts 1:8; Mark 13:32-37).

In its acceptance of these teachings the Reformed Church maintains an unashamed interest in "things to come." It believes, as we
have seen, that they have begun to come already. This is a guarantee
that the others are to follow. For the Christian then the best is yet
to come (1 Cor. 2:9; Rom. 8:18). Now knowledge and vision are
imperfect; someday imperfection will be gone (1 Cor. 13:9-12). The
Christian cherishes this hope and it becomes a part of his motivation
as he lives before the face of God from day to day. One may
legitimately meditate on the future life during this pilgrimage, as
Calvin urged his readers to do (*Inst.,* III. ix),[24] but as he does so he
also remembers that this present world is his Father's world which
he is called upon to use, to understand, and enjoy with thanksgiving
to its Creator (1 Tim. 4:4).

The Right Use of This Present World

The last suggestion requires amplification, for there are many
whose understanding of Christianity gives them little appreciation
for the present world. Their interest is in the world to come, and
they believe that serious concern with the present order is a betrayal
of Christ. There have been periods in the history of the church,
particularly in times of persecution, when this position was adopted
by many. Outstanding church leaders have been quoted in defense of
this conception, Calvin among them. For did not the Reformer,
along with others, write disparagingly of this world and our lot in it?
Some need only to read his chapter on "Meditation on the Future
Life" to get this impression. For there they read in the first paragraph of the necessity "to accustom ourselves to contempt for the
present life"; that it is only "blockishness" that allows us to be
"stunned by the empty dazzlement of riches, power, and honors";

that it is folly to pant after fleeting riches; and that this life, judged in itself, is "troubled, turbulent, and unhappy in countless ways." The development of this theme enables Calvin to speak repeatedly of a "contempt" for the present world and to affirm that believers should judge mortal life as being nothing but misery (*Inst.*, III. ix. 1-4).[25]

Such selective quotation from the Reformer is unfair, however. Interspersed throughout the negative judgments noted above, and others like them, are equally strong statements of world acceptance and affirmation. Moreover, other sections of Calvin's treatment of the right use of this present life demonstrate that aspect of his thought even more clearly. His meaning, he shows, is that if the

> earthly life is compared with the heavenly, it is doubtless to be at once despised and trampled under foot. Of course it is never to be hated except in so far as it holds us subject to sin; although not even hatred of that condition may ever properly be turned against life itself (*Inst.*, III. ix. 4).

Nor should our weariness of it even suggest murmuring or impatience inasmuch as we are willing to abide in this life at our Lord's pleasure. The fact is that there is much that is glorious and good about this present world and the life that we live in it. Calvin had written rhapsodically about the glory of God manifest in creation earlier in the *Institutes* (I. v), and in his chapter on the use of this present life, and elsewhere, he further shows his appreciation for the here and now.

The principles that Calvin lays down for the Christian use of the things of this world are drawn from scripture and represent Calvin's sane interpretation and practical interest. First, we should use God's gifts for the end for which they were created for us. When we ponder the purpose for which he created food, we find that it was delight and good cheer as well as need. The purpose of clothing was not only necessity but also comeliness and decency; the reason for grasses, herbs, and trees is beauty and fragrance. If this were not true,

> Scripture would not have reminded us repeatedly, in commending his kindness, that he gave all such things to men. And the natural qualities themselves of things demonstrate sufficiently to what *end* and extent we may enjoy them. Has the Lord clothed the flowers with the great beauty that greets our eyes, the sweetness of smell that is wafted upon our nostrils, and yet will it be unlawful for our eyes to be affected by that

beauty, or our sense of smell by the sweetness of that odor?
What? Did he not so distinguish colors as to make some more
lovely than others? What? Did he not endow gold and silver,
ivory and marble, with a loveliness that renders them more
precious than other metals or stones? Did he not, in short,
render many things attractive to us, apart from their necessary
use? (*Inst.*, III. x. 2).

This quotation serves to illustrate Calvin's point and to destroy the
myth that he was lacking in an esthetic sense. Since God has given us
all of creation to use *and enjoy,* "away, then, with that inhuman
philosophy" which would deprive us of it (III. x. 3). All things are
ours if we use them in accordance with the divine intention.

The second principle Calvin sets forth about the right use of this
world is that the things of the world must be used with gratitude.
What recognition of God is there when men's minds become fixed
on a thing and forget its creator who gave it to them?

Many are so delighted with marble, gold, and pictures that
they become marble, they turn, as it were, into metals and are
like painted pictures. The smell of the kitchen or the sweetness
of its odors so stupefies others that they are unable to smell
anything spiritual (*Inst.*, III. x. 3).

Those who have not been blessed with material abundance should
beware lest they develop an immodest desire for it inasmuch as other
vices accompany the coveting of earthly things. It is important for
the Christian to recognize that whatever he has, has been entrusted
to him and that he must be a faithful as well as grateful steward.
Someday he will be asked to give an account of his stewardship and
then the importance of the spirit in which he received and used
God's gifts will be evident (*Inst.*, III. x. 5). With these last principles, the warning against coveting the world's goods and the statement of Christian stewardship, Calvin completed his discussion. He
had demonstrated his positive appreciation for creation and the way
in which God intended it to be used and enjoyed.

The Example of Christ

In seeking to live as a Christian in the world one learns that his
principal concern is not a set of rules or ethical maxims but a person,
not an idea but a life. In Jesus Christ God became a man who lived
and taught, healed and preached among us. Having returned to
heaven after he had accomplished man's redemption, Jesus sent the

promised Spirit who makes him contemporary and relevant to his disciples. Through the action of the Holy Spirit the risen Savior becomes real to believers to a degree that the world cannot imagine or understand. Jesus Christ reveals his living presence to those who find their hope in him so that he becomes a dynamic force in their lives. This is the meaning of grace or the gift of the Holy Spirit. The Spirit does more than reveal the teachings of Christ; he sets Christ himself before the mind of the believers. The gospel comes alive so that what happened "once for all" comes near and the chief character in the drama of redemption addresses us. This real Christ is the Christian's example. He is the perfect example because he is the holy Son of God and the new, heaven-sent head of the human race. He is the unique one, "the one quite unspotted life that has been lived within our sinful race," as Mackintosh declares.

> No miracle of Christ equals the miracle of His sinless life. To be holy in all thought and feeling; never to fail in duty to others, never to transgress the law of perfect love to God or man, never to exceed or to come short — this is a condition outstripping the power of imagination and almost of belief. Here is a casement opening on a Diviner world.[26]

Had Christ been sinful, imperfect, the disciples would have known it. In their concourse with him over the hours and days and years, when they had staked all on his claim to divine insight and personality, they would have detected weaknesses and flaws if there had been such in him. They had observed and studied him carefully. Yet when he asked his closest associates which of them would convict him of sin, none dared make reply. For they knew that Jesus taught the way men should live with divine authority and that he lived that way himself to the full. Much that he said and did filled his disciples with wonder but nothing was more impressive than his life itself. What Jesus taught, he was and did. Thus he became the master example as well as teacher of his disciples, and he could command them to seek to imitate him.

> Take my yoke upon you, and learn from me (Matt. 11:29).
>
> If any man would come after me, let him deny himself, and take up his cross and follow me (Matt. 16:24).
>
> You call me Teacher and Lord; and you are right, for so I am....I have given you an example, that you also should do as I have done to you. Truly, truly, I say to you, a servant is not greater than his master (John 13:13, 15f.).

The first leaders in the church took these words of Christ to
heart, and there are frequent exhortations to follow Christ in the
apostolic writings.[27] When the church at Corinth needed correction
and encouragement because of its condition, Paul even suggested
that Christians there might seek to imitate him. He dared to suggest
this because of his own faithfulness to the Lord. Moreover, he says,
he is having Timothy convey this advice to all the churches (1 Cor.
4:15-17; 2 Cor. 11:21-31; cf. Phil. 4:9). The objective is that every
man may grow unto the likeness of Jesus Christ, the one incompa-
rable example set before the Christian.

In its witness in the world the church has continually looked back
to Christ for inspiration and a renewal of the picture that he gave it
of himself. W. E. H. Lecky, writing from a nineteenth-century background that could not accept the supernatural element in Christianity or understand the stupendous influence that Christ has had
on his disciples, does not exaggerate when he states:

> It was reserved for Christianity to present to the world an ideal
> character, which through all the changes of eighteen centuries
> has inspired the hearts of men with an impassioned love; has
> shown itself capable of acting on all ages, nations, tempera-
> ments, and conditions; has been not only the highest pattern
> of virtue but the strongest incentive to its practice; and has
> exercised so deep an influence that it may be truly said that
> the simple record of three short years of active life has done
> more to regenerate and to soften mankind than all the disquisi-
> tions of philosophers, and all the exhortations of moralists.
> This has indeed been the well-spring of whatever is best and
> purest in the Christian life. Amid all the sins and failings, amid
> all the priestcraft and persecution and fanaticism that have
> defaced the Church, it has preserved, in the character and
> example of its Founder, an enduring principle of regener-
> ation.[28]

The high christology of the Reformed Church must not diminish
its appreciation of the necessity for its members to imitate Christ.
Christ must be embraced as the eternal Son of God, but also as a
high priest who can be touched with the feeling of our infirmity
since he has been made like us in all points, sin excepted. Nor must
belief in the persistence of sin in the lives of Christians be an excuse
for the neglect of this teaching. Some may consider Charles M.
Sheldon's *In His Steps* to be a naive presentation of Christianity
hardly consistent with the ambiguities of life in which Christians
find themselves, and others, floating with the stream; they may

decry "do-goodism" as a cheap substitute for the gospel, but the fact is that refusal to follow the example of Jesus is a denial of him. "Whoever does not bear his own cross and come after me, cannot be my disciple" (Luke 14:27).

The Law of God

With the example of Christ before him it might be asked if there need be any place in the life of the Christian for the law of God. To put the matter more sharply we may ask whether there *can* be any place for the law once it has shown a person his sin and has led him to Jesus Christ for salvation.

There are many who would answer this question with a resounding No. They would say that after a person has come to know Christ to go back to law would be to fall into a new legalism, the very error that Paul condemned in his letter to the Galatians. It would be to abandon the divine Savior as example and norm in favor of a sub-Christian standard and an enslavement to the elementary principles and commandments from which a Christian has been set free. It would be a new burdening of the conscience with the requirements of law when Christ has already satisfied those requirements for his people. An appeal is made to such scripture as the following:

> The law was given through Moses: grace and truth came through Jesus Christ (John 1:17).

> For freedom Christ has set us free; stand fast therefore, and do not submit again to a yoke of slavery (Gal. 5:1).

> Christ is the end of the law, that every one who has faith may be justified (Rom. 10:4).

> You are not under law but under grace (Rom. 6:14).

Since Christ is an all-sufficient Savior, it is said, there is no need for anything else. In the Old Testament one reads about law; in the New Testament we encounter grace. So many

> have protested against any construction of the Christian religion which, by introducing legal conceptions, seems to blur the splendor of the Gospel as the affirmation of the free and unconditioned grace of God to sinful men or to question the complete adequacy of a life directed inwardly by the Spirit in independence of external authority of any kind.[29]

This is taught by a considerable portion of conservative Christianity of the fundamentalist variety, by much of Lutheranism, by a strong new school of moral theology, and even by some within the Reformed tradition.

The phrase "*even* by some in the Reformed tradition" is intentional. For if there is any point of doctrine and practice that has distinguished the Reformed Church from other Christian confessions it is precisely this one concerning the place of the law in the life of the Christian. From the time of Calvin the Reformed tradition has taught that besides the civil use of the law in society and its pedagogical use by which sinners are led to Christ, there is a third use of the law: its function as a guide in the life of the Christian. As an expression of the perfect will of God the law shows the believer how he ought to live in gratitude for the salvation given him.

The essence of the law is given in its summary, cited by Jesus from the Old Testament (Deut. 6:5; Lev. 19:18; Mark 12:28-31), and can be stated in one word: love. The statutes of human government fill many volumes. Even so, they are proverbially indefinite, and attempts to condense them only make the uncertainty worse. But the whole law of God is set forth by Jesus in two sentences enjoining love for God and man, and the essence of the divine mandate can be reduced to one word. Love, then, heaven's greatest gift and man's chief blessing, is God's will for us; and all the other commandments in the New Testament are but an elaboration in one way or another of this fundamental one.

How can men misunderstand this? How can they reproach the Reformed Church for its deep interest in law when that interest only reflects a concern to honor God by striving to be what he would have us be? Yet a prominent theologian writes:

> Where the strict separation between law and gospel is not carried out with Lutheran doctrine, where the article of justification is no longer the key which alone opens the door to the whole Bible, there there is a usage of scripture which we can no longer acknowledge as correct. With all respect for the profound moral earnestness which lies behind the position of the old Reformed Church about the law of Christ, we Lutherans can only consider the use of scripture by that church concerning the question about the divine commandments for the particulars of church order, worship, and of congregational life as an unevangelical misuse of the Bible. Here, according to our judgment, the Reformed Church remains stuck fast in the legalism of the Roman Church while she levels the analogous reproach against us with respect to the Lord's supper.[30]

If the Reformed Church is legalistic, so are the gospels, which give instruction about the divine will for us and are thus of the nature of law. The Sermon on the Mount is an example. So is Paul, who speaks about being "under the Law of Christ" (1 Cor. 9:21), who settled a dispute by "a command of the Lord" (1 Cor. 14:37), who asked converts to "fulfill the law of Christ" (Gal. 6:2), who declares that "the law is holy, and . . . the commandment is holy and just and good" (Rom. 7:12) and that the law is not overthrown by faith in the gospel but rather upheld (Rom. 3:31). If the Reformed Church is legalistic because of its belief in the usefulness of the law in the life of the Christian, so is our Lord himself who said that he had not come "to abolish the law and the prophets...but to fulfill them" (Matt. 5:17), who gave his disciples commandments (John 15:12), and whose gospel concerned the kingdom of God, a concept that implies obligation, authority, and law (Mark 1:14).

The fact is that the Reformed Church is "legalistic" in the same sense that the New Testament is "legalistic." It is true, as opponents of the Reformed position have said, that much of the New Testament looks at the law negatively, but this is in response to the misinterpretation of it by some in the first century, who tried to make it a means of salvation. God had never intended that it should be such, and in its correction of that error the New Testament seems to set the law over against grace, whereas in reality an underlying synthesis exists between them. It was in his grace that God gave the law so that men might know his will. The Old Testament sets forth both grace and law and the New Testament does the same. Men were saved by grace under the old covenant by believing that God *would* fulfill his promise of redemption and men are saved by grace under the new covenant by believing that God *has* fulfilled that promise. In Jesus Christ both law and grace, and the Old and New Testaments, are bound together.

The important place given the law of God in Reformed thinking is seen nowhere more clearly than in the Heidelberg Catechism. This is indeed "the glory of the catechism," as John Hesselink has called it.[31] Unlike Luther's catechism, which treats the law in its first part and is then through with it as it moves into an exposition of the gospel, the Heidelberg Catechism gives only the summary of the law in its first section where the need of salvation is shown, whereas the exposition of the law is found in the third part which treats of gratitude shown by obedience. Obedience, however, requires a knowledge of the will of God and this is revealed in his commandments. After its exposition of the Ten Commandments in which both the negative and positive sides of each commandment are

shown, the catechism asks whether Christians can keep them perfectly. The response is as follows:

> No, for even the holiest of them make only a small beginning
> in obedience in this life. Nevertheless, they begin with serious
> purpose to conform not only to some, but to all the com-
> mandments of God.
>
> *Why, then, does God have the ten commandments preached so*
> *strictly since no one can keep them in this life?*
>
> First, that all our life long we may become increasingly aware
> of our sinfulness, and therefore more eagerly seek forgiveness
> of sins and righteousness in Christ. Second, that we may
> constantly and diligently pray to God for the grace of the
> Holy Spirit, so that more and more we may be renewed in the
> image of God, until we attain the goal of full perfection after
> this life (Q. 114, 115).

This is the language of the Reformed Church. One sees in this
exposition of the law, particularly in the above questions, something
of the sensitiveness to sin and desire to be conformed to the image
of Christ, of the interest in sanctification and ethics, and of the
discipline that has characterizeed that church, where it has been true
to itself, throughout its history. The law of God, personified in Jesus
Christ who is also its fulfillment, serves the Christian as a guide
through life. In his journey the Christian looks to Jesus who has
traveled this way. A wise traveler listens to him and obeys. Since
Christ is no longer with us in person he guides through his Word and
Spirit. Through scripture the Holy Spirit points out the only Savior
and how men ought to live while on their journey. There are, in
short, "rules in the book" to help us. These should be received
gratefully and used with faithfulness. In the words of the Psalmist
the Christian can say,

> Oh, how I love thy law!
>   It is my meditation all the day.
> Thy commandment makes me wiser than my enemies,
>   for it is ever with me.
> I have more understanding than all my teachers,
>   for thy testimonies are my meditation.
> I understand more than the aged,
>   for I keep thy precepts.
> I hold back my feet from every evil way,
>   in order to keep thy word.
> I do not turn aside from thy ordinances;
>   for thou hast taught me.

> How sweet are thy words to my taste,
>   sweeter than honey to my mouth!
> Through thy precepts I get understanding;
>   therefore I hate every false way.
>
> Thy word is a lamp to my feet
>   and a light to my path (Ps. 119:97-105).

A word of caution remains, however. The Reformed Church has frequently been charged with legalism and, unfortunately, there has been reason for that accusation. Legalism is the disjointed elevation of law to a position where it is absolutized and observed for its own sake. The rule becomes the thing. If it is observed, no matter how formally, all is well. Its relation to Christ and the Holy Spirit is forgotten and unknown. Christian living has degenerated to this in some communities in the history of the church and preaching has sunk to this level in some pulpits. Salvation has, in effect, come to be seen in terms of works-righteousness and the gospel is lost. This was the error of the Galatian Christians who evoked a deserved tongue-lashing from Paul (Gal. 2:18f.; 3:1–5:14). The freedom that believers have in Christ was lost in a welter of detail much of which had become irrelevant with the introduction of the new covenant.

Abuse does not invalidate use, however, and misunderstanding here does not justify the discarding of the use of law in Christian living altogether. Finding in Christ salvation from the "curse of the law," the Christian soon discovers that the law he had feared "is holy and just and good" (Rom. 7:12). It is the mirror that shows him his true appearance, the standard that helps him discover his fault. As it had once driven him to Christ to escape its terrors, it has now become a helpful friend. In this manner the church proclaims the law as a help in the life of the Christian. It remembers that before his ascension Jesus gave his disciples their marching orders. They were to teach and to baptize all nations so that they might observe all things that he had "commanded" them (Matt. 28:19f.). A short time before that he had said,

> If you keep my commandments, you will abide in my love, just as I have kept my Father's commandments and abide in his love....This is my commandment, that you love one another as I have loved you....You are my friends if you do what I command you (John 15:10, 12, 14).

Years later the last of the apostles wrote,

> By this we know that we love the children of God, when we love God and obey his commandments. For this is the love of

God, that we keep his commandments. And his commandments are not burdensome (1 John 5:2f.).

The Calling of the Christian

In the ordering of life the Reformed tradition has followed
Luther and Calvin in their appreciation of the doctrine of vocation,
or the calling of the Christian to service in society so that he may
glorify God. In the pre-Reformation church the ordinary Christian
was not considered to have a particular call of God. This was
reserved for monks and others who took vows to renounce this
world in favor of the world to come. They were the spiritual people
because they heard and obeyed God's call while other Christians, not
so favored, only made a living with no spiritual significance being
attached to their work. The church was divided dualistically between
those who had been called to God's service and the multitudes of
rank and file Christians who had not.

In an essay on the history of the word "calling" Karl Holl affirms
that Martin Luther had personally experienced what that word had
signified before his time and the new meaning that he gave it. "It is
possible to portray his whole inner development as a struggle with
this conception."[32] After his years in the cloister and his discovery
of the gospel Luther became convinced that monasticism rests upon
a false presupposition. As Holl put it,

> The monk believes that through his vow he is bringing some-
> thing to God and traveling the sure road to salvation. But that
> militates against the conception of God in the gospel. Man
> cannot bring God anything from himself but, conversely, God
> is always the first one who gives. With that discovery the
> monastic vow lost its validity for Luther once and for all and
> also faith in a special call which monks were to receive....In
> God's eyes all the work of monks has no more significance
> than the ordinary labor of a farmer or a housewife done in
> true faith.[33]

This momentous conviction of Luther, which became a part of
his doctrine of the universal priesthood of all believers, was accepted
by Calvin, who worked it out just as thoroughly (and perhaps more
activistically). For Calvin, as for Luther, man lives *coram Deo,*
before the face of God. Because man is not his own but belongs to
his Lord who created and has redeemed him, he ought to live wholly
to his glory.

> Now the great thing is this: we are consecrated and dedicated
> to God in order that we may thereafter think, speak, meditate,
> and do, nothing except to his glory....If we, then, are not our
> own (cf. 1 Cor. 6:19) but the Lord's, it is clear what error we
> must flee, and whither we must direct all the acts of our life.
>
> We are not our own: let not our reason nor our will, there-
> fore, sway our plans and deeds. We are not our own: let us
> therefore not set it as our goal to seek what is expedient for us
> according to the flesh. We are not our own: insofar as we can,
> let us therefore forget ourselves and all that is ours.
>
> Conversely, we are God's: let us therefore live for him and die
> for him. We are God's: let his wisdom and will therefore rule
> all our actions. We are God's: let all the parts of our life
> accordingly strive toward him as our only lawful goal (*Inst.,*
> III. vii. 1).[34]

Here one has a view into the heart of Calvin; this is the center of his
interest. Man exists, not for himself, but for God, and he finds his
true humanity only when he finds him.[35] The contrast between this
and the prevailing views of our day is striking. Here God is at the
center and is given his due; in most current thought he exists, if at
all, for the sake of man who occupies the center of the stage and for
whose interests all else finds its *raison d'être*. Because we are not our
own but belong to God, and because God's providence regulates our
lives, each of us should be mindful of his divine calling. The importance of this teaching in Calvin and in Protestant history is sufficient
to note the chief statement of it in the *Institutes,* although this is by
no means the only place where it is found in his writings:

> The Lord bids each one of us in all life's actions to look to his
> calling. For he knows with what great restlessness human
> nature flames, with what fickleness it is borne hither and
> thither, how its ambition longs to embrace various things at
> once. Therefore, lest through our stupidity and rashness every-
> thing be turned topsy-turvy, he has appointed duties for every
> man in his particular way of life. And that no one may
> thoughtlessly transgress his limits, he has named these various
> kinds of living "callings." Therefore each individual has his
> own kind of living assigned to him by the Lord as a sort of
> sentry post so that he may not heedlessly wander about
> throughout life....
>
> But I will not delay to list examples. It is enough if we know
> that the Lord's calling is in everything the beginning and
> foundation of well-doing. And if there is anyone who will not
> direct himself to it, he will never hold to the straight path in

his duties. Perhaps, sometimes, he could contrive something laudable in appearance; but whatever it may be in the eyes of men, it will be rejected before God's throne. Besides, there will be no harmony among the several parts of his life. Accordingly, your life will then be best ordered when it is directed to this goal. For no one, impelled by his own rashness, will attempt more than his calling will permit, because he will know that it is not lawful to exceed its bounds. A man of obscure station will lead a private life ungrudgingly so as not to leave the rank in which he has been placed by God. Again, it will be no slight relief from cares, labors, troubles, and other burdens for a man to know that God is his guide in all these things. The magistrate will discharge his functions more willingly; the head of the household will confine himself to his duty; each man will bear and swallow the discomforts, vexations, weariness, and anxieties in his way of life, when he has been persuaded that the burden was laid upon him by God. From this will arise also a singular consolation: that no task will be so sordid and base, provided you obey your calling in it, that it will not shine and be reckoned very precious in God's sight (III. x. 6).[36]

It would be impossible to exaggerate the significance of this teaching, found first in the writings of the Reformers, proclaimed from hundreds of pulpits, and accepted by multitudes of Christians who heard the new teaching. It gave strength to the Christian ethic and cheer to the hearts of men. It encouraged the sick and feeble, gave hope to the forgotten, and wrought iron into the souls of many. Peasants bound to the soil found their toil to have become meaningful, women felt less the drudgery of their tasks, and people everywhere came to see that the worth of labor depends not on office or station in life but rather on the spirit of consecration in which it is performed. Called to service *coram Deo,* before the face of God, they believed the tasks of a day to be filled with blessing when done "unto him."

The Practice of Piety

In the light of the discussion of the last two chapters it is evident that there has been a marked emphasis on what has been called the "practice of piety" in the Reformed tradition. Professor S. vander Linde calls attention to this fact and claims that virile piety has been the distinguishing characteristic of Reformed Protestantism. Taking issue with those who stress only its objective side and with others who hold that the Calvinistic Reformation was chiefly a political or scientific movement, he declares that it was preeminently religious in nature. It is characterized more sharply by its piety than by its theology, he avers, and surely more so than by its political aspirations.[37] In development of this thesis he writes:

> The most sensitive, most vulnerable, and at the same time the most distinguishing traits of Reformed folk do not lie in the more objective sphere of dogmatics or ethics, but in what follows from the practice of faith. Consequently the work of the Holy Spirit has a great and wholesome emphasis in Calvin and the Reformed pietists.[38]

Although there are some who would disagree with this judgment, in particular those who are rationalistically inclined and consequently give slight place to the more subjective, mystical side of the Christian faith, we believe that it can be sustained. We have already shown that doctrine is not an end in itself but that it is rather a means to holy living before the face of God. Likewise scripture has an instrumental function; its purpose is to call men to the service of the Lord.

> All scripture is inspired by God and profitable for teaching, for reproof, for correction, and for training in righteousness, that the man of God may be complete, equipped for every good work (2 Tim. 3:16f.).

The means used is divine teaching; the end is living in fellowship with God. There is nothing more central in the Christian faith than the practice of piety, and the Reformed Church has honored that practice from the sixteenth century until today. From the very beginning, as Ernst Troeltsch declares, Calvinism aimed at the creation of a "holy community."[39] Its interest was a people who should be redeemed from all iniquity and purified unto God as his own possession, zealous for good deeds (Titus 2:14). This was the emphasis of Voetius, first professor of Utrecht University, who believed in the equal importance of sound doctrine and sound piety; of the leaders of the Church of Scotland in days of renewal; of the leaders of revival and reform in England, Switzerland, and Hungary; and of the leaders of the Great Awakening in the American colonies. Puritanism, which stems from the Reformed tradition, and Methodism, which has strong ties with it, bear witness to its concern for a daily walk with the Lord and the creation of a holy community. Whether the church has retained that vision is the question beyond all others on which its future well-being depends.

Interestingly, a church in our day whose virile emphasis on the practice of piety is reminiscent of the Reformed Church is the Roman Catholic Church of the Netherlands. A witness to this similarity of emphasis is the latter's "new catechism," whose stress throughout its five hundred pages on the necessity of devotional habits for Christians and their seeking to live the Christian life from day to day is one of its chief characteristics. Although it existed as a minority church for centuries and did not have a bishop in the post-Reformation era until 1853, the Dutch Roman Catholic Church today includes over forty percent of the population and, on several counts including devotional practices, is one of the strongest churches in the world. Its leaders have been generous in their expressions of indebtedness to the Reformed Church of the Netherlands for all that they have learned from it. Not the least important of the lessons learned is the *"praktijk der godzaligheid,"* the practice of piety which, as Vander Linde has shown, came to be a hallmark of the Dutch church late in the Reformation period and remained such for centuries.

NOTES TO CHAPTER V

1 "Preliminary Principles; The Form of Government," *The Constitution of the United Presbyterian Church in the United States of America* (Philadelphia: The Office of the General Assembly of the United Presbyterian Church in the United States of America, 1958), p. 117. This statement is unchanged since the year 1788.

2 Van Ruler, *De Vervulling van de Wet,* pp. 152, 185.

3 Krusche, *Das Wirken des Heiligen Geistes nach Calvin,* p. 266 *et passim,* and Vander Linde, *De Leer van den Heiligen Geist bij Calvijn.* pp. 118ff. *et passim,* demonstrate its central importance in his teaching.

4 The Holy Spirit is mentioned explicitly in questions 1, 8, 21, 24, 25, 31, 49, 51, 53, 54, 65, 67, 69, 70, 71, 72, 76, 79, 80, 86, 103, 109, 115, 116, 123, 127, with corresponding significance in the overall structure of the doctrine presented.

5 *The Idea of Perfection in Christian Theology* (London: Oxford University Press, 1934), p. 335.

6 *Christian Holiness* (New York: Harper, 1960), p. 37.

7 Warfield, *Perfectionism,* pp. 457-8; quoted in Neill, *op. cit.,* p. 40.

8 *The History of England* (New York: Harper, 1856), Vol. I, p. 91.

9 Quoted by Henry Bast, *Ordination Vows of Ministers and Elders* (Grand Rapids: Evangelical Fund, 1947), p. 58.

142   THE SPIRIT OF THE REFORMED TRADITION

10 *Dogmatik* (Amsterdam: Scheffer, 1887), pp. 504, 507.

11 *The Reformed Doctrine of Justification* (Grand Rapids: Eerdmans, 1946), p. 275.

12 *Ibid.,* p. 278.

13 *Ibid.,* p. 308.

14 *Forgiveness and Reconciliation* (London: Macmillan, 1948), p. 57.

15 *Ibid.,* p. 66.

16 *Ibid.,* p. 69.

17 G. C. Berkouwer, *Faith and Justification* (Grand Rapids: Eerdmans, 1954), p. 83.

18 "The True Method of Giving Peace to Christendom and Reforming the Church," *Tracts,* tr. Henry Beveridge (Edinburgh: Calvin Translation Society, 1851), Vol. III, p. 244; "Acts of the Council of Trent: with the Antidote," *ibid.,* p. 115; cf. "The Adultero-German Interim," *ibid.,* pp. 197, 201 (*C.R.* 35, 595, 448, 556, 559f.); *Inst.,* III. xi. 11; xiii. 5; and *Commentaries passim.*

19 *Tracts,* Vol. III, pp. 116, 114 (*C.R.* 35, 448f., 447).

20 *Ibid.,* Vol. III, p. 248 (*C.R.* 35, 598).

21 *The Works of Mr. Richard Hooker* (Oxford: The University Press, 1850), Vol. II, p. 606.

22 *The Divine Imperative* (Philadelphia: Westminster, 1947), p. 80; cf. Otto Piper, "Justification and Christian Ethics," and "Faith and Life," *God and Caesar* (Minneapolis: Augsburg, 1959), pp. 173ff.

23 "Acts of the Council of Trent: with the Antidote" (*C.R.* 35, 448). Cf. *Inst.,* III. xvi. 2; xvii. 5 (*C.R.* 30, 587, 593); Karl Barth, *Church Dogmatics* (Edinburgh: T. & T. Clark, 1958), Vol. IV/2, pp. 503ff.; 584ff.

24 Recently Jürgen Moltmann, a Reformed theologian, has set forth this dimension in *A Theology of Hope* (New York: Harper, 1967).

25 Cf. Doumergue, *Jean Calvin,* Vol. IV, pp. 305ff.; and J. Bohatec, *Calvinstudien* (Leipzig: Rudolph Haupt, 1909), pp. 427f., who defend Calvin against this charge.

26 Hugh Ross Mackintosh, *The Doctrine of the Person of Jesus Christ* (Edinburgh: T. & T. Clark, 1948), pp. 400f., 403.

27 See, for example, Eph. 4:13, 15, 20f.; 5:1f., 25; Phil. 2:5; 3:8-14; Col. 3:17; Heb. 12:2; 1 Pet. 2:21ff.

28 *History of European Morals* (New York: Longmans, Green, and Co., 1913), Vol. II, pp. 8f.

29 C. H. Dodd, *Gospel and Law* (Cambridge: University Press, 1951), p. 65.

30 Sasse, *Was heisst Lutherisch?* pp. 95f.

31 In *Guilt, Grace and Gratitude,* ed. Donald J. Bruggink (New York: Half Moon Press, 1963), p. 194.

32 Karl Holl, "Die Geschichte des Worts Beruf," *Gesammelte Aufsätze zur Kirchengeschichte,* p. 213.

33 *Ibid.,* pp. 216f.

34 Cf. Bohatec, *op. cit.,* pp. 397ff.

35 Andre Bieler, *The Social Humanism of Calvin,* tr. Paul T. Fuhrmann (Richmond: John Knox, 1964), pp. 13ff.

36 Citations from Calvin's other writings are given in W. J. Aalders, *Roeping en Beroep bij Calvijn* (Amsterdam: Noord-Hollandsche Uitgevers Maatschappij, 1943).

37 *Het Gereformeerd Protestantisme* (Nijkerk: G. F. Callenbach, 1957), p. 5.

38 *Ibid.,* p. 12.

39 *The Social Teaching of the Christian Churches,* tr. Olive Wyon (New York: Harper, 1960), Vol. II, p. 718.

VI

the christian and the social order

Our discussion of the life of the Christian is not yet complete, for we have taken no account of the Christian's interpersonal relationships. Man is a social creature who has been made for fellowship with others. Inasmuch as man's nature is reflected in this fellowship, a Christian brings with him into his relations with other persons the nature he has received from God. Having been raised with Christ into newness of life he must "seek the things that are above" and mortify his old nature. Whatever he does, in word or deed, must be done gratefully with reference to the Lord (Col. 3:1-17; cf. Heid. Cat., Q. 88-90). Since he is not his own, his aim must be to glorify his creator and redeemer (1 Cor. 6:20).

We have seen the importance of the doctrine of the calling of the Christian in the teaching of the Reformers. They held that every believer has a vocation to serve God in his daily task. To serve believingly, *coram Deo,* as in God's presence, is to glorify him. Although this is emphasized in both Luther and Calvin, its social implications were carried out more completely in the Calvinistic tradition. One reason for this is that as Calvin labored to restore the church and society he had ever before him the vision of Old Testament Israel called to be a covenant community consecrated to God. Under the old covenant every area of life was holy; nothing might be withheld from God. Under the new covenant shadow has been replaced by substance (Heb. 10:1; Col. 2:17), and no less a condition should prevail. The ideal that the prophet pictured was that someday there would be written on the bells of the horses "Holy to the Lord" and that every pot and bowl would be sacred to

144

him (Zech. 14:20ff.). Calvin's ideal, never realized perfectly but ever to be sought, is a holy community of persons serving God in every area of life. One of the ablest students of the subject asserts that precisely here "the difference between Lutheranism and Calvinism is most manifest." He continues,

> Calvinism aimed consciously and systematically at the creation of a Holy Community. It co-ordinated the activity of the individual and of the community into a conscious and systematic form. And since the Church as a whole could not be fully constituted without the help of the political and economic service of the secular community, it was urged that all callings ought to be ordered, purified, and enkindled as means for attaining the ends of the Holy Community. Thus the ideal was now no longer one of surrender to a static vocational system, directed by Providence, but the free use of vocational work as the method of realizing the purpose of the Holy Community. The varied secular callings do not simply constitute the existing framework within which brotherly love is exercised and faith is preserved, but they are means to be handled with freedom, through whose thoughtful and wise use love alone becomes possible and faith a real thing.[1]

Men deliberately sought to carry their convictions into life with them and to exert themselves to bring this world under the reign of God and of Christ. In Calvin they found the teaching needed to erect a new social philosophy. Its components were a new doctrine of man, of grace, of social responsibility, and the call to serve God *in* the world.

(1) Concerning man Calvin taught as clearly as Pascal and Dostoevski—and more fundamentally if not as dramatically—man's almost infinite possibilities for good or evil. These possibilities are his by virtue of his creation in God's image and subsequent fall. He came from the hand of God and is restored by grace. He is like a lieutenant of God in governing the world with gifts shared by no other creature. His well-being, however, is dependent on his faithfulness to God. When he gives God obedience in love, he is free to fellowship with him and to share his blessedness; when he goes his own way of selfishness and pride, he becomes a slave to sin which, in its vileness, hatred, and lust, eventually destroys him. Unaware of his true plight, fallen man fancies himself to be the master of his fate, the captain of his soul, whereas in reality his existence is a miserable slavery. The tragedy is that man mistakes this slavery for freedom.

The man whom we moderns know—the man whom we analyze, the man of psychology, the man whom science examines, the man of literature, and the man of profane humanism—is not the authentic man. He is only a pale shadow, a counterfeit, a caricature of man. This man has no hope whatever of reaching anything. In spite of his marvelous gifts which still witness in him to the majesty of the work of God, everything that the man of today undertakes is devoted to death and ends in death.

The desperate analysis of man so lucidly given by the Camus of any period is more just, more realistic, and more evangelical than the analysis given by religious and profane idealists. Although not intending to do so, these idealists deceive natural man by having him believe that merely imagining what a man wishes to become actually changes him into what he wants to be![2]

(2) Calvin's realistic appraisal of man is balanced by his understanding of divine grace. The unexpected has happened. In the person of Jesus Christ, God has stepped into the midst of man's miserable condition *as a man* to set men free and to lead them in the way of blessedness, peace, and love. Through the gift of the Holy Spirit that Christ bestows on his disciples they receive a new nature enabling them to live as his ambassadors in the world that he once redeemed and now rules. In him, God's man, humanity finds its new head and a suggestion of its own future beatitude.

Salvation, as Calvin conceived it, is not an experience that an individual enjoys alone. Rather it is an experience that he shares with others in the bosom of the church so that he and they can be God's agents to bring it to the world. Men exist in society and redeemed men become members of the body of Christ so that they may share fellowship and blessing with the Head and with each other. Salvation, therefore, is a social as well as an individual experience. Calvin states it well in discussing the meaning of the "communion of saints": "If truly convinced that God is the common Father of all and Christ the common Head, being united in brotherly love, they cannot but share their benefits with one another" (*Inst.*, IV. i. 3).

(3) Moreover, men are saved so that, by word and deed, they may influence others by the quality of the new life they have received from God. To speak more precisely, Christ saves men and gives them the Holy Spirit so that he may use them in his purpose to save the world. Christians, then, have a responsibility to the world

outside the church. This is a much emphasized theme in our day and a much needed one.

(4) The responsibility that Christians bear towards the world needs a forceful statement in our time for three reasons. The *first* reason is that Christians are called to be agents of reconciliation in the world individually and corporately. Christians are called to serve; the church likewise exists to preach the gospel in word and deed. This runs throughout scripture and it has been the peculiar glory of the Reformed tradition to understand that simple message and to try, however imperfectly, to relate the gospel to the world about it. Perhaps the most encouraging phenomenon in the church in our times, next to the biblical and theological revival, is the rediscovery of this fact of the church's responsibility to seek to fulfill its mission. A hopeful sign in the present concern of the church to rediscover and more faithfully to discharge that responsibility is self-criticism. An example is a study-paper prepared for the Eighteenth General Council of the World Alliance of Reformed Churches.

Addressing itself to the subject "The Reformed Faith and the World of Today," it states the responsibility of the church to proclaim the gospel to the world and then laments as follows:

> *We confess with shame, however, that the Reformed witness to the world, while never completely obscured, has tended to fade and diminish both in its content and in its passion.* We have been content to judge the world, to condemn it, to deny it, and thus virtually to stand aloof and remain apart from it. We have embraced a personal pietism, good in itself, but too often isolated from and insulated against the world in which we live. We have developed an ethical morality bordering on legalism which knows how to denounce and how to frown but is unskilled and inept at restoring or healing. We have so projected the Christian hope into the future as to make us other-worldly in a wrong and misguided way. We have become so fearful of secularism both outside and inside the Church that we have lost our vision of service to and in the world.
>
> The baleful result of our dimmed vision is that we no longer really know the world, and the world for its part no longer pays us heed or looks to us for help. In such a situation neither the Church's judgment upon the world nor its message of redemption for the world can be trenchant or creative.[3]

The introversion of the church referred to in this statement is the *second* reason that Christian responsibility to the world is a needed emphasis. The church *has* become a refuge from the world for many, an escape from duty, and a sickly substitute for the dynamic witness *in the world* that it was intended to be. "It has been tacitly understood," says Arnold B. Come, "that the only really saving, redeeming, reconciling work is that of converting and holding sinners within the church."[4] The fact that they have been saved to serve as ambassadors in the world is neglected or forgotten.

The *third* reason for emphasizing Christian social responsibility is the lamentable secularism of our time. It was not always so. During the high Middle Ages and the Reformation era, living conscious of Christian realities was common and natural. In every phase of human activity—social, economic, political—life's spiritual dimension was real. During the last three centuries, however, the western world has experienced a gradual lessening of Christian influence as "the acids of modernity" have eaten away at the older foundations.

Secularism began in the thinking of men. Philosophers, scientists, moralists, and theologians rested their case with unaided reason rather than with God and repudiated certain fundamental Christian convictions. The speed with which that tendency moved in the last quarter of the seventeenth century, and its spread in the eighteenth and nineteenth centuries, would be incredible if the history were not there for all to read. In an essay on the foundations of culture, the Dutch scholar G. van der Leeuw speaks about the great process of reduction that has been going on—a *vermagerings-proces*, a thinning or watering down—with the result that Christianity and culture have become this-worldly, secularized, and humanized.[5] An American sociologist has written:

> Religion is faced with a kind of threat that is more powerful even than the combined police force of the totalitarian states. This threat is the rise of secularism. A point of view rather than a specific doctrine, secularism has been gradually increasing in extent and intensity. The basic characteristic of the secular outlook is the belief that human problems are primarily *social,* rather than *religious.* The secular attitude is a worldly attitude, not in the sense of superficial sophistication, but rather in its insistence that human affairs should be governed by reason rather than faith.[6]

The present time is often referred to in Europe as the post-Christian era, and America, despite its numerically high church membership, is little better off spiritually, as has been amply shown.[7] The situation undoubtedly reflects man's spiritual myopia and lethargy but also the judgment of God on the church for its excessive self-concern and failure to address itself to the needs of the world in which it is called to witness.

There is agreement that Calvin and the Reformed tradition have caught the biblical emphasis on the responsibility of Christians to bring the gospel to the world in word and deed, but there is a difference of opinion among Calvinists on how best to minister to society. Some would advocate such identification with the world that the distinction between church and world would disappear and the church might lose its character as church; others emphasize a large measure of social separation. In the name of Calvinism it is argued that separate organization should be achieved in as many areas of social intercourse as possible. So an "absolute principial break with the world," on the basis of the "absolute antithesis" between Christian and non-Christian, is proposed.[8] One wonders to what extent such a program, if widely adopted, would benefit society when one's contacts outside his own circle of like-minded Christians are reduced to a minimum.[9]

The spirit of Calvin and of the Reformed tradition has little in common with a separatistic social philosophy, however. In times of apostasy and the persecution of believers it may be temporarily necessary for Christians to withdraw from social involvement in part, but this is never the ideal or normal posture for Christians. Since the Reformed Christian knows that this is his Father's world, he feels no need to flee from it. Rather, remembering that "God was in Christ reconciling the world to himself," and that Christians "are ambassadors for Christ, God making his appeal through [them]" (2 Cor. 5:19f.), the Reformed Christian feels it to be his peculiar privilege and duty to seek to permeate society in the name and strength of his master. The avenues of social intercourse become opportunities for him to make Christ and the Christian way of life known. He is not to make light of evil but to relate it to the devil whence it came. However, he is to fight evil and the devil *in* the world, not *out* of it. How can it be otherwise, since Christians are still a part of society? It is obvious that underlying such a social ethic is a spirit of strenuous activity. As Dakin points out, "Men are encouraged to live, sent out to live. They are to master the world, dominate it, bend it indeed to their supreme religious aim."[10]

The fact is that at certain periods in European and American history this social ethic was put to work in the life of the people and its accomplishments have made it a favorite theme in the writing of that history. It is agreed that the application of the Calvinistic social ethic to society resulted in the greatest penetration into society of

Christian principles that the world has ever seen and that the benefits of this penetration are still being felt in our age. Concluding his discussion of this subject Troeltsch makes the following judgment:

> Along with the organic and patriarchal fundamental theory of the medieval idea of Society, Calvinism has become the second great Christian definite social ideal of European Society.... Indeed, the great importance of the Calvinistic social theory does not consist merely in the fact that it is one great type of Christian social doctrine, its significance is due to the fact that it is one of the great types of sociological thought in general. In inner significance and historical power the types of the French optimistic equalitarian democracy, of State Socialism, of proletarian Communist Socialism, and of the mere theory of power, are, in comparison with Calvinism, far behind.[11]

This is the judgment of the historian concerning the influence of the Reformed tradition upon society in another age. For us, the strength of that tradition to discharge its social responsibility in the present time is a more important question. From among the profusion of social problems confronting us today—race and class hatred, poverty and the economic system, overpopulation, the pollution of natural resources, the dissolution of the home, disrespect for law and authority, the international order, the state, education, to name only the most obvious—we shall discuss the last two mentioned in order to illustrate the need to apply Christian thought to social problems in general. The problems of the state and of education are selected because of the long interest that the Reformed Church has had in them as well as their present relevance.

A. THE CHRISTIAN AND THE STATE

An area of social concern that has come to demand more and more attention is the state. The added duties and functions that the state assumes in a shrinking and increasingly complex world make it a problem for all of us, not only those who live under totalitarian forms of government but persons in the free world as well. The reason that this becomes so important a problem for the citizen is that the state wields power. It can coerce. One may have this brought home to him if he fails to pay his taxes or exceeds the speed limit. The magistrate "does not bear the sword in vain," the apostle says, and then adds that he is "the servant of God" in the discharge of his duties (Rom. 13:4). For Paul the state is rooted in the ordinance of God.

> There is no authority except God, and those that exist have been instituted by God. Therefore he who resists the authorities resists what God has appointed, and those who resist will incur judgment (Rom. 13:1f.).

The state has authority; that authority is derivative; it comes from God. And the state, represented by its magistrates, is responsible to God. These were the main ingredients in the political theory of "Christian" society for a millennium and more. The implications of this view changed the conditions of life for whole nations. Where authority was believed to derive from God, human sovereigns were not supposed to rule arbitrarily. The law of the realm should reflect the law of God. King John learned this lesson the hard way when, after a decade of struggle, he was made to sign the *Magna Carta* at Runnymede in 1215. In countless other political incidents, great and small, there is evidence of a general conviction that all authority, including that of the state and its representatives, comes from God and that men might make their final appeal to him.

The rapid erosion of these ideas, which no longer mold political theory or determine action,[12] began in the Renaissance and received powerful assistance from certain developments in the seventeenth century. The first of these developments was within the church itself. It was carried out by radical, left-wing Puritans and independents bent on achieving a separation of church and state, in itself a laudable objective. Oliver Cromwell's army came to be made up largely of these. According to James H. Nichols, when a frightened Parliament sought to disband that army in 1647 because of the radical ideas rife within it and the army refused to go home, modern democracy was born. "Democratic left-wing Puritanism had challenged theocratic right-wing Calvinism." A year later Parliament was purged of Presbyterians and the "army democracy" prepared to organize a new state and a new church system for England.[13] The establishment of any and all churches was forbidden and separation of church and state was proclaimed on the dubious ground that whereas the church lives in the sphere of grace the state should be guided by reason and natural law.

The doctrine of natural law and reason, which, it was held, is understood by all rational men, was worked out by political philosophers of this period. Troeltsch traces the development of these ideas and shows particularly the great influence of John Locke on

Anglo-American political thinking. Although he was a son of the Calvinist-Puritan tradition, Locke's theory of the state is far removed from the older theological formulation. Troeltsch sketches it as follows:

> He blends the various ingredients which composed the previous theories of Natural Law in an entirely fresh way; he starts neither from Stoic rationalism nor from Scriptural revelation, but from a utilitarian empiricism, from which, however, he often reverts towards the older ideas. His Natural Law results psychologically from the idea of the equality and freedom of all mankind in the Primitive State; in his conception the state of Nature was one in which peace and reason prevailed; men possessed equal natural rights to life, liberty, and property, and, in order to maintain these rights, the individuals, by means of a social contract, formed a body politic. This body had the power to protect these natural rights of man; and out of this social contract there arose the forms of government which individuals found necessary for their welfare. This Natural Law is under Divine guidance, it is true, and is Divinely reiterated in the Decalogue, and is thus in agreement with Revelation; but that which it produces is solely for the good of individuals, and not for the glory of God.
>
> The ecclesiastical communities stand completely alongside of the State, and are free associations which in all political and moral questions must adjust themselves to the order of the State....Further, Locke regarded the ruling authorities which have emerged from the process of history as-directly-appointed by God, and he was a firm supporter of the positive law of that period, which to him in England seemed to be a particularly happy incorporation of Constitutional Natural Law, and which also implicitly contains this Natural Law as its own presupposition, and its own standard. But these loud echoes of the Calvinistic Christian Natural Law do not drown the underlying tones, which are quite different: the complete removal of the idea of the glory of God as the religious end of the State, the idea of the sole sovereignty of God, of the theoretical inequality of individuals, and their obedient adjustment to things as they are. Here in Locke's theory the dominating idea is rather one of the most versatile individualistic rationalism, purely utilitarian and secular in character, which can be abstracted as it stands from the religious setting of Locke's theory; at a later date this often actually took place. This rationalism rests upon such an independent basis, both in philosophy and in public law, and corresponds so closely to

the secular idea of progress, and to the political necessities of the day, that its inclusion in the religious framework no longer had much inward significance. It stands alongside this framework, not within it, just as the religious associations exist alongside of the State. That, however, is the spirit of the Enlightenment and not the spirit of Calvinism.[14]

Locke was a Christian and a philosopher who, in certain respects, cut himself loose from the old moorings. Other Christians who were leaders in the church came to share similar political ideas after his time. Nichols discusses this in connection with the contribution of eighteenth-century evangelicalism to political thinking. After observing the faltering political interest of the evangelicals in their preoccupation with experimental religion he notes the omission of the "Puritan urge to theocracy, the demand for a common life integrated by the Word." This, however, has been quietly dropped.

If the evangelicals were Puritans, they were Puritans of the radical left wing....They had accepted the compartmentalization of religion from economics and politics and science, and in these latter areas even men like Jonathan Edwards and Wesley were rationalists, sons of the Enlightenment. Their political and economical thought and practice were no longer related to revelation, but to the laws of nature.[15]

In practice left-wing Puritans and evangelicals may have been as theistically motivated as their grandparents had been; in theory they had severed their thinking about the state from theological foundations. This autonomy of political theory was to have far-reaching consequences in a later day.

That day has arrived. The last traces of the older theological foundations were erased by the positivistic philosophy of the last half of the nineteenth century, so that today the state has no transcendental connections. It is autonomous, free, and, as Brunner has said, "this freedom has been its ruin."[16] The ruin is seen in political developments in every area of the globe. It is seen when a clique gets control of a country and does as it pleases with nothing to curb it except opposing power. It is seen in the totalitarian forms of government in our day. Who would have dreamed a century ago that ours would be an age of political totalitarianism? Then men were talking and writing about the brave, new world that soon would be. Victor Hugo believed that in the twentieth century war would be dead, sin would be dead, and that man would live; Karl Marx muttered that in the age of Communism the state would eventually wither away because it would have outlived its usefulness.

Yet today men are more conscious of the state as a real or potential evil than they have been for centuries, and there has never been greater confusion in political theory.

We live in a day when the secular state is magnified, glorified, and deified. One sees the beginnings of this development in the modern world in the writings of certain German philosophers a century and a half ago. Subsequent history has shown the world the damage that resulted when this evil idea was accepted widely and worked out in practice. Yet most countries today follow an unenlightened policy of self-interest with nothing more ultimate than their own welfare or that of those in power. With the dissolving of transcendental foundations international law has practically disappeared and the world political picture is one of near chaos. What is needed is an adequate foundation on which a doctrine of the state can be built, one of our most urgent political tasks today.

In our judgment that foundation must be derived from principles found in scripture. Here men learn that God is the Lord and that all authority and blessing derive from him. Reformed Christians should be especially interested in laying such a foundation because of their historic social concern and willingness to occupy themselves with theoretical questions. But as we look back into history for guidelines in our thinking, we shall have to look beyond the evangelicals of the eighteenth century and the negativism of the Anabaptist tradition. The tone was struck for the latter in the Schleitheim Confession of 1527, which refers to the magistrate's office as belonging "to the flesh," wherefore "it is not appropriate for a Christian to serve as a magistrate." The magistrate's sword must be rejected by Christians inasmuch as it is "outside the perfection of Christ."[17] This was sheer heresy to Calvin, who looked upon politics as holy work and magistrates as "vicars of God" who "are occupied not with profane affairs or those alien to a servant of God, but with a most holy office, since they are serving as God's deputies" (*Inst.*, IV. xx. 6). Calvin's teaching is so clear and fundamental in the matter before us that sons and daughters of the Reformed tradition who have an interest in it can do no better than to start their thinking with his exposition of the doctrine of the state in the last chapter in the *Institutes.* When they learn from there that the state is a gift from God and that it must be used as an instrument in his service, they will have learned their most important lesson.

But this clashes with the modern idea of the state as autonomous and without transcendental religious connections. The modern view will have nothing of the older, "theocratic" political conception.[18]

Here, as elsewhere, however, the long view of history has its advantages. "The most significant thing about the modern state," one author quips, "is that it is *modern,* dating back only a few hundred years." Only since then has there developed a wholly secular or autonomous political theory.[19]

This development in the area of political theory was of one piece with the secularization of other areas of life. It occurred when modern man cut himself off from God and determined to live by and for himself. It is understandable that those outside the church should hold such a political philosophy, but today there are many leaders *within* the church who embrace such a doctrine of the state. A Roman Catholic justice of the United States Supreme Court has lauded a previous decision of that court which stated that "man's relation to his God was made no concern of the state" in the drafting and adoption of the fundamental law of the country. [20] Furthermore the General Assembly of one of the largest Reformed churches has gone on record approving the doctrine of the "neutral" state and affirming that the practice whereby "ministers serve as military chaplains, paid by the state, raises serious questions." [21] This latter position is consistent with the doctrine in vogue in current political theory and conceivable as a *modus vivendi* in a pluralistic society but, in our judgment, it should not be set forth as the ideal, or the approved, doctrine of the church.

No Christian is neutral in his service to God in any walk in life. He is called to seek first of all the kingdom of God, that is, his reign. This is true in politics as well as elsewhere. The state is composed of men, and every man is responsible to God for the quality and the degree of his service. The ideal of Christians in the political sphere can never be a "godless" state but one in which men recognize him in theory as well as in practice as the living Lord. This is not to argue for a "state church," or the establishment of religion, but that Christian commitment should influence political theory.

The alternative position, carried out consistently, would eliminate all religion from public life and confine it to the church and home, a possibility that no right-thinking believer would accept. To stop with the elimination of devotions in public schools is a half-way position which consistent secularists will never allow. Their conception of state neutrality in religion calls for its total exclusion from all civic endeavor, and would have to eliminate, among other things, the words "under God" from the pledge to the flag, the motto "In God We Trust" from our coins, the last stanza of "America" which begins with the words "Our fathers' God, to Thee," public oath-taking on the Bible, state-paid chaplains in military service and chaplains in congress, state legislatures, and other governmental units, any invocation of God or recognition of him in a public meeting.[22]

Such radical changes in the structure of western civilization should be resisted, particularly by those who bear the name Reformed. No less an authority than John T. McNeill is quoted as having declared that John Calvin "would never have countenanced the secularization of the state, and that the exclusion of religion from education would have seemed madness to him."[23] That judgment ought to be weighed by Calvin's spiritual heirs today.

Calvin would never have countenanced the secularization of the state because he knew from whence all political authority is derived. Its source for him was *not* the will of the people, but God. The former position was that of the French Revolution and is widely accepted today. It allows no appeal beyond the will of the majority and knows no moral norms beyond its own. Its "justice" is drawn from its own resources, including its prejudices, with no recourse to eternal standards of value which, for the French revolutionaries, did not exist. Moreover, the purpose of justice can easily be subordinated to a given program, as was true during the French Revolution.

Calvin saw both government and people responsible to a higher authority. The importance of this conviction cannot be exaggerated. Its absence during the French Revolution allowed the revolutionaries in control to guillotine nineteen thousand of their opponents with apparently no qualms of conscience, and it enables totalitarian governments today to liquidate those who stand in the way of "progress." Thus the Nazi government in Germany could wipe out six million Jews and the Russian and Chinese Communist governments could murder millions of their own countrymen who opposed the party program. Fifteen thousand Polish army officers could be shot to death by their Russian captors in Katyn Forest[24] and top-flight party men and governmental leaders can be murdered in cold blood when it suits the will of the majority.

The elimination of Lavrenti Beria is worth mentioning in this connection since Nikita Khrushchev, who condemned Stalin for brutality, injustice, and terrorism, has given the reason and apparent justification for it. After the death of Stalin the bosses in the Politburo became suspicious that Beria, the head of the secret police, was plotting against them. They decided that they had better get him first so one day the Presidium, of which they were members, held a special meeting and questioned Beria for hours. As narrated by Khrushchev and related by *Look* magazine, November 19, 1963, the following ensued:

> At that time we did not have at our disposal a sufficient amount of juridical evidence of his guilt and we found ourselves in a difficult position. Evidence for his assignment to a court we did not have, yet to leave him at liberty was impossible. We came to the conclusion that the only correct measure for the defense of the republic was to shoot him immediately. This decision was adopted by us and carried out on the spot.

This shocking crime, and countless others like it, was not perpetrated in antiquity, but in our time! It was not planned and executed by small-time thugs but by the leaders of a great state including the head of state who told it to the world with the conviction that it was the thing to do. It shows to what level government can sink when it cuts itself loose from the living Lord.

What we need, Otto Piper has said in another connection, "is a militant approach to secular thought . . . . We are under obligation to unmask the superficiality and shortcomings of modern world views which pretend to be based upon science and infallible reason."[25] To leave God out of our national and public life is impossible, for God has to do with nations and with cultures, not only with the church. To relate the lordship of God only to his people and the kingship of Christ only to the church is a pietistic error that is wholly contrary to the Reformed tradition. God is the God of nations as well. He made Israel his people and promised that someday Egypt and Assyria would worship him too (Isa. 19:21-25). America and Russia, China and Chile are called to serve God, and their "authorities are ministers of God, attending to this very thing" (Rom. 13:6), i.e., governing the people. In their "most holy office" (Calvin) they must seek God's help and praise as they rule in his stead.

> All the kings of the earth shall praise thee, O Lord,
>   for they have heard the words of thy mouth;
> And they shall sing of the ways of the Lord,
>   for great is the glory of the Lord (Ps. 138:4f.).

It is well that in its social concern the Reformed Church, following Calvin, has seen the import of a doctrine of the state which does not eliminate God and that it appreciates the dignity attaching to those who hold civil office. Calvin writes,

> No one ought to doubt that civil authority is a calling, not only holy and lawful before God, but also the most sacred and

by far the most honorable of all callings in the whole life of mortal men (*Inst.*, IV. xx. 4).

In commenting on the tradition that stemmed from Calvin, Dakin, a Baptist, writes,

Calvinism claims the State in a much more emphatic way than do the rest of the Free Churches, or, for that matter, than does Lutheranism. The State not less than the Church is also an instrument in the hand of God even though its allotted task is different. [26]

A contemporary Reformed scholar who shares Calvin's high appreciation for the state and its spiritual contribution to culture is A. A. van Ruler. "The question whether the state serves the living God or its own gods is of decisive significance," he writes, and then points out that it will be one or the other. In reality, he affirms, the fancied "neutrality of the state is a naivete of the grossest kind." It would be better for the state to persecute the church than to pretend neutrality, he says, perhaps overstating the case slightly, for then its position is at least made clear. [27] In harmony with this position the General Synod of the Netherlands Reformed Church adopted a statement in 1950 which, in its article on the state, reads in part as follows:

. . . governments in fulfilling their calling may not be neutral nor adopt world views of their own choosing, but rather in their ruling, they must seek to represent God's kingly rule, and honor Jesus Christ as Supreme Ruler of earthly kings. Then men will see that the service of a true humanity is found only where the service of God is sought. [28]

The majority of Christian opinion in America is far from the position taken here. But that doctrine of the state results largely from the religious pluralism in the United States and has been molded by the spirit of the Baptist and similar churches rather than by those of the Reformed tradition. [29] The Reformed Church is in a favorable position to contribute to contemporary thinking in the relation of the state to its spiritual foundations. At one with the rest of American Christianity in opposing the establishment of any one church in the land, it may yet speak a needed word about the derivation of all authority from God and the responsibility of the state to remember that fact and to honor norms established by him. "Blessed is the nation whose God is the Lord" (Ps. 33:12).

B. THE CHRISTIAN AND EDUCATION

A second contemporary problem that illustrates the need for the application of Christian thought to society is public education, the process whereby the minds of tomorrow's men and women are molded. In today's world, where the home no longer plays the determinative role and education is entrusted to the state, the public school is the most significant single factor in that process. A century ago Charles Hodge predicted the possibility of the American public school system becoming

> the most efficient instrument for the propagation of atheism which the world has ever seen. If every party in the state has the right of excluding from the public schools whatever he does not believe to be true, then he that believes most must give way to him that believes least, and he that believes least must give way to him that believes nothing, no matter in how small a minority the atheists and agnostics may be.[30]

It would seem that the prediction of Hodge may be fulfilled in our time. At least, there is a small minority of citizens who would like to see it fulfilled. But complete religious neutrality in education, as in politics, is impossible and the influence of many educators with Christian convictions continues. Nevertheless, recent court rulings have accelerated the secularization of state-subsidized education in this country and altered the character of the public school in a great number of school districts. The effects of this trend on the future of American culture have become the concern of people in every area of life. Many of them were unaware of the growth of secularism in western society during the last three centuries and assumed that America was still a "Christian" nation. They failed to realize that connections with theological beliefs had already been severed in prevailing political and educational theory and that they were fast being severed in practice.

Hence, while it is true that American culture has in it a large residue of Christian thought shared by millions of believers, the prevailing materialistic, secular philosophy in which theories of education and the state are rooted is not so very different from, let us say, that of a Communist country. In the Soviet Union, for example, there are millions of believers, just as there are here. According to recent surveys, a majority of Russians profess belief in God. Perhaps our differences in theory and in practice are not as great as some imagine. The naive judgment that certain symbols, such as pious phrases on our coins and in the pledge to the flag, are evidences of a

Christian culture, may be our greatest danger. Those who think so should examine and ponder the ideological substructure of the American way of life and the part that public education has in forming it.

In this connection the dissenting opinion of Justice Potter Stewart of the United State Supreme Court in the Murray-Schempp case is interesting. It reads in part:

> If religious exercises are held to be an impermissible activity in schools, religion is placed at an artificial and state-created disadvantage. Viewed in this light, permission of such exercises for those who want them is necessary if the schools are truly to be neutral in the matter of religion. And a refusal to permit religious exercises thus is seen, not as the realization of state neutrality, but rather as the establishment of a religion of secularism, or at the least, as government support of the beliefs of those who think that religious exercises should be conducted only in private.[31]

That "the establishment of a religion of secularism," to use Justice Stewart's words, is not altogether a remote possibility seems evident today and education may be a means in its achievement. In this religion, democracy becomes a substitute for God, since it claims first allegiance, and patriotic ritual such as the pledge to the flag assumes the character of devotional exercises. Moreover, the Supreme Court has stated repeatedly in recent rulings that the law of the land commits the American nation to a position of "wholesome neutrality" with respect to religion in theory and in practice.

In the light of this it is interesting to note that in its majority opinion in the famous Murray-Schempp case on the question of devotional exercises in public schools the court based its judgment on the need for a *secular* legislative purpose that must be fulfilled if the Constitution is to be interpreted properly. In that opinion one reads,

> To withstand the stricture of the Establishment Clause [of the first amendment] there must be a secular legislative purpose and a primary effect that neither advances nor inhibits religion.[32]

In its use of the adjective *secular* the court undoubtedly meant nothing more than that it would not favor any religion. Nevertheless, the use of the word forces the whole issue into the area of philosophy and theology where it belongs. The fact is that neutrality here is impossible; secular legislation provides for secular education. It is more than a little puzzling then to read that the "primary effect" conjoined to the secular legislative purpose desired is to be one which "neither advances nor inhibits religion." One is led to ask how a *secular* legislative purpose can fail to inhibit religion. It would seem bound to do so.

With all respect, and with appreciation for other sections of the court's opinion—those, for example, that speak of the firm place of religion in our national culture—we may say that, in asserting its advocacy of a secular legislative purpose, the majority, in effect, stands perilously close to those who would eliminate all mention of God from public life.[33] This is true regardless of the court's denial that it is thereby helping to establish a "religion of secularism."[34]

A secular philosophy of life or of education was not the intention of the framers of our Constitution and its first amendment, however. It is well known that the intention of the first amendment is to prohibit the establishment of any one church as *the* church and to guarantee the free exercise of religion. It is also common knowledge that there was no intention to drive a wedge between belief in God and fidelity to the state, as the court has made clear in its majority and concurring opinions. On the day that the first amendment to the Constitution was adopted, September 25, 1789, a resolution was passed in the House of Representatives calling for a day of thanksgiving and prayer to thank God for his blessings. The effect of contemporary developments, however, is to make the doctrine of the separation of church and state mean the separation of the state from God. Is this the political doctrine that we hold, or desire? Where *do* we stand in fundamentals?

Perhaps Americans stand at the crossroads where they will have to decide whether they are going to support the prevailing secularism in their culture or throw their weight behind a firm belief in God and in man as God's creature. Those were the convictions on which western democracy was built.[35] The Justice who wrote the majority opinion in the Murray-Schempp case is a professing Christian and a member of a Reformed church. One of the nationally-known ministers in that communion, George A. Buttrick, has written as follows:

> In our fear of indoctrination we have practiced a worse indoctrination: *by our silence in secular education we have indoctrinated children to believe that God does not exist and that Jesus Christ does not matter.* In protecting the scruples of agnostics we have trampled roughshod over the convictions of believers. This debacle has come so slowly that most people still do not realize its iconoclastic import.[36]

Those words were written before the court decisions referred to above but those decisions would probably not serve to make the author soften his language.

In the pluralistic society of America there seem to be three alternatives: (1) a return to a religious orientation in the schools of the land, an admittedly difficult, if not impossible, course in our present society; (2) the establishment all along the line of a system of separate "Christian schools" operating independently of the public school system; or (3) the establishment of Christian schools that function in cooperation with public schools in their respective neighborhoods. In the latter arrangement certain work would be taken by all students together and some of it separately. Neither this latter nor the alternative of separate Christian schools operating independently of the public school system is ideal, but preferable to a system embodying a secularist philosophy of education.

Some would claim that separate Christian schools are the ideal. But social separation is never the ideal for biblical, least of all for Reformed, Christianity. As we have shown above, Christians are intended to be society's leaven. To abstract Christians from society would be to remove from society the leaven that God intends to use there and to reduce Christianity to a ghetto-culture here and there. The place for Christians, insofar as it is possible, is *in* society where they may work. This should be the ideal in education as well as elsewhere.

It is well to remember, as one wrestles with this problem, that there is no perfect solution and that it is necessary to work for the best that is possible. If one feels that his convictions lead him to the acceptance of a Christian philosophy of education and also to the view of social involvement given above, he may have to decide whether to give the preference to the one or the other. One's philosophy of education—his conception of the goals of education, his scale of value, the nature of the child and of reality, and of the child's relation to it—ought not to be sacrificed. How can it be any more than his philosophy of life, if it has been thought through? A Christian should seek to honor God and Christian values *as Christian values* in education just as he does in the rest of life. He may feel required, therefore, to seek a means of educating his children consistent with his basic convictions about life. If he also has convictions about his responsibility to society, however, he will regret his inability to cooperate with it completely in its educational program. He may then conclude that a system of dual attendance whereby some work is taken together in public schools and some is taken separately would be the best arrangement.

That the Reformed tradition has had a deep stake in Christian education is not only evident in the activity of John Calvin and others in the more remote history of the church but in the establishment of Christian colleges and in the departments of Christian education in every denomination and almost every local church. In my own denomination, typical of others, there have been repeated expressions of concern by the General Synod about day school education.[37] On the local level, an example of this concern can be found in the establishment of the Reformed Church in Michigan. The Holland Classis took action on at least four occasions in the first ten years of its existence to encourage the founding of "parochial schools."[38] The founder of the Holland Colony and Hope College, the Rev. A. C. Van Raalte, was a strong proponent of Christian education. Sharply critical of a secular philosophy of education, Van Raalte held that "we must never sacrifice the principle that the fear of God must be the soul of our education; our Christian color must come out everywhere." Preston J. Stegenga concludes his treatment of the subject as follows:

> Van Raalte, the great advocate of Christian education, was ever alert to the changing needs of the settlement, and as soon as the Pioneer School was established, he began to visualize an even greater field for a Christian training program. During the first few years of the school's existence, a combined parochial-civil educational program was continued. It rapidly expanded into a completely church-controlled educational program extending from the elementary level, through the secondary school, and culminating in Hope College which offered a complete four-year college curriculum. [39]

We have stated that the Reformed Church has a special call to provide leadership in working at a solution to the problems that confront society. Some of these are in the field of education. The profound interest in both the philosophy of education and in social responsibility that marks the Reformed tradition places those who are in it in a unique position in Protestantism. The history of their tradition should give them courage for their task. With the love of God for man reflected in them, and a firm resolution to carry the principles of a Christian philosophy of education into the world, they may work as God gives them opportunity for the improvement of the educational picture as broadly and as intensively as they are able.

NOTES TO CHAPTER VI

1 Troeltsch, *The Social Teaching of the Christian Churches,* Vol. II, pp. 610f.

2 Bieler, *The Social Humanism of Calvin,* p. 15.

3 *Theology Today,* XVI (1959), 309.

4 *Agents of Reconciliation* (Philadelphia: Westminster, 1960), p. 169.

5 G. van der Leeuw, *Balans van het Christendom* (Amsterdam: H. J. Paris, 1940), p. 28.

6 Frances E. Merrill, *Society and Culture* (Englewood Cliffs, N.J.: Prentice-Hall, 1965), p. 379.

7 See, e.g., Martin E. Marty, *The New Shape of American Religion* (New York: Harper, 1959); John A. Gates, *Christendom Revisited: A Kierkegaardian View of the Church Today* (Philadelphia: Westminster, 1963).

8 H. Evan Runner, "Does Christian Social Action Demand an Absolute Break?" *Torch and Trumpet,* III (1953), 3. A series of articles, *ibid.,* IV (1954), includes one entitled "Christian Witness Requires Christian Organization." On the same subject, see Runner, *ibid.,* V, Nos. 1-5 (1955); R. B. Kuiper, "Scripture on the Antithesis," IX, No. 2 (1959); H. J. Kuiper, "The Antithesis, as a Cornerstone of Christian Life and Action," X, No. 3 (1960).

9 Leonard Verduin uses *reductio ad absurdum* to criticize this theory: "Since there is not an inch of ground which the regenerate and unregenerate can share, it is quite natural that someone on this side of the Atlantic has proposed that it is high time that we organize a counterpart to the Dutch *Vereeniging voor Geitenfokkerij op Gereformeerde Grondslag*—A Society for Goat-Breeding on a Reformed Basis." "The 'Absolute' Antithesis," *Reformed Journal,* III (June 1953). A colleague has informed me that in the village of three thousand persons in which he once lived in the Netherlands there were three societies for raising goats, one for the Roman Catholics, one religiously neutral, and one organized "on a Reformed Basis." However, for reasons of economy, the three societies had a billy goat in common. It would seem to this observer that the kids raised under such an arrangement could hardly be considered orthodox to any of the societies.

10 Dakin, *Calvinism,* p. 203.

11 *Op. cit.,* p. 621; cf. H. Richard Niebuhr, *Christ and Culture* (New York: Harper, 1951), pp. 217f.

12 Cf. Will Herberg, *Protestant-Catholic-Jew* (Garden City, New York: Doubleday, 1960), pp. 1f.

13 *Democracy and the Churches* (Philadelphia: Westminster, 1951), p. 31; cf. Troeltsch, *op. cit.,* pp. 668ff.

14 *Op. cit..* pp. 637-639.

15 *Op. cit.,* p. 62.

16 Brunner, *The Divine Imperative*, p. 441.

17 *Baptist Confessions of Faith,* ed. William L. Lumpkin (Philadelphia: Judson, 1959), pp. 27f.

18 The best exposition of this position that I know is in the writings of A. A. van Ruler, *Religie en Politiek* (Nijkerk: Callenbach, 1945) and *Droom en Gestalte* (Holland: Uitgeversmaatschappij te Amsterdam, 1947).

[19] Alden D. Kelley, *Christianity and Political Responsibility* (Philadelphia: Westminster, 1961), p. 65.

[20] William J. Brennan, Jr., in a concurring opinion in the "Abington School District v. Schempp," *United States Supreme Court Reports*, Vol. 373, US 203, Lawyers' Edition, 10, second series (Rochester, New York: The Lawyers Co-operative Publishing Company, 1964), p. 871.

[21] *Presbyterian Life,* June 15, 1963, p. 11.

[22] Justice Brennan does not think so. In his concurrent opinion in the case cited above he speaks, e.g., about "the various patriotic exercises and activities used in the public schools and elsewhere, which, whatever may have been their origins, no longer have a religious purpose or meaning. The reference to divinity in the revised pledge of allegiance, for example, may merely recognize the historical fact that our nation was believed to have been founded under God." *Op. cit.,* p. 904.

[23] *The Church Herald,* May 1, 1964, p. 7; cf. George F. Hunt, ed. *Calvinism and the Political Order* (Philadelphia: Westminster, 1965), p. 176.

[24] See J. K. Zawodny, *Death in the Forest* (Notre Dame, Ind.: University of Notre Dame Press, 1962).

[25] "Protestant Theology's Predicament," *Theology Today,* XX (1964), 483.

[26] *Op. cit.,* p. 210.

[27] *Religie en Politiek,* p. 236.

[28] *Foundations and Perspectives of Confession* (New Brunswick, New Jersey: New Brunswick Theological Seminary, 1955), p. 26.

[29] E.g., Winthrop S. Hudson, *The Great Tradition of the American Churches* (New York: Harper, 1953).

[30] Quoted by Louis Cassels, United Press International, March 10, 1961.

[31] *United States Supreme Court Reports,* Vol. 373, US 203, p. 910.

[32] *Ibid.,* p. 858.

[33] Only Justice Tom C. Clark, who wrote the majority opinion, and Justices Warren, Black, and White agreed on the ground for declaring why public school devotions are unconstitutional. Justices Brennan, Douglas, and Goldberg wrote separate concurring opinions, with Justice Harlan agreeing with that written by Goldberg. Justice Brennan stated: "Our decision in these cases does not clearly forecast anything about the constitutionality of other types of interdependence between religious and other public institutions." *Ibid.,* p. 899. Agreeing with the majority in the unconstitutionality of devotional exercises in public schools, he nevertheless writes: "Any attempt to impose rigid limits upon the mention of God or reference to the Bible in the classroom would be fraught with dangers." Objective (*sic*) teaching of religion is approved and encouraged in both Justice Brennan's and Justice Clark's opinions. *Ibid.,* pp. 902f., 860.

[34] *Ibid.,* p. 860.

[35] That western democracy was built on the Christian doctrine of man as God's creature has been shown by students of political science. See, e.g., Ernest Barker, *Principles of Social and Political Theory* (New York: Oxford, 1951). In an essay entitled "Pluralism and Christianity: the Political Thought

of Ernest Barker," Randall B. Ripley writes: "It has long been a point of dispute among students of political theory whether the Christian doctrines have added anything to political thought that the Stoics had not already said. The thought of Ernest Barker offers evidence in a modern setting that Christian doctrines have independent political value." *The Christian Scholar,* XLVI, No. 4 (Winter 1963), 311. Associate Justice Felix Frankfurter of the United States Supreme Court once wrote: "Ours is the only country in the world's history where men are bound together by a common territory, not by a common racial source, or a single body of theological beliefs. We are bound together by a sense of the ultimate simple decency of human dignity. Nothing binds us together but this sense of frail, fallible, aspiring human beings." Religious News Service, Dec. 8, 1952, quoted by G. Elson Ruff in *The Dilemma of Church and State* (Philadelphia: Muhlenberg Press, 1954), p. 86. The question is whence arises this sense of "the ultimate simple decency of human dignity" of which the Justice speaks.

36 George A. Buttrick, *Christ and Man's Dilemma* (Nashville: Abingdon-Cokesbury, 1946), pp. 134f. Italics his.

37 The statement of the General Synod of the Reformed Church in America of 1809 is worth reading. *The Acts and Proceedings of the General Synod of the Reformed Protestant Dutch Church in North America,* Vol. I, pp. 296ff., 397ff. At the meetings of the General Synod in 1962 and 1964 the church was urged "to stubbornly resist all attempts to deprive our children of the religious symbols of Bible reading and prayer in our public educational systems." *Ibid.,* Vol. XLIV, No. 2, p. 224, re-affirmed in 1964.

38 In an action of June 20, 1848, the judgment of the classis was that "the schools must be promoted and cared for by the churches, as being an important part of the Christian calling of God's church on earth. All luke-warmness and coldness toward that cause must be condemned and rebuked." *Classis Holland: Minutes 1848-1858,* Translated by a Joint Committee of the Christian Reformed Church and the Reformed Church in America (Grand Rapids: Grand Rapids Printing Company, 1943), p. 26. In an action of April 13, 1854, the classis resolved the following: "With respect to Parochial Schools, it is the judgment of the assembly that the churches ought to take care that their children are taught in schools where they are brought under definitely Christian influence, and that consequently wherever there is an overwhelming influence of unbelief and superstition, it is emphatically a duty to establish congregational schools." *Ibid.,* p. 157; cf. pp. 174f., 232.

39 *Anchor of Hope* (Grand Rapids: Eerdmans, 1954), p. 39.

VII

the spirit of the reformed tradition

In the foregoing discussion we have given attention to some of the chief characteristics of the Reformed tradition. We have seen that it is a tradition within the church of Jesus Christ and that it has sought to understand God's Word to the church: that is why long ago there was a Reformation. We have seen further that at the heart of that tradition there is an awareness of living in the presence of God, which has consequences for the personal and social life of the Christian. There are religious and theological reasons for the sharp accent on ethics and Christian living in the Reformed Church.

The Reformed tradition then is not first of all a system of theology or of doctrine. Nor is it a particular type of church government, or belief in "the five points of Calvinism." As important as these are, they do not constitute that tradition, nor do they reveal its heart. The spirit of the Reformed tradition is more subtle, more profound than any of these.

Many have attempted to describe, or characterize, that spirit. One such effort seeks to discover the legacy that Calvin, a chief architect in the Reformed tradition, left the church. The author's conclusion is that

> Calvin's true legacy is, indeed, not a system but a method, the method of striving to see everything—man, Christ, faith, the world, the Bible, religion, life . . . —not from man's point of view but from the viewpoint of God.[1]

167

The historian John T. McNeill, who is probably the foremost Calvin scholar in the western hemisphere, struggles to capture and express the spirit of Calvin's tradition. His conclusions can be applied to the Reformed tradition as a whole inasmuch as the heart and mind of Calvin made a great and lasting impression on it. After a lifetime of study he affirms that the spirit of Calvinism is "found in faithful response to the Scripture revelation of a sovereign and redeeming God." Then, after exploring that spirit further and noting its suffusion in churches beyond those usually identified with the Reformed tradition, he finds it in "a type of piety familiar in the old Calvinism and once distinctive of it." He continues:

> This is a piety not much identified with peculiar words and rites of worship. It is characterized by a combination of God-consciousness with an urgent sense of mission. The triune God, Sovereign Creator, Redeemer, and Comforter, is an ever-present reality through both prosperity and disaster. Guilt is real, but it is submerged under grace. The Calvinist may not know how it happens; he may be a very simple-minded theologian; but he is conscious that God commands his will and deed as well as his thought and prayer. This is what makes him a reformer and a dangerous character to encounter on moral and political issues. He is a man with a mission to bring to realization the will of God in human society. . . . when he knows what is God's will, and how it is to be translated into action of the hour, he will espouse it with courage, energy, and tenacity. God has not given him the spirit of fear.[2]

There is indeed a spirit of the Reformed tradition. Reduced to a minimum, it is a consciousness of being in God's presence with a call to live unto him. The consecration of life, personally and in its social relationships, is the Christian's mandate and privilege. It also becomes the dynamic by which he lives, for it brings him into fellowship with God whose resources are infinite.

The world needs this dynamic, a power greater and more revolutionary than any mere human philosophy and more benign than the most constructive accomplishments of men. There was a time when this power was manifest in the Reformed tradition. A leading historian mentions it:

> If Communism is revolutionary, it hardly exceeds sixteenth-century Calvinism in its energy as a militant, missionary, expanding creed. As the headquarters of international revolution, the Geneva of Calvin presents important features which make it a remarkable anticipation of modern times.[3]

Our revolutionary times need to recapture that spirit. They need an adequate way of life, a faith, a philosophy that grips men's hearts and empowers them for their tasks. There is no lack of offers: secularism, scientism, materialism, Communism—these and others are held out to men, but they cannot satisfy. Nor will half-heartedness or half-measures win the day. Any program lacking in ambition or aggressive execution is bound to fail. The church has the program; it was given by its Lord. The question is whether it will carry out that program in obedience to Christ. Presently other movements have the initiative. Abroad Communism fans flames of hatred and mouths its false promises as it regiments men in a program fore-doomed to failure. At home secularism siphons off the energies of people so that even Christians have little left for God. Numberless sects evangelize with a vigor that puts the church to shame. The renewal of Roman Catholicism continues as one of the great phenomena of our time. It has led so stalwart an opponent as Karl Barth to ask some searching questions about the future of Protestantism in relation to it.[4] In the midst of it all, where is the church of Jesus Christ which has been reformed according to the Word of God? Is it still *ecclesia semper reformanda,* an ever reforming church, capable of molding the future through its hidden, transcendent power, or has that honor gone to Rome? The expressions *ecclesia reformanda* and *ecclesia reformata* have been frequently ascribed to her in the last few years by her own sons because of the powerful movement that has been transforming so much of her thought and life.

The future under God belongs to those who are determined to mold it. With the resources which it has at its disposal the Christian church can lead the world into a new day with the sky the limit. If history means anything, the Reformed Church should share in that victory. It will share in it if that church receives a new outpouring of the Holy Spirit to equip it for its task. The Spirit is given in response to our request. Jesus said,

> Ask, and it will be given you; seek and you will find; knock and it will be opened to you. . . . If you then, who are evil, know how to give good gifts to your children, how much more will the heavenly Father give the Holy Spirit to those who ask him? (Luke 11:9, 13).

NOTES TO CHAPTER VII

[1] Paul T. Fuhrmann, *God-Centered Religion* (Grand Rapids: Zondervan, 1942), p. 23.

[2] *The History and Character of Calvinism,* pp. 433, 436f.

[3] Herbert Butterfield, *Christianity, Diplomacy and War* (Nashville: Abingdon-Cokesbury, 1953), p. 104.

[4] *The Ecumenical Review*, XV, No. 4 (July 1963), 365.

appendix

the name "Reformed"

In the early history of the Reformation various names were used to designate the reforming people. Those in opposition were quick to use nicknames to stigmatize the new movement. The first names used by the opposing party were "Lutheran" or "Zwinglian" and, later, "Calvinist." In the literature of the first years of the movement one meets various equivalents for the names "Lutheran" and "Lutheranism."[1] The Roman Catholic apologist Eck, and the scholar Erasmus are among those who used these expressions. As the advocates of reform labeled their opponents Papists, they were labeled with the name of their leader by those who continued with Rome. In *The Apology of the Augsburg Confession*, for example, one finds Melanchthon lamenting the fact that his opponents "call the dear, holy Gospel Lutheran."[2]

The earliest name used by the Reformers of themselves and their people was "Evangelical," and that name soon came to be used of their churches and doctrine as well. Erasmus wrote in a letter of a group whom he called "the evangelicals," and then said parenthetically, "for so they rejoice to be called."[3] An observer in Italy reported that in the years 1526 and 1527 the evangelical faith was preached so widely and publicly that "one could see the number of Lutherans who had taken the name Evangelicals increase daily."[4] The First Helvetic Confession, written in 1536, has a chapter on "The Purpose of Evangelical Doctrine."[5] As this name was the earliest, so it is also the most common found in the literature of the period. Other names that were used are "Protestant," after 1529, and "Adherents of the Augsburg Confession," after 1530.[6]

171

In the early years of the Reformation its advocates also frequently spoke of their church as having recovered the original divine order and life, of being a church "reformed," "corrected," "cleansed,"[7] although the expressions were not used in any formal, titular sense. Thus in the Augsburg Confession of 1540 Melanchthon used the designation "corrected church,"[8] and, from the great frequency with which one meets the expression "reformed church" in later literature of that century as one which is well understood and fixed, it is fair to infer that it was frequently used earlier in Reformation history. The necessity of reform was often on the lips of churchmen, so that the word and its cognates were much in use. An example is Lambert of Avignon in the first of his one hundred fifty-eight theses posted on the church door and subsequently read at the first session of the Synod of Homberg in 1526. "All things must be reformed," he declared, "which have been deformed."[9]

The Reformers at first did not speak of their church as anything other than the church of Christ, the Christian church, the true church, the church, the French church, or by a similar expression. This is understandable in view of the fact that their opponents were accusing them of having separated from the one church of Christ and of having become sectarians. That is why the name "Lutheran" is not used by followers of Luther in any symbolical or official sense until near the the end of the century and that one searches in vain in the writings of Calvin for use of the name "Reformed" until near the end of the Reformer's life. He speaks of the church constantly but he keeps clear of any name that may appear sectarian or other than that of the one church of Jesus Christ. What was true of Calvin was true of the other Reformers.

The earliest known official usage of the name "Reformed" is in 1561 at the Colloquy of Poissy in France. At this meeting, called by French royalty at a critical juncture in French history, Theodore Beza served as spokesman for the Protestant delegation. On September 26, after addresses had already been given by the leading Roman Catholic prelates and by Beza, the latter read a statement in the presence of Catherine de'Medici, the Queen Mother and actual sovereign of the realm. In it reference is made to the doctrine of transubstantiation, "which is disapproved of by the common accord of all the reformed churches both in Germany and elsewhere."[10] In his history of this period Beza makes mention of the "reformed religion," or the "reformed church," prior to the narration of this incident,[11] but the account itself was written subsequent to the conference at Poissy and does not provide us with an actual earlier instance of the usage, although the name "reformed" undoubtedly was used commonly and perhaps even ecclesiastically by 1561.

In a document written by the counselors of the French king, Charles IX, known as the Edict of January (January 17, 1562), the first official recognition of French Protestantism, there is no use of the name "reformed" whatsoever. There are, however, a number of references to "all those of the new religion," or to "those of the said new religion," or to "ministers and principals of the new religion." [12] In the subsequent "Advice and Council of the Assembled Ministers and Deputies of the Churches of France on the Execution and Observance of the Principal Clauses of the Edict of January," the evangelicals refer to themselves again as "the reformed church," and "the reformed churches." [13] The qualifying adjective is omitted where simply "Churches of France" appears.

After the Colloquy at Poissy the adjective "reformed" was used frequently. A letter dated November 27, 1561, from the French congregation-in-exile in Frankfurt-am-Main to the magistrate of the city makes reference to the "reformed Churches"; [14] a letter of Louis of Bourbon, Prince of Condy, written July 5, 1562, contains the same expression; [15] letters of Calvin to Bullinger on April 8, 1563, and to the Duchess of Ferrara on January 8, 1564, mention "reformed religion" and "a church duly reformed"; [16] and the correspondence of Queen Elizabeth of England to continental princes makes frequent mention of the reformed religion when ecclesiastical matters are being considered. An interesting instance appears in her letter to the Prince of the Palatinate in 1577 concerning the meetings of the German Lutheran princes that resulted in the appearance of the Form of Concord: "The most serene Queen takes this assembly of theologians most seriously because, while as a result of it many persons will be experiencing difficulties, no one will be acquiring any benefit therefrom except the common Papist enemies of the reformed religion, who consider Lutherans and Zwinglians one and the same." [17]

A point of significance in the queen's letter is its inclusive use of the name "reformed." Both Lutherans and Zwinglians are comprehended by it since both are a part of the same Reformation. The evidence is clear that the term was widely used in at least the last four decades of the sixteenth century. An example is a conference on the issue of images held at St. Germain shortly after the Colloquy at Poissy, between certain theologians of the Sorbonne and evangelical ministers. At its conclusion the four ministers, led by Beza, presented a written statement to Catherine de'Medici in which mention is made of "all the reformed churches of this kingdom, and we hope not less of those outside, that is to say, of the Churches of England, of Scotland, of Denmark, Sweden, Germany, Poland, Switzerland and Grisons."[18]

Further evidence of an inclusive usage of the word is that it was employed by the followers of Luther in Germany as well as by those of Calvin in Switzerland or in France. In the fall of 1570 leading princes in Germany sent an emissary to Paris to intercede for the persecuted Huguenots. They asked the king not to listen to the counsel of those who would have him believe that the reformed religion could not exist alongside another in a kingdom. Experience showed, they said, that not only in Germany, but also in other kingdoms and countries both religions (the reformed or evangelical and the Catholic) existed peacefully alongside each other, and that also thereby bloodshed and persecution had been averted and general peace and proper obedience had been maintained until the present.[19]

In both preparatory statements of the Form of Concord of the Lutheran churches there is an introductory section that states that "our reformed churches have been separated from the Papist and other dissolute and accursed sects and heresies."[20] The theologians of Lübeck, Hamburg and Lüneburg drew up and signed the Formula of Torgau in 1576, which, it states, is not intended to abrogate the old confessions but rather to witness publicly to their doctrine, which has been known in these environs "ever since the beginning of the reformed religion."[21] Without adducing other evidence it is interesting to note that the Book of Concord itself calls its church "reformed." This strict Lutheran statement, written in opposition to Melanchthonian-Calvinistic teaching in the German churches, designates that church as "our reformed church" in the introduction to the Form of Concord.[22]

This usage continued through the rest of the sixteenth and into the seventeenth century. Leonhard Hutter, most orthodox of the orthodox Lutherans and sworn enemy of Calvinistic teaching, was a professor of theology at Wittenberg at the end of the sixteenth century. In his exposition of the Form of Concord there is "an apologetic preface to all the German churches truly reformed."[23] So also Calixtus used the designation "Reformed" as synonymous with Protestant, Lutheran, or Evangelical in 1634[24] and in 1641.[25] There is ample evidence of the fact that Lutheran writers called themselves Reformed until the end of the sixteenth century, as Heppe indicates. He argues that the expression "Lutheran Church" was wholly unknown in Hesse until the beginning of the seventeenth century, and that at the turn of the century some of the advocates of the Form of Concord disfavored using that expression of themselves, preferring to continue to designate their church as the evangelical or reformed church. One source offered as proof is the writing of a Marburg Professor named Winckelmann, who, Heppe says, became known as a fanatical Lutheran and zealous enemy of Calvinism. He guards against using the name "Lutheran," which he calls a sectarian name given by Rome; his church is "no new one, but a reformed Church."[26] The Form of Concord itself never uses the word "Lutheran," nor was that term used in an official sense by any evangelical writer until after the appearance of the Form of Concord in 1580. The commonly used name preferred by Protestants was "Reformed" and only in a later period did this name come to be restricted to those of Calvinist, or non-Lutheran, persuasion.

It was the sacramentarian controversy that eventually caused the name "Reformed" to be descriptive of only the non-Lutheran element in the churches of the Reformation. After the death of Melanchthon the dogmatic quarrels caused the expressions "Lutheran," "Calvinist," "Zwinglian," "Philippist," and "Reformed" to be used in a sectarian and controversial manner. This can be seen, for example, in a letter written in 1563 by Frederick III of the Palatinate to the Landgrave Philip. Frederick writes that it was indeed the "Lutherans" who deviate from the text of the words of institution in the doctrine of the Lord's Supper.[27] He had previously been accused of being "Calvinist" in his position on the doctrine by fellow German princes.[28] The Form of Concord described the Calvinists as "the most pernicious of all sacramentarians."[29]

In the Palatinate after 1584 "Lutheran" came to have a symbolical-confessional meaning;[30] in Württemburg in 1590 it became customary for evangelicals to use "Lutheran" of themselves and their doctrine, and the same became true in Electoral Saxony in 1591.[31] In Strasbourg after 1598 "Lutheran" came to have a symbolical meaning,[32] and between 1592-1599 the name "Reformed" came to have the meaning of "Calvinist" in Wittenberg while "Lutheran" came to mean those of the persuasion of the Form of Concord.[33] In a polemical writing entitled "Christianity, Papism and Calvinism," published in Dresden in 1602 and written by an extreme Lutheran named Leyser, the same fixed use of the names is evident. In speaking about religious controversy he mentions "Evangelicals, who are called Lutherans and the other, the Calvinists, who call themselves Reformed."[34] Latter he avers that the Calvinistic God is more similar to the devil than to the true God and that the Calvinists are "falsely named Reformed."[35] He seems reluctant to give over the name "Reformed" to the other party and a bit hesitant to accept the name "Lutheran" in view of its earlier use by opponents of the evangelical cause for he writes "we Lutherans, as men call us."[36]

As the sacramentarian controversy continued, and as some of the German evangelical churches made further steps in the reformation of worship and the elimination of practices that were customary in the Roman Catholic Church, the name "Reformed" came to be associated with the churches that followed Calvin in their sacramentology and in the further reform of worship, while the name "Lutheran" was attached to those who abode by the decisions of the Form of Concord and opposed Calvinistic tendencies in the church. Sometimes, in connection with the further reform of worship, the proponents of Calvin's ideas would speak of their church as "Reformed according to the Word of God" and for them that expression came to denote more thorough reformation.

In the year 1578 the expression "Reformed" is seen here and there to be used in a relationship of opposition to tendencies that were later known within Protestantism as "Lutheranism."[37] But it was not until the end of the century that "Reformed" was used as a designation of the non-Lutheran Churches of Germany. In dogmatics the name "Reformed" came to be used in a non-Lutheran sense in 1598 when Ursinus' Commentary on the Heidelberg Catechism, which was famous as a Calvinist creed, was published by his student Pareus under the title *Corpus doctrinae Christianae ecclesiarum a papatu reformatarum, etc.* In England, however, until the Thirty Year War (1618-1648) "Reformed" meant Evangelical Protestantism.[38] Thereafter the terms "Reformed" and "Lutheran" had clear symbolical meaning.[39]

NOTES TO APPENDIX

[1] *Luteriana, Lutheranus, Luthericus, Lutheranismus, Lutheriain, Lutherien, Lutherisch, Martinisten.*

[2] *"Das liebe, heilige Evangelium nennen sie Lutherisch."* Quoted by Heinrich Heppe, *Ursprung und Geschichte der Bezeichnungen "reformirte" und "lutherische" Kirche* (Gotha: Verlag von Friedrich Andreas Perthes,

1859), p. 12. My indebtedness to Heppe in the early usage of the name "Reformed" is evident. Cf. Sasse, *Was heisst Lutherisch?* p. 24.

3 *". . .evangelicos, sic enim appellari gaudent."* Heppe, *op. cit.*, p. 2.

4 *". . .l'on voyait augmenter tous les jours le nombre des Lutheriens, qui avoient pris le nom d'Evangeliques."* *Ibid.*, p. 3.

5 *"Was der Zweck der evangelischen Lehre Sei: Scopus Evangelicae Doctrinae."* Schaff, *The Creeds of Christendom*, Vol. III, p. 217.

6 *"Verwandte der Augsburgischen Confession."* Heppe, *op. cit.*, pp. 12ff.

7 *". . .reformata, emendata, repurgata. . . ." Ibid.*

8 *"ecclesia emendata." Ibid.*

9 *". . . omnia reformanda, qua deformata sunt." Ibid.*, p. 2.

10 *". . . laquelle est réprouvée par le commun accord de toutes les églises réformées, tant en Allemagne, qu'ailleurs."* Theodore de Beze, *Histoire Ecclésiastique des Églises Réformées au Royaume de France* (Lille: Imprimerie de Leleux, Grand Place, 1841), Vol. I, p. 374.

11 E.g., pp. 126, 133ff., 139, 309, 327.

12 *"nouvelle religion. . . .la dite nouvelle religion. . . ." Ibid.*, pp. 425f.

13 *Ibid.*, pp. 429ff., Articles 1 and 8.

14 Heppe, *op. cit.*, p. 14.

15 Beze, *op. cit.*, Vol. II, p. 640.

16 *". . . religionis quam ipsi reformatam vocant"; "église deuement réformée." C.R.* 47. 691; 48, 232.

17 *"Serenissima Regina grauius de hoc Theologorum instituto sentit, quod quum multi incommoda hinc experturi sint, nulli commoda sint relaturi praeter Pontificios communes reformatae religionis hostes, qui Lutheranos et Zwinglianos eodem loco habent."* Heppe, *op. cit.*, p. 17.

18 Beze, *op. cit.*, Vol. I, p. 450. There were 2150 congregations of the Reformed Church in France at the time.

19 Heppe, *op. cit.*, p. 19.

20 *"Unsere reformirten Kirchen von den Papisten und anderen verworfenen und verdammten sekten und Ketzereien absondert worden." Ibid.*

21 *"vom Anfange der reformirten Religion an." Ibid.*, p. 20.

22 *"unsere reformirte Kirche." Ibid.*

23 *"Praefatio apologetica ad universas Germaniae ecclesias vere reformatas." Ibid.*

24 *"eadem, (fide) qua nos hodie, qui Protestantes vel Reformati dicimur." Ibid.*

25 *"Diese disputatio kann ohne Nachteil der reformirten Kirche und Vorteil der Papisten nicht eingestellt werden." Ibid.*, pp. 20f.

26 *"Wir haben sectirerische Namen und werden Lutherisch genannt, dargegen mag er wissen, dass ob wir wol Lutheri nicht schamen, noch seiner Bekenntnis und Lehre,—dass doch wir nicht von ihm Lutherisch nennen, sondern wir mussen solches von euch Papisten leiden. . . .wir sind keine neue, sondern eine reformirte Kirche." Ibid.*, p. 41.

27 *Ibid.*, p. 16.

28 John Calvin, *Commentaries on the Book of the Prophet Jeremiah and the Lamentations,* Dedication to Frederick III (Edinburgh: Calvin Translation Society, 1850), pp. xvii, xxii.

29 Schaff, *The Creeds of Christendom,* Vol. I, p. 317.

30 Heppe, *op. cit.,* p. 36.

31 *Ibid.,* p. 30.

32 *Ibid.,* p. 38.

33 *Ibid.,* p. 35.

34 *"Evangelischen, die man die Lutherischen nennt, die andere der Calvinisten, die sich die Reformirten. . .nennen." Ibid.,* p. 40.

35 *". . .den Calvinisten und falsch genannten Reformirten. . . ." Ibid.*

36 *"wir Lutherischen (wie man uns nennt)." Ibid.*

37 *Ibid.,* pp. 70, 72f., and 84ff.

38 *Ibid.,* p. 94.

39 *Ibid.,* p. 96.

annotateð select bibliography

CHAPTER I – THE REFORMATION OF THE CHURCH

Althaus, Paul. *The Theology of Martin Luther.* Philadelphia: Fortress, 1966. A summary of Luther's theology by one who has been a student of the subject for half a century.

Bainton, Roland H. *Here I Stand: A Life of Martin Luther.* Nashville: Abingdon-Cokesbury, 1950. One of the best-written biographies of Luther, illustrated with old wood-cuts. An excellent bibliography is appended.

Boehmer, Heinrich. *Road to Reformation.* Philadelphia: Muhlenberg, 1946. A study of Martin Luther to the year 1521.

Bornkamm, Heinrich. *Luther's World of Thought.* St. Louis: Concordia, 1958. A selection of main themes in the thought of Luther, showing the importance he attached to them and his influence on his contemporaries and later generations. The present relevance of each theme is portrayed.

Courvoisier, Jacques. *Zwingli.* Richmond: John Knox, 1963. A good brief survey of the life and thought of the first Swiss reformer.

Daniel-Rops, H. *The Catholic Reformation.* New York: E. P. Dutton, 1962. An interpretation of history during the sixteenth century by a Roman Catholic scholar who sees what happened to his church as much more than a mere "Counter-Reformation."

Fairbairn, A. M. "Calvin and the Reformed Church," in *The Cambridge Modern History,* Vol. II. An excellent, brief portrait of the Genevan Reformer.

Gerrish, B. A., editor. *Reformers in Profile.* Philadelphia: Fortress, 1967. Short characterizations of Wyclif, Pierre d'Ailly, Erasmus, Luther, Zwingli, Calvin, Cranmer, Menno Simons, Muentzer, and Loyola by various scholars. A bibliography is appended to each chapter.

Hershberger, Guy F., editor. *The Recovery of the Anabaptist Vision.* Scottdale, Pa.: Mennonite Publishing House, 1957. An evaluation of various aspects of the radical reformation, showing strengths and weaknesses of a tradition whose importance is recently being appreciated.

Kooiman, W. J. *By Faith Alone.* New York: Philosophical Library, 1955. A chronicle of the life of Luther and an evaluation of his significance.

Lau, Franz. *Luther.* Philadelphia: Westminster, 1963. A good, brief sketch of Luther's significance as a Reformer.

Loane, Marcus L. *Masters of the English Reformation.* London: Church Book Room Press, 1954. Well-written narratives of the lives of five English Reformers: Bilney, Tyndale, Latimer, Ridley, and Cranmer.

Lortz, Joseph. *The Reformation in Germany* (2 volumes). New York: Herder and Herder, 1968. An excellent interpretation of Luther by a Roman Catholic scholar who finds reasons for the Reformation within the Roman Catholic Church of the sixteenth century.

Luther's Works, edited by Jaroslav Pelikan, Helmut T. Lehmann *et al.,* fifty-five volumes. St. Louis: Concordia, and Philadelphia: Muhlenberg, 1955–. This American edition of Luther's writings is a selection of all of Luther's more important writings and includes helpful introductions, notes, and indices.

McSorley, Harry J. *Luther: Right or Wrong?* New York: Newman, and Minneapolis: Augsburg, 1969. This study of Luther's doctrine of the will by a Roman Catholic theologian holds that Luther was right in attacking the semi-pelagianism in the theology of his day and that, in spite of his exaggerated language and failure to distinguish between natural and acquired freedom, his intention was sound and his concern "clearly Catholic." McSorley challenges Luther's condemnation and criticizes the popes of his day.

Murray, Iain. *The Reformation of the Church: A Collection of Reformed and Puritan Documents on Church Issues.* London: Banner of Truth Trust, 1965. A helpful collation of writings relating to the Bible and reformation, the need for reformation, church government, and the unity of the church.

Nygaard, Norman E. *A Mighty Fortress.* Grand Rapids: Zondervan, 1964. A young people's life of Luther.

Pelikan, Jaroslav. *Obedient Rebels.* London: SCM Press, 1964. Essays showing "the catholic substance and Protestant principle in Luther's reformation," with an assessment of Roman Catholic-Protestant theological relationships today.

Pollard, A. F. "National Opposition to Rome in Germany," "Social Revolution and Catholic Reaction in Germany," "The Conflict of Creeds and Parties in Germany," and "Religious War in Germany," in *The Cambridge Modern History*. These concise essays give insight into the Lutheran Reformation and a perceptive appraisal of the great Reformer and the issues he had to face. The entire volume contains good essays on Reformation themes.

Rupp, Ernest Gordon. *The Righteousness of God.* London: Hodder and Stoughton, 1953. An excellent appraisal of Luther and his work with helpful citation of sources and a good bibliography of Luther studies until 1953.

Patterns of Reformation. London: Epworth, 1969. A study of some secondary figures of the Reformation: Oecolampadius, Karlstadt, Müntzer, Vadianus and Johannes Kessler, by an excellent Reformation scholar.

"Luther and the German Reformation to 1529," in *The New Cambridge Modern History,* Vol. II. A concise statement of the views and activity of the Reformer through the first dozen years of reform. This entire volume consists of excellent essays on aspects of life in the sixteenth century.

Schaff, Philip. *History of the Christian Church,* Volumes 7 and 8. New York: Scribner's, 1904, reprinted Grand Rapids: Eerdmans, 1962. A standard treatment on the history of the German and Swiss reformations by America's greatest church historian.

Schwiebert, Ernest G. *Luther and His Times.* St. Louis: Concordia, 1950. A thorough treatment with helpful apparatus for further study.

Thiel, Rudolf. *Luther*. Philadelphia: Muhlenberg, 1955. A good, popular narrative of the story of the great Reformer without notes or critical apparatus.

Thompson, Bard. "Zwingli Study Since 1918," in *Church History*, XIX (1950), 116-128. A comprehensive bibliography of writings on Zwingli from 1918-1949.

Verduin, Leonard. *The Reformers and Their Stepchildren*. Grand Rapids: Eerdmans, 1964. A thorough and sympathetic treatment of the radical wing of the Reformation. Verduin sets weaknesses of the primary Reformers in focus, but fails to do the same with respect to the Anabaptists.

CHAPTER II – THE REFORMED CHURCH

Ainslie, James L. *The Doctrines of Ministerial Order in the Reformed Churches of the 16th and 17th Centuries*. Edinburgh: T. & T. Clark, 1940. This best work on the subject treats the historical constitution of the ministry of the Reformed Church, the duties and powers of the ministry, the equality of the ministry, ordination and its effects, apostolic succession, call to the ministry, and the concept of valid ministry.

Baird, C. W. *The Presbyterian Liturgies*. Grand Rapids: Baker, 1957. A selection of Reformed orders of worship from Calvin and various Reformed churches. An introduction is included in each chapter.

Bannerman, James. *The Church of Christ*, two volumes. Edinburgh: T. & T. Clark, 1868. A rather definitive treatise on the nature, powers, ordinances, discipline, and government of the church from the Reformed perspective.

Bast, Henry. *Ordination Vows of Ministers and Elders*. Grand Rapids: Evangelical Fund, 1947. A discussion of the crisis in the church because of doctrinal indifference and the dereliction of duty by church officers sworn to proclaim and defend the gospel.

Bieler, Andre. *The Social Humanism of Calvin*. Richmond: John Knox, 1964. A brief popularization of a larger work in French in which the social and economic thought of Calvin is shown to be rooted in the Bible and relevant today.

Bohatec, Josef. *Bude und Calvin*. Graz: Hermann Böhlaus, 1950. This single title is given of a study on Calvin's relation to French humanism in order to mention a scholar whose Calvin studies are all excellent contributions to Calviniana.

Bratt, John H., editor. *The Rise and Development of Calvinism*. Grand Rapids: Eerdmans, 1959. A brief treatment of the life of Calvin and the spread of Calvinism in Europe and America.

Calvin, John. *Institutes of the Christian Religion*, two volumes, edited by John T. McNeill and translated and indexed by Ford Lewis Battles. Philadelphia: Westminster, 1960. The notes, bibliographies, references, and indices help make this the most valuable tool for an understanding of the Reformed tradition. Part of the Library of Christian Classics series.

Clasen, Claus-Peter. *The Palatinate in European History, 1559-1660*. Oxford: Basil Blackwell, 1963. A survey of the foreign relations and political policy of Germany's most militant state during the period of the Reformation. Clasen shows the importance of the Palatinate and its capital, Heidelberg, when it was a leading Reformed principality.

Daken, A. *Calvinism*. Philadelphia: Westminster, 1946. A summary of the doctrine of the *Institutes* is followed by discussions of Calvinism as an ecclesiastical system in Europe and America, and various aspects of Calvinism: its view of authority and Scripture, its way of life, attitude towards society, and church and state.

Davies, Horton. *The Worship of the English Puritans.* Glasgow: Dacre Press, 1948. An excellent discussion of the liturgical principles and practices of an influential Reformed tradition.

Doumergue, Emile. *Jean Calvin: Les Hommes et les choses de son temps,* seven volumes. Lausanne: Georges Bridel, 1910. Volume Four of this definitive study of Calvin and his work treats his thought.

Duffield, G. E., editor. *John Calvin.* Grand Rapids: Eerdmans, 1966. A fine collection of essays on the work and thought of the Genevan Reformer.

Ganoczy, Alexandre. *Calvin, Theologien de L'Eglise et du Ministere.* Paris: Les Editions du Cerf, 1964. A good exposition of Calvin's doctrine of the ministry of the church by a Roman Catholic scholar.

Good, James I. *History of the Swiss Reformed Church Since the Reformation.* Philadelphia: The Reformed Church in the United States, 1913. A narrative of events in the life of the Swiss Reformed Church from the late sixteenth through the nineteenth century.

Goodykoontz, Harry G. *The Minister in the Reformed Tradition.* Richmond: John Knox, 1963. A helpful discussion of the office of the minister of the Word of God in the Reformed Church in history and today.

Heideman, Eugene P. *Reformed Bishops and Catholic Elders.* Grand Rapids: Eerdmans, 1970. A helpful contemporary discussion of the ministry and offices of the church in the light of ecumenical development.

Henderson, G. D. *Presbyterianism.* Aberdeen: The University Press, 1954. A good discussion of the offices of the church in the Reformed tradition.

Küng, Hans. *The Church.* New York: Sheed and Ward, 1967. Perhaps the best recent treatment on the doctrine of the church. Written by a prominent Roman Catholic theologian, it is representative of Reformed teaching in almost all aspects of the subject treated.

Kuyper, Abraham. *Lectures on Calvinism.* Grand Rapids: Eerdmans, 1931. Calvinism as a life system, and its relation to religion, politics, science, art, and the future are discussed by one of the giants of the Reformed tradition. Originally given as lectures at Princeton in 1898.

Manson, T. W. *The Church's Ministry.* Philadelphia: Westminster, 1948. This answer to the exclusive claims of high church episcopacy shows that the only essential ministry is the perpetual ministry of the risen Christ and that all other ministries are dependent, derivative, and functional. It is Christ's call that validates any ministry.

Marcel, P. Ch. *The Biblical Doctrine of Infant Baptism.* London: James Clarke, 1953. A good discussion of the biblical doctrine of the sacrament of the covenant of grace from a Reformed perspective.

Maxwell, W. D. "The Elements of Liturgy: Reformed," in *Ways of Worship: The Report of a Theological Commission of Faith and Order,* edd. P. Edwall, E. Hayman and W. D. Maxwell. London: SCM, 1951. An excellent contribution in a symposium on the meaning and ways of worship in the church.

McAfee, Cleland Boyd. *The Ruling Elder.* Philadelphia: Presbyterian Board of Education, 1931. One of the best discussions of the office and duties of the elder in the Reformed tradition.

McDonnell, Kilian. *John Calvin, the Church, and the Eucharist.* Princeton:

Princeton University Press, 1967. An excellent discussion of the subject by a Roman Catholic scholar who sees Calvin's criticism of Roman Catholic dogma as having present relevance for ecumenical discussion.

McNeill, John T. *The History and Character of Calvinism.* New York: Oxford University Press, 1954. The best recent treatment of the subject, with a helpful book list appended.

―――. "The Church in Sixteenth-Century Reformed Theology," *Journal of Religion,* XXII (1942), 251-269; "The Church in Post-Reformation Reformed Theology," *Journal of Religion,* XXIV (1944), 96-107; "The Doctrine of the Ministry in Reformed Theology," *Church History,* XII (1943), 77-97; "The Significance of the Word of God for Calvin," *Church History,* XXVIII (1959), 140-145; "Thirty Years of Calvin Study," *Church History,* XVII (1948), 232-235. Helpful short essays on the subjects by a leading authority.

―――. *Unitive Protestantism.* Richmond: John Knox, 1964. A discussion of the unitive principle in the Reformation movement including Protestant catholicity and conciliarism, and the union and reunion activities of the Reformers and their successors down the centuries. A unique treatment contradicting popular ideas concerning the Reformers.

Niesel, Wilhelm. *The Theology of Calvin.* London: Lutterworth, 1956. A treatment of the subject by a Calvin specialist.

Nijenhuis, W. *Calvinus Oecumenicus.* The Hague: Martinus Nijhoff, 1959. A demonstration of the ecumenical interests, relationships, and endeavors of Calvin.

Parker, T. H. L. *The Oracles of God: An Introduction to the Preaching of John Calvin,* London: Lutterworth, 1947; *The Doctrine of the Knowledge of God: A Study in the Theology of John Calvin,* Edinburgh: Oliver and Boyd, 1952; "A Bibliography and Survey of the British Study of Calvin, 1900-1940," *The Evangelical Quarterly,* XVIII (1946), 123-131. Very useful essays and a helpful bibligraphy for Calvin study.

Torrance, T. F. *Conflict and Agreement in the Church,* two volumes. London: Lutterworth, 1959-60. Addresses and papers by a leading Reformed theologian concerning doctrine and polity.

―――. *The School of Faith: The Catechisms of the Reformed Church.* London: James Clarke, 1959. An excellent introduction of 120 pages preceding the ten catechisms discusses the general method, principles, and doctrinal tendencies of the catechisms, and the nature of theology. The importance which the author sees in catechetical instruction gives occasion to cite a quaint tale related by the chaplain assigned to the British ambassador to The Hague at the time of the Synod of Dordt. Charged to learn all he could about the synod, John Hales wrote Ambassador Dudley Carlton on November 19, 1618, as follows: "Doubtless the most effectual way of all the rest to bring young persons to learn their catechisme, was that which was related by one of the Helvetian Deputies. For he told us that in his country the manner was that all young persons that meant to marry were to repair, both he and she, unto their Minister, a little before they meant to marry, and by him to be examined how well they had conned their Catechism; if they had not done it perfectly to his mind, he had power to defer their Marriage till they had better learnt their lessons. I was much affected to this course when I heard it, and I thought that doubtless it was a speedy way to make all young persons, excepting myself and two or three more that mean not overhastily to marry, to be skilful in their Catechism. The Synod shall be ill advised if they make no use of it." (*Golden Remains of the Memorable Mr. John Hales*. London: Tho. Newcomb, 1673, Vol. II, p. 11.)

Wendel, Francois. *Calvin: The Origins and Development of His Religious Thought*. New York: Harper, 1963. An excellent study of the subject.

CHAPTER III – REFORMED ACCORDING TO THE WORD OF GOD

Berkouwer, G. C. *De Heilige Schrift,* two volumes. Kampen: J. H. Kok, 1967. This work, soon to appear in English, is a continuation of the kind of treatment that one finds in Herman Bavinck's dogmatics. One of the best discussions of the Reformed doctrine of Scripture, it is marked by careful scholarship, thorough analysis of problems, and judicious emphasis.

Dowey, Edward A., Jr. *The Knowledge of God in Calvin's Theology*. New York: Columbia University Press, 1952. An able discussion of a central theme in the Reformer's thought.

Kooiman, Willem Jan. *Luther and the Bible*. Philadelphia: Muhlenberg, 1961. An able exposition of the Reformer's doctrine of Scripture shows that he did not have the tight doctrine of inerrancy in all detail adopted by later Lutheran orthodoxy.

Murray, John. *Calvin on Scripture and Divine Sovereignty*. Philadelphia: Presbyterian and Reformed, 1960. A brief statement of fundamentals by an able scholar.

Ramm, Bernard. *Special Revelation and the Word of God*. Grand Rapids: Eerdmans, 1961. A useful statement of the subject which acknowledges its indebtedness to Abraham Kuyper's *Principles of Sacred Theology*.

Reid, J. K. S. *The Authority of Scripture*. New York: Harper & Brothers, n.d. A useful study of Reformation and post-Reformation understanding of the Bible, which is weak in recognizing the objective authority of Scripture.

Rogers, Jack Bartlett. *Scripture in the Westminster Confession*. Grand Rapids: Eerdmans, 1967. This careful study argues and documents the thesis that later Reformed orthodoxy, as in the Princeton School of Hodge and Warfield, narrowed and thus misinterpreted the doctrine of Scripture of the Westminster divines while claiming to hold and to amplify that position. The Westminster doctrine is advocated.

Rossouw, H. W. *Klaarheid en Interpretasie*. Amsterdam: Drukkerij en Uitgeverij Jacob Van Campen, 1963. An excellent exposition of the doctrine of the perspicuity, or clarity, of Scripture, showing what the Reformers meant and did not mean by it.

Warfield, Benjamin B. *The Inspiration and Authority of the Bible*. Philadelphia: Presbyterian and Reformed, 1948. The doctrine of plenary verbal inerrancy is expounded by its ablest spokesman.

CHAPTER IV – IN THE PRESENCE OF GOD

Augustine. *Confessions,* translated by Vernon J. Bourke, in *The Fathers of the Church,* volume 21, Roy Joseph Deferrari, editor. New York: Fathers of the Church, Inc., 1953. A classic by one of the greatest of churchmen and Christian thinkers.

Bakker, J. T. *Coram Deo: Bijdrage tot het Onderzoek naar de Structuur van Luthers Theologie*. Kampen: J. H. Kok, 1956. Luther's profound sense of

God is said to be the main motivation of his labors in this well-done thesis.

Barrois, Georges A., editor. *Pathways of the Inner Life: An Anthology of Christian Spirituality.* Indianapolis: Bobbs-Merrill, 1956. A selection of brief devotional writings from a wide range of Christian authors from about A.D. 400 to today.

Benoit, Pierre, *et al. The Presence of God,* in *Concilium: Theology in the Age of Renewal,* volume 50. New York: Paulist Press, 1969. A helpful symposium by contemporary Roman Catholic scholars.

Bevan, Frances. *Hymns of Ter Steegen, Suso, and Others,* two volumes. London: Nisbet, 1901. The great hymnology of the church is a rich source for the study of Christian devotion. This is very evident in these volumes.

Brother Lawrence. *The Practice of the Presence of God;* and *Selections From the Little Flowers of St. Francis,* edited by High Martin. London: SCM Press, 1956. Two brief works that deserve their acclaim.

Brunner, Emil. *The Divine-Human Encounter.* Philadelphia: Westminster, 1943. This key to an understanding of Brunner's thought shows his conception of the Christian's dynamic relationship to God.

Cadier, Jean. *The Man God Mastered,* translated by O. R. Johnston. London: Inter-Varsity, 1960. This brief biography of Calvin shows his interest in living with a sense of God's presence.

Daniélou, Jean. *God and Us,* translated by Walter Roberts. London: Mowbray, 1957. A study by a fine Roman Catholic scholar, which moves from general conceptions of God in religion through Christian thought to the values of Christian mysticism.

Herrmann, Wilhelm. *The Communion of the Christian With God,* translated by J. Sandys Stanyon. New York: Putnam, 1913. In spite of his inadequate conception of theology, Herrmann strikes a note that he found in the Reformers. A needed corrective to the anti-mysticism of his day and ours.

Kierkegaard, Søren. *Purity of Heart Is To Will One Thing,* translated by Douglass V. Steere. New York: Harper, 1938; *Training in Christianity,* translated by Walter Lowrie. Princeton: Princeton University Press, 1947. These two writings of the great Dane show his interest in fellowship with God.

Küng, Hans, editor. *The Unknown God?* New York: Sheed and Ward, 1966. Essays on the search and encounter with God by Roman Catholic scholars Joseph Möller, Herbert Haag, and Gotthold Hasenhüttl.

Murray, Andrew. *The Inner Chamber and the Inner Life.* London: Revell, 1905. One of many volumes written by a Christian with a keen sense of God's presence.

Pascal, Blaise. *Pensees.* New York: Random House (The Modern Library), 1941. A suggestive, inspiring work by one of the great Christians of the church.

Thomas à Kempis. *The Imitation of Christ.* New York: Dutton, 1947. A classic on Christian devotion and the sense of the divine.

CHAPTER V – THE LIFE OF THE CHRISTIAN

Baillie, D. M. *Faith in God and Its Christian Consummation.* London: Faber and Faber, 1964. A good discussion of the meaning and content of faith in general and the uniqueness of Christian faith.

Bavinck, J. H., *Faith and Its Difficulties,* translated by Wm. B. Eerdmans, Sr.

Grand Rapids: Eerdmans, 1959. A helpful discussion of man, God, and the delicate nature of their relationship to each other.

Berkouwer, G. C., *Studies in Dogmatics. The Providence of God; Faith and Sanctification; Faith and Justification; Faith and Perseverance; Divine Election.* Grand Rapids: Eerdmans, 1952–. Good studies by an eminent Reformed theologian.

Bruggink, Donald J., editor. *Guilt, Grace, and Gratitude.* New York: Half Moon, 1963. A commentary on the Heidelberg Catechism discussing aspects of the life of the Christian.

Brunner, Emil. *The Divine Imperative,* translated by Olive Wyon. Philadelphia: Westminster, 1947. An excellent treatise on Christian ethics, which deals with several subjects discussed in this chapter on the life of the Christian.

Chamberlain, William Douglas. *The Meaning of Repentance.* Philadelphia: Westminster, 1943. A good discussion of a neglected subject.

Fisher, Fred L. *The Purpose of God and the Christian Life.* Philadelphia: Westminster, 1962. The author relates God's purpose to various aspects of salvation history and the individual's life in a helpful way.

Küng, Hans. *Justification.* New York: Nelson, 1964. A good exposition of Karl Barth's teaching on justification by a prominent Roman Catholic. Küng agrees with Reformation teaching on justification.

Moltmann, Jürgen. *A Theology of Hope.* New York: Harper, 1967. An excellent treatment of this important aspect of the Christian faith in its relation to other doctrine and life.

Smith, C. Ryder. *The Bible Doctrine of Grace.* London: Epworth, 1956. Grace is expounded and related to various doctrines in a clear, helpful manner by an able author.

Stewart, James S. *A Man in Christ.* New York: Harper, n.d. An unusually good discussion of union with Christ, a subject that is at the heart of the soteriology of Paul and John Calvin.

Stoeffler, F. Ernest. *The Rise of Evangelical Pietism.* Leiden: Brill, 1965. An important study with information on Reformed pietism.

Tanis, James. *Dutch Calvinistic Pietism in the Middle Colonies.* The Hague: Martinus Nijhoff, 1967. A good study of the life and theology of T. J. Frelinghuysen and the early Reformed Church in America.

Wallace, Ronald S. *Calvin's Doctrine of the Christian Life.* Grand Rapids: Eerdmans, 1959. A helpful summary of the subject without evaluation of Calvin's teaching.

Warfield, Benjamin B. *Studies in Perfectionism,* two volumes. New York: Oxford University Press, 1931. Learned discussions that show the danger of unbiblical teaching of freedom from sin in this life. Probably the best work in the field.

CHAPTER VI – THE CHRISTIAN AND THE SOCIAL ORDER

Cave, Sydney. *The Christian Way.* London: Nisbet, 1949. A good, general discussion of the subject with a helpful section on life in community.

Gardner, E. Clinton. *Biblical Faith and Social Ethics.* New York: Harper, 1960. Excellent discussions of contemporary socio-ethical problems.

Gustafson, James M. *Christ and the Moral Life.* New York: Harper, 1968. An excellent discussion of the meaning of Christ for Christian life in its moral dimensions.

Niebuhr, H. Richard. *Christ and Culture.* New York: Harper, 1951. A clear treatment of various attitudes of Christian thinkers towards society. Niebuhr holds that view of Reformed theology which believes that the gospel of Christ must enter and transform culture.

Niebuhr, Reinhold. *Christianity and Power Politics.* New York: Scribners, 1940. Valuable in its treatment of pacifism, the roots of democracy, and the state.

———. *Faith and Politics.* New York: George Braziller, 1968. A collation of Niebuhr's essays on ethical, social, political, and economic subjects. A very useful volume of writings by an able student of society and its problems.

Ruff, G. Elson. *The Dilemma of Church and State.* Philadelphia: Muhlenberg, 1954. A good, brief presentation of one of society's vexing problems.

Troeltsch, Ernst. *The Social Teaching of the Christian Churches,* two volumes. New York: Harper, 1960. An excellent historical treatment of the subject.

index